The Rise of the
Anti-Corporate Movement

THE RISE OF THE ANTI-CORPORATE MOVEMENT

Corporations and the People
Who Hate Them

Evan Osborne

Westport, Connecticut
London

Library of Congress Cataloging-in-Publication Data

Osborne, Evan, 1964–
   The rise of the anti-corporate movement : corporations and the people who hate them /
Evan Osborne.
      p. cm.
   Includes bibliographical references and index.
   ISBN-13: 978–0–275–99786–1 (alk. paper)
1. Corporations. 2. Anti-globalization movement. 3. Corporate profits. 4. Corporate
power. 5. Corporate culture. I. Title: Anti-corporate movement. II. Title: Corporations
and the people who hate them. III. Title.
   HD2731.O83 2007
   306.3´4—dc22   2007020591

British Library Cataloguing in Publication Data is available.

Library of Congress Catalog Card Number: 2007020591
ISBN-13: 978–0–275–99786–1

First published in 2007

Praeger Publishers, 88 Post Road West, Westport, CT 06881
An imprint of Greenwood Publishing Group, Inc.
www.praeger.com

Printed in the United States of America

The paper used in this book complies with the
Permanent Paper Standard issued by the National
Information Standards Organization (Z39.48–1984).

10 9 8 7 6 5 4 3 2 1

To Weymar and Victoria, for always asking such good questions.

And especially to Toyoko, my most important shareholder.

Contents

Preface

On January 31, 2007, an odd incident occurred in Boston. The Cartoon Network, a cable channel devoted to animated shows, had engaged in a bit of guerrilla marketing by placing small devices at well-known locations around town. The devices had small lights showing a cartoon character from a new show they were seeking to promote and had visible wires to boot. To some citizens of a country consumed by fear of terrorism, they seemed potentially dangerous and thus caused inconvenience and even chaos in the city as police officers both sought to defuse them and sought to search for others possibly undiscovered. By the end of the day, the network's parent company, Turner Broadcasting System, had sheepishly informed the police that it was responsible. The mayor of Boston, Thomas Menino, was understandably upset about this waste of his police department's time and the anxiety that the stunt generated among city residents all day. But in the wake of the incident, he said, among other things, something very strange—that the incident was "all about corporate greed."

Let us stipulate that this action was, at best, selfish and foolish; someone at the Cartoon Network made a dumb and possibly criminal mistake. But Mayor Menino, a politician whose job depends on knowing what kind of language stirs or scares enough of the public to keep him popular, chose a surprising term—"corporate"—to describe what had happened. Either the incident fit comfortably into a mental model he was already using to think about how the world works or he suspected that talking that way would enhance his reputation with Boston voters. Whether chosen out of anger or careful consideration, his use of "corporate" in this manner is instructive. He could have spoken in terms of individual employees or of this company in particular or even just of plain old "greed," a sin as old as mankind. But he chose instead to say that the event was the fault of "corporate" malfeasance. That mindset—the turning of the word "corporate" into a generic adjective of scorn, and of corporations into the dominant force in society—is what this book is about.

The anti-corporate movement whose development it traces is no longer the province merely of disgruntled contrarians in the academy or people mourning the death of 1960s dreams. It is a growing movement that is increasingly influential in politics, particularly in the United States and Europe. Many of its most rhetorically gifted advocates do not simply believe that corporations frequently commit crimes, or need to be reined in, or that they are run by and for the rich. They believe something far larger—that corporations are driven by costly incentives mistakenly encoded into corporate law over a century ago and that the monsters these laws created have been driven inexorably to more and more control the world.

In the course of researching this book, I had many occasions to order one of the growing mass of anti-corporate books from my local book superstore. On one occasion, when telling a clerk the title of one of them, which suggested that corporations control the world, she (an employee herself of a major corporation) looked at me and, stating it more as fact than question, said "They do, don't they?" So simple, yet so complete as an explanation for why things are as they are—this is the new anti-corporatism. The French have a wonderful phrase that is underused in English—*idée fixe,* which Merriam-Webster defines as "an idea that dominates one's mind, especially for a prolonged period." That, I think, is where we are. We live in a world of tremendous change—culturally, economically, politically. Change being as unsettling as it is, many find themselves in need of a comprehensive narrative to explain it all. And corporations, especially large ones, increasingly provide for many the sturdiest ground in which to plant their narrative.

Despite its rapid growth, hostility to corporations is a phenomenon that has seldom if ever been extensively studied. The purpose of this book is to provide for the reader with an interest in corporations and their role in the world a thorough and, I hope, fair guide to what anti-corporate thinking is, a history of where it came from, an exploration of the truth of its main claims (which, it is probably best to say right up front, I view skeptically), and some speculation on what might happen if it becomes sufficiently influential. In doing so, I hope to contribute to understanding of a movement that has expanded very rapidly relative to what we know about it.

Writing a book, even one written primarily for the sheer intellectual joy of it, is a very enjoyable but demanding task. There were many whose help and guidance were indispensable in bringing this book to fruition.

The idea to write it came to me while I was at the Osaka University Institute of Social and Economic Research, and the research support they provide to their visiting scholars is outstanding. I am particularly grateful to Atsushi Tsuneki for his willingness to host an unknown scholar and to tolerate his eccentric research. I must also thank Jeff Olson and Nick Philipson at Praeger/Greenwood for helping shepherd the work of an inexperienced author through to completion, Vijayakumar Subramanian and (on short notice) Anne Beer for first-rate editorial work, and Ellen Geiger for helpful advice on publishing. I am also intellectually indebted to the reading group at the Raj Soin College of Business at Wright State University for discussing and helping me develop some of my thoughts in this book. Joe Petrick, Maggie Houston, and John Blair were particularly helpful in constantly holding me to account. Jeff Carlisle, Zach Selden, and Charles Wharton of The Policy Hut were selfless (and sometimes brutally honest) in their assessments of the work while it was in progress. My greatest intellectual debt is to the late Jack Hirshleifer, who impressed upon me the importance of making an argument accessible, of economics for understanding human behavior, and of the problem of understanding when people do and don't get along with one another. His patience, curiosity, and genius were always an inspiration.

Finally, I would be unable to achieve anything (let alone this book) without my family, who mean everything to me. Toyoko has put with far too many late nights at the office and gripes about the book-writing process. She listens without protest to all my wild ideas, projects, plans, and dreams. For Weymar and Victoria, from whom I have learned so much, I hope that by the time you're old enough to read and fully understand this fruit of your dad's labor you think he is saying something worth listening to.

Chapter 1

The Concept of the Corporate Regime

So there seems to be nothing to prevent the transnational corporations taking possession of the planet and subjecting humanity to the dictatorship of capital...Controlling virtually all the means of information and communication, they meet with only localized and sporadic resistance as they compete relentlessly for monopoly control of the markets.

—Christian de Brie, editor, *Le Monde Diplomatique*[1]

In the summer of 2004, Paramount Pictures released a film about a candidate for Vice President of the United States who is a bona fide war hero, groomed for years for high office. Unbeknownst to the candidate, he is actually a pawn in a larger scheme by a secret group with evil designs and global reach to gain control of the U.S. government. These puppet-masters are a gigantic organization known as Manchurian Global, which is involved with such mysterious and seemingly unrelated activities as "medical biotherapeutics," "urban commercial property reclamation," and "complex text recognition nanotechnology." The firm engages in all manner of what on the surface appear to be unobjectionable and even noble acts, but which invariably occur in regions plagued by both political instability and a bounty of oil and other natural resources.[2] Like something out of a James Bond movie, its secret goal is to rule the world and is depicted as a villain *par excellence* not simply because of what it does but because of how easily it is able to deceive a seemingly free society.

The striking thing about *The Manchurian Candidate* is that we have literally seen this movie before. It is a remake of a film from an earlier era, when fear was also great but what was feared was quite different.

The general story outline—secret plotters manipulating decision-makers at the highest levels of the U.S. government to achieve ultimate power—is retained, but there is a new villain in the early years of the 21st century. Whereas the 1962 version, written at the height of the Cold War, revolved around a plot by Communists, now it is a multinational corporation that seeks to undermine the Republic. Astonishingly, the movie even implies that the fictional corporation is responsible for a factual event (the September 11 attack on the Pentagon) for which a real person (Osama bin Laden) has in the real world actually taken public credit. To preserve the linkage to an earlier era, even the name of the corporation evokes, however clumsily, the original film.

That a more recent version of an admired film from an earlier era casts a corporation rather than an international communist movement as a conspiratorial mastermind is, as it were, no coincidence. It is rather a sign of an idea that is increasingly prominent in modern American and global public conversation. The idea is of large for-profit corporations as dark plotters exerting more and more control over the lives of average citizens—as marauding conquerors of the public space, desperately in need of control or even elimination by governments around the world. The idea and the movement it has spawned have not been much studied to date. But they merit such study because of their growing appeal.

There is fiction, of which *The Manchurian Candidate* is hardly the only example,[3] and then there is nonfiction. In 2002, the U.N. Commission on Human Rights published a document submitted to it by a variety of pressure groups. It alleges the following *modus operandi* for the world's multinational corporations:

a) the promoting of wars of aggression and interethnic conflicts in order to control the natural resources of the planet—in particular energy sources and strategic minerals—and to foster the growth and the profits of the war industry;

b) the violation of workers' rights and human rights in general;

c) the degradation of the environment (air, water, and soil included) and in particular the active and well-financed opposition by the Global Climate Coalition, comprising, among others Ford, GM (General Motors), Mobil, and Union Carbide, with the unflagging support of the government of the United States, to any limitation of emission of greenhouse gases (Kyoto Protocol);

d) the bribing of civil servants to take over essential public services (such as the supply of drinking water) through their fraudulent privatization and thus the elimination of the rights of present and potential users;

e) the appropriation—formally legal or illegal—of ancestral, technical, and scientific knowledge, which are by nature social entities;

f) the corruption of political and intellectual elites and of leaders of civil society;

g) the monopolization of the principal means of communication, purveyors of the dominant ideology and mass cultural products, in order to manipulate and condition public opinion and thus change the habits and behavior of people;

h) financing dictators, the overthrow of governments, and other criminal activities.[4]

The list of charges is startling in its breadth and its malevolent characterization of its targets. This idea that corporations control the world is an idea that, while of recent vintage, is carefully constructed, rapidly gathering strength, ultimately fallacious, and in the meantime very dangerous. To be sure, the idea that big business and the wealthy wield excessive influence is not new. Thomas Jefferson, among many other prominent Americans during the republic's infancy, was deeply skeptical of moneyed interests, which he felt threatened the agrarian foundations of individualism and hence of liberty itself. The following, from a letter to then Secretary of War (and later Secretary of the Treasury) William H. Crawford in June of 1816, is fairly representative of his sentiments:

The exercise, by our own citizens, of so much commerce as may suffice to exchange our superfluities for our wants, may be advantageous for the whole. But, it does not follow, that with a territory so boundless, it is the interest of the whole to become a mere city of London, to carry on the business of one half the world at the expense of eternal war with the other half. The agricultural capacities of our country constitute its distinguishing feature; and the adapting our policy and pursuits to that, is more likely to make us a numerous and happy people, than the mimicry of an Amsterdam, a Hamburgh, or a city of London. Every society has a right to fix the fundamental principles of its association, and to say to all individuals, that, if they contemplate pursuits beyond the limits of these principles, and involving dangers which the society chooses to avoid, they must go somewhere else for their exercise; that we want no citizens, and still less ephemeral and pseudocitizens, on such terms. We may exclude them from our territory, as we do persons infected with disease. Such is the situation of our country. We have most abundant resources of happiness within ourselves, which we may enjoy in peace and safety, without permitting a few citizens, infected with the mania of rambling and gambling, to bring danger on the great mass engaged in innocent and safe pursuits at home.[5]

Opposition to wealthy financial interests also loomed large in the support for Andrew Jackson, William Jennings Bryan, and other towering figures of American politics. But the issue this book explores is different in several respects, some of which are illustrated in Jefferson's letter above. In recent years, there has emerged an odd sort of ideology I will call (without claiming any particular originality of coinage) anti-corporatism. The new anti-corporatism harnesses the old tradition, as vivid in the United States as elsewhere, of skepticism of great wealth and merges it with ideology developed in subsequent years, partly rooted in the ideas of the 1960s New Left and even of Marxism. In the course of absorbing these belief systems, the ideology has become something new, a belief that the corporate form in particular is disastrous for human society. Taken to its limit, the new anti-corporatism depicts corporations as the central organizing fact of global governance and social life. Decent people must work to fight corporate dominance because the very nature of corporations requires their managers and owners to be loyal to Mammon at the expense of country or other higher moral purposes, incentives that do not drive other social groups. As Jefferson's attack on "ephemeral and pseudocitizens" demonstrates, there is some historical precedent for this idea. But in the new anti-corporatism, corporations, uniquely among all pressure groups, seek with increasing success to dominate governments, commerce, and other key institutions of society. They seek to subvert traditional social order, destroy democracy, promote irresponsible consumption, and even persuade states to wage wars on their behalf.

THE BIRTH OF A WORLDVIEW

The long-standing theme of the need for a crusade against a more general plutocracy has thus become the belief that large corporations in particular are the controllers of public policy, all-seeing and all-knowing, with the rest of society—workers, consumers, parents, children, the schools, the military—utterly in their thrall. Thus it is that the anti-corporate campaigner Lee Drutman can ask, in a fairly common remark, "How did corporations become the dominant institutions in our society, powerful behemoths with a hand in every almost every aspect of our lives?"[6] The use of an adjective such as "dominant," which like words such as "tyranny," "dictatorship," and "pathology" is found throughout the movement's literature, is striking. Corporations do not force us to buy their products, they do not conscript armies, they do not have the power to assess taxes under the penalty of imprisonment for nonpayment, they do not tell us whom we may marry or how many children we may have. They do not, in short, have disproportionate "power" if that term is taken to mean the ability to limit one's control over one's own life.[7] Their "power" arguably pales into insignificance next to that of peers, family, church, or state. As will be seen, there is some evidence that even in the political arena, their influence is far from excessive.

To be sure, there are many cases in which there are clear conflicts between the interests of some corporations and those of some other American interest groups—labor-management conflicts, pollution standards, who should pay how much in taxes, and the like. But what distinguishes anti-corporatism is its propensity to see the hidden hand of corporations in American or global problems far-flung from any obvious immediate concern of those firms, and even in fundamental reorganization of the way we live. Corporations are seen as the single most or even the only powerful force in governing the world. Such extreme anti-corporatism is rapidly metastasizing into more mainstream outlets as an explanation for why American and global society is the way it is.

And so global childhood obesity is increasing not because of broad changes in lifestyle involving exercise, the ready availability of calories, or other seemingly more direct causes but because of the pernicious effects of corporate advertising on parents and children.[8] Corporations with ties to the incumbent political establishment deviously manipulate electronic voting to steal U.S. elections.[9] Information corporations—movies, music, publishing, news, etc.—seek to crush distinct local cultural forms. The titanic, forty-year struggle that was the Cold War was fought, like most U.S. wars, for corporate interests rather than out of any devotion to profound political principles or more conventional national-security concerns.[10] On more recent questions of war and peace, corporate interests are also more and more said to call the tune.

Thus a writer for the eminently mainstream British newspaper *The Guardian* claims that the attack on Yugoslavia in 1999 by the North Atlantic Treaty Organization was not, as sensible people might suppose, because of exasperation over the inability to end violence against Kosovar Albanians by means other than war, or for the usual *raisons d'état*. Rather, it was because of a desire to hand the province's economy over to large mining and other corporations.[11] The argument requires, absurdly, that the governments of NATO were prepared to send their armed forces (primarily from the United States) into battle at tremendous expense to obtain control over one of the poorest areas of Europe, after having gone to great, temporizing lengths to avoid war in the months leading up to the bombing. That naval flotillas would be deployed and armed forces in Europe put on a war footing for such meager payoffs seem wildly implausible, yet these sorts of interpretations of recent military history, analogous to other interpretations of larger social trends, are gaining disturbing traction among intellectuals and activists worldwide.

Even September 11, and the dramatic change it brought in the willingness of the U.S. government and public to invoke military force independently of any sinister manipulation of the state by corporate forces,
is refracted, however tortuously, through the cracked prism of anti-
corporatism. The Iraq war is the clearest example. Many proponents
of the war in Iraq depicted it as a necessary campaign to construct a
consensually governed society in the heart of Arabia. Those inclined
toward a *realpolitik* theory of nation-state behavior argued that its primary
purpose, in conjunction with the war in Afghanistan, was to place over
100,000 troops in the center of an unstable Middle East. On the other
hand, many opponents argued that the war was fought without giving
diplomacy a chance, that it would sow chaos, that it violated international
law and the human rights of Iraqis, that it was conducted with insufficient
deference to the interests of other powers, and the like. These are all
reasonable arguments, and history may vindicate some or all of them.
But anti-corporate thinking sees Iraq entirely through the lens of corporate
interests. The placement in high national-security positions in the
government of many people with experience in military contracting is
not, as one might suppose, a way to capitalize on valuable expertise
but instead a chance for those officials to conspiratorially promote an
ever-expanding appetite for military hardware, where wars serve both to
test new weapons platforms and to use up weapons stockpiles, promoting
an unceasing demand for yet more weapons.[12]

John Kenneth Galbraith, the late professor of economics at Harvard,
was always something of an outsider looking in with bemusement on
the mainstream of his profession. But he was for decades one of the most
well-known and widely read economists in the English-language world,
justly celebrated for the ingenuity of his insights and the quality of his
writing. He was not an orthodox economist, but he was a distinguished
public intellectual. And based on personal experience and the (accurate)
observation that former corporate executives are not hard to find at the
highest reaches of U.S. government, he in his last years deduced that
corporations are a prime driving force behind U.S. government decisions
on war and peace:

> The corporate appropriation of public initiative and authority is
> unpleasantly visible in its effect on the environment, and dangerous
> as regards military and foreign policy. Wars are a major threat to
> civilized existence, and a corporate commitment to weapons pro-
> curement and use nurtures this threat. It accords legitimacy, and
> even heroic virtue, to devastation and death...As the corporate
> interest moves to power in what was the public sector, it serves
> the corporate interest. It is most clearly evident in the largest
> such movement, that of nominally private firms into the defense

establishment. From this comes a primary influence on the military budget, on foreign policy, military commitment and, ultimately, military action. War. Although this is a normal and expected use of money and its power, the full effect is disguised by almost all conventional expression.[13]

Indeed, corporations are on occasion simultaneously blamed both for geopolitical X and –X, as when the Unocal corporation and the American government purportedly doing its bidding were vilified first for propping up the Taliban so as to promote the construction of an oil pipeline, then for overthrowing the Taliban so as to promote the construction of an oil pipeline. In March 2001, six months before the September 11 attacks, Reuel Marc Gerecht could argue in an opinion piece in *The New York Times* that, "In 1996, it seemed possible that American-built gas and oil pipelines from Central Asia could run through an Afghanistan ruled by one leader. Cruelty to women aside, we did not condemn the Taliban juggernaut rolling across the country." Meanwhile, having reported on October 7, 2001, literally hours before the U.S. attack on Afghanistan began, that the U.S. government in fact had long supported the Taliban in order to facilitate a pipeline, the same news agency, Agence France-Presse, could then report on October 11, once the attack had begun, that "experts say the end of the Islamic militia could spell the start of more lucrative opportunities for Western oil companies."[14]

That respectable news organizations could so uncritically relay such compellingly dark and often contradictory charges of corporate malfeasance is a key part of the story told in these pages. One could hardly imagine a charge about other groups in the United States orchestrating government policy to such a degree not undergoing more scrutiny. To be sure, the American political conversation always been full of voices making astonishing claims about the ability of this or that sinister group to dictate, often behind the scenes, American and global public policy and the nature of life in the United States. But anti-corporatism has respectability and influence that these other voices do not. It is difficult to imagine assertions about the power of the Socialist International (which still exists and is still a focus of marginal conspiracist tales about American politics), Jews, the United Nations, or the other usual suspects in the more outlandish theories about how the world *really* works achieving such a respectable presence.

This view would thus be of little interest if it were as far out on the fringe as these other conspiracy theories. But the anti-corporatist theme is far more prevalent both in the media and in the academy than other analogous theories of all-controlling forces.

The belief in corporate control of the government, of universities, of the media, and of the other most consequential institutions of American society is by no means a majority one, but it is on the rise. And the public footprint of anti-corporatism is larger than its current prevalence in politics suggests, owing to the extent to which it is believed by those who traffic in ideas—journalists, intellectuals, and the like. There are, for example, hundreds of American university syllabi skeptically invoking the phrase "corporate power." In the primary debates during the nomination process for the 2004 Democratic nominee, "corporate," "the corporate culture," "corporate agriculture," and "big corporate America" were among the favorite terms of opprobrium. In a May, 2003, debate in Columbia, South Carolina, for instance, four candidates—John Edwards, Richard Gephardt, Howard Dean, and John Kerry—used some variation of the word "corporate" seventeen times. Sen. Edwards led the pack with twelve uses, including four uses (in addition to "pharmaceutical companies," "big insurance companies," and "big HMOs") in a single answer to a question that originally asked how access to health care might be increased.

Given that politicians now generally use such statements only after they have been carefully rehearsed using the modern technology of political campaigns, it is no surprise that there is broader disquiet among the public as well. A survey of Americans released in October, 2005, by the Pew Center for the People and the Press found that 45 percent of Americans had a very or mostly unfavorable view of corporations, a number that has been rising since 1997 and is at the highest level in the twenty years in which they have asked the question. Another Pew Center survey in 2003 found that 77 percent of Americans completely or partly believed that "too much power is concentrated in the hands of a few big companies." While this number has been constant since 1987, the number of true believers, those who completely (rather than partly) agree with the statement (a number indicating hard-line anti-corporate sentiment), has risen over the same interval from 27 to 40 percent. And anti-corporatism may have some force as a wedge issue. In the 2003 survey, two-thirds of independents said they believe "business corporations make too much profit," as compared with 72 percent of Democrats and only 46 percent of Republicans. Somewhat astonishingly, given that the former can only use the information to sell products and the latter can use it to put someone in prison, 77 percent of respondents were "concerned that business is collecting too much information on me," while only 57 percent believed the same about government.[15] Government of course already collects vast, non-anonymous employment and financial information as an indispensable part of the American tax code, as any perusal of the 1040 forms quickly illustrates. Objections to the income tax are seldom expressed in privacy terms, although if the same standard is applied to government as is applied to corporations, they certainly should be.

To be fair, responses to simple polling questions such as these are not the same as complete acceptance of anti-corporatism as it will be portrayed here. But their increasing prevalence nonetheless suggests a bullish future for that more extreme ideology, particularly in certain ideological communities in the industrialized world. In addition, even if the movement itself fades into insignificance, its relatively rapid coalescence around a few themes, and the prominence it has quickly achieved among intellectuals, makes it worthy of contemporaneous documentation. The chances that it will fade away in the near future are slight. If anything, political pressure for global regulation of corporate conduct, in ways that would never be contemplated for any other pressure group in society, is growing. The United Nations, for example, is currently contemplating whether it should establish norms governing corporate conduct and whether those norms will have the same legal force under international law as more traditional treaty obligations do. (There is no contemplation of similar regulation of labor unions, ethnic-advocacy groups, religious organizations, etc.) If anti-corporatism informs these deliberations (and it does), its views are important.

Anti-corporate views do not coincide perfectly with traditional ideological categories. To the extent that the left/right continuum is a useful way to talk about the issue (in that in the United States, "left" and "right" mean different things than in other industrial democracies), anti-corporatism is in the United States mostly associated with the left. But in recent years, elements of the American right have also latched onto anti-corporatism, jettisoning the standard position of modern American conservatism that favors limited regulation of business. Patrick J. Buchanan's three presidential campaigns were built in part on right-wing populism, and in particular a belief that corporate desire to increase profits combined with corporate control of the U.S. government led them to promote globalization and its alphabet soup of enforcement bodies—the North American Free Trade Area, the World Trade Organization, etc. Unlike the left, which is concerned about corporate despoiling of the environment, elimination of global cultural diversity, and excessive wealth held by a small minority, the anti-corporate right is concerned about dilution of American identity and culture through globalization, in addition to the punishment of the working class when factories and people in search of work and opportunity easily move from one end of the earth to another.

But both wings of the ACM (anti-corporate movement) find themselves united in their concern about the loss of "national sovereignty" to the largest global corporations. This term typically means the ability of national governments to regulate and manage the behavior of their citizens, which has allegedly been surrendered to multilateral organizations ruled by multinational corporations. But both wish the government to exercise its sovereignty in different ways. What the left-wing and the right-wing anti-corporatists would do if they gained the ability to use the "sovereign" power of the American government differs, but their beliefs about what stands in their way is the same—Exxon/Mobil, Microsoft, and GM. To be fair, despite some sense of common cause in curbing corporate power, some on the currently more prominent anti-corporate left have expressed concern about the dangers of allying with a nativist right.[16] But the core beliefs about the nature of corporations—that they are disloyal, even traitorous, and control many if not most major world governments and the various international institutions responsible for managing the global economy—are the same in both camps, and so the assessment of those claims will affect equally the conclusions that both wings of the anti-corporatist movement draw.

HOW TO SOLVE PROBLEMS

The anti-corporate view is at its heart driven by a particular notion of how best to solve human problems. There are two ways to solve any particular political/economic problem, whatever it may be—vulnerability to military attack, inadequate allocations of medical treatment, giving citizens more living space than they currently possess, an improved national performance in the Olympic Games, *anything* that involves the use of scarce resources whose best use people disagree over. One approach is to rely on what goes by such terms as "the market," the "private sector," "property rights," "the price system," or "capitalism." In this approach, legal procedures are defined and enforced to give individuals meaningful control over a resource—the right to use it as they see fit or to transfer those rights to someone else to do as he sees fit. Reliance on this system to, say, improve disease treatment would require those who wish to see the problem addressed (not just patients, but insurance companies or charities) to make offers to resource owners to use those resources for that purpose—by funding research, by employing people to develop and distribute medicine, by hiring people to treat patients, and so on. Resources cannot be employed for any purpose without the consent of the people who own them. This consent requires giving the owner compensation— sometimes money, sometimes not—that provides more value to him than the use to which he would otherwise put these resources. Doctors and drug salesmen must be paid compensation that justifies the value of their time, insurers must pay out less in costs from covering a treatment than they ultimately pay by not covering it, donors to medical charities must feel that the emotional satisfaction from their generosity exceeds that from the alternate use to which the money would be put, and so on.

The other approach is to rely on politics, which presents a theoretical opportunity to implement the "public will," if such a thing exists. Indeed, in the eyes of its advocates, this is its strongest advantage. The market, in contrast, can only put resources to whatever uses their scattered, individual owners can be persuaded to accept. An airline, for example, will only provide wide seats and free champagne to passengers willing to pay great sums of money, in the form of first-class tickets. For everyone willing only to buy an economy-class ticket, travel will be less comfortable but (in historical terms) astonishingly reliable, safe, and affordable. The government, in contrast, may have the power (subject to the legal code in the particular country) to require that resources be used for particular purposes and on particular terms—that airlines not bump passengers without offering a full refund, that workers in any occupation earn at least a certain amount per hour, that ceilings be imposed on the prices of drugs, etc. Resources may even be devoted to this purpose or that based on an official vote of the public authorities, who may, for example, opt to nationalize private property or build an interstate highway system.

Of course no society operates in absolutes. In the United States, there are substantial rights to private property, but factory owners may not pollute at will, landowners may be prevented from using the property for particular purposes because of zoning codes, and so on. Even in a largely state-directed society like Cuba or North Korea some activities are relegated (sometimes unofficially) to the market, and other rationing devices—political influence, bribes paid, etc.—still determine how nominally state-directed resources are deployed. And so it is not a question of one or the other but of the degree of each.

Corporations are clearly a way, and an unusually efficient way, as will be demonstrated in Chapter 4, of relying on the market to decide who gets what. The primary defect of the market in the eyes of many is that it provides too many benefits to the rich or that resource owners otherwise make the "wrong" choices from the perspective of the broader society. How they are wrong is often not made clear; the choices are clearly right to the constituents of the corporation who buy from and sell (including sell their labor) to it. But one way of thinking about "wrong" is that in the eyes of a sufficiently large percentage of the public, resources could be better used. When individuals transacting through the market make such "wrong" choices, the power of the state may be used to alter them.

But it turns out that markets have a number of strengths, which are amplified in the corporate form. Markets allow people to capitalize on private knowledge that an official operating under government supervision would miss; a truck-company manager who notices that there are so many grocery deliveries to a particular location that it is straining the company's resources may choose to buy more trucks for use on that route, lowering the waiting time or the money price, or both, that consumers pay for groceries at that location. Such knowledge will be invisible to the head of a government trucking ministry, and indeed the public-sector equivalent of a private-sector trucking manager may find that he is punished rather than rewarded for making this inefficiency known. This kind of waste of local knowledge is part of the reason why communist societies historically used resources so badly and were thus so poor.

Markets also quickly liquidate mistakes. If the trucking company continually sends out trucks half-empty and refuses to change, it will be out-competed by companies that deliver the goods more efficiently. Waste—resource uses that deliver relatively little value at relatively high cost—is not tolerated when there is competition. And so it will turn out that the market generally does a much better job than politics of delivering and improving medicine and medical procedures, of allowing people or goods to get from point A to point B most efficiently, of making sure that excess goods that would otherwise ultimately go unsold and be thrown away aren't produced, and that there are no long waiting times for goods desired by other people. And it has the philosophical advantage of giving people the freedom to navigate their way through life by acquiring the consensual cooperation of others, as opposed to engaging in conflict with their fellow citizens to get the government to make this choice instead of that.

This last effect reflects another critical difference between solving problems through politics and through the market—the former emphasizes what economists call zero-sum thinking, and the other positive-sum. In zero-sum thinking, bad things happen to you because good things have happened to someone else, and your improvement can only come by damaging others. In positive-sum environments, people cooperate effectively for mutual gain. By definition, interaction in the market makes participants better off (although it might damage others not involved in a particular trade). Indeed, the extent to which such cooperation for mutual advantage has advanced human possibilities through economic progress is a story not as widely understood as it should be. Politics, in contrast, usually lends itself to zero-sum thinking and action. Because the tools of government so readily lend themselves to redistributing resources and privileges from one class of citizens to another, channeling activity into politics runs the risk of aggravating social conflict and of turning the society more into us vs. them. Whereas the market suggests that if an individual earns too little, he go out and seek other offers (or make choices that put him in a position to get better offers), politics tends to make him desire to go out and take earnings that, in his view, unfairly go to someone else. This group conflict is encoded into the very language of politics— the rich vs. the poor and the middle class, "big business" vs. "working people," "people of faith" vs. "secularists," men vs. women, and so on. There is a reason that politicians so often promise to "fight for" this or that constituency—because divide-and-conquer is frequently a successful strategy for politicians.

If we assume that cooperation is generally a good thing and conflict generally a thing to be avoided, it stands to reason that, other things equal, we prefer people to resolve their problems creatively and competitively through voluntary cooperation rather than in the I'm-up-you're-down logic that is inherent in politics. This is not to say that politics can never serve the general good. Sometimes, in circumstances outlined later, it is essential. But often reacting to and even creating or exacerbating social conflict is the order of the day in politics. It takes overwhelming competition among political jurisdictions or overwhelming public support to allow governments to break completely free from such factional warfare. Much long-standing government policy—the guarantees of individual rights, the provision of social insurance through the welfare state, etc.—is of this type. (The gradual global enactment of corporate law, it will be seen, is one such exception.)

But the market has many perceived weaknesses in the eyes of some—it provides too little of such goods as housing and medical care to the poor, it encourages people to buy things they don't really need, it generates excessive monopoly power for large corporations, etc. And so politics in this view should partly or even substantially substitute for the market—the law should require that firm size should be limited, that all corporate "stakeholders" have a guaranteed voice in running the corporation, that international trade be "fair," that the government actually own some productive facilities, etc. And the comparison of politics and the market as a way of solving problems however humans define them is a major theme of this book. The ACM believes in general that politics outperforms the market in solving human problems. I believe the opposite.

THE BOOK'S PLAN OF ATTACK

Anti-corporatism is a relatively new social movement, a distinct set of claims requiring a particular plan of analysis. Readers who are at least somewhat familiar with the charges made against corporations, without being as familiar with their historic and economic context, will benefit from understanding precisely what a corporation is and why it is so fervently criticized. Chapters 2 and 3 lay out the history of the corporation and the ACM. Chapters 4–7 analyze the movement's most important claims. Chapter 4 both presents widely accepted and some new economic analysis of corporations, which is generally but not entirely positive. Chapter 5 explores the claim that corporations dominate democracy, Chapter 6 investigates globalization and the corporate role in it, and Chapter 7 investigates the corporate rule in culture, broadly defined.

The ACM relies, whether it knows it or not, on a number of questionable assumptions that will come up again and again in the analysis; it is best to present those themes now. While not empirical claims in and of themselves, these often unexamined beliefs motivate the claims the movement makes, even if they are unacknowledged within its literature. The movement first has a deep, almost romantic attachment to *local self-reliance* as the ideal form of human social organization. The moral society is small, personal, and self-sufficient; it does not depend on anonymous corporate production from the other side of the world. To acquire a mass-produced product from someone in China to whom you have no cultural connection is a strange and immoral act when compared to buying things produced locally, ideally by people you know and at a minimum by people who are close enough so that a nearby government can regulate your commercial dealings. Locality *is* morality, and one of the primary themes of anti-corporate criticism is that the very structure of multinational corporate trading networks disrupts these precious local ties.

Fear of standardization is a second theme. One of the primary indictments of a corporate-run world is its imposition of a single cultural pattern on a diverse humanity. In addition, the penetration of corporate brands throughout the world is seen as insidious and dehumanizing. In both cases, there is a profound hunger for distinctions and diversity, which corporations are forced by their very nature to destroy. Cultural uniformity isn't simply an unfortunate by-product of corporate marketing to consumers, but an actual corporate-designed and corporate-desired outcome.

And this is why Laura Barnett, a performance artist in New York City, can create an exhibit in which people publicly display anonymous confessions from their private lives and thoughts, and describe one of the exhibit's virtues as is its contribution to fighting dreary corporate-imposed uniformity. "My goal was to have people reveal their innermost thoughts and in a way that is entirely confidential," she notes. "What I found through this project is that no matter how much corporate culture tries to homogenize its citizens, people to the core try to reveal themselves on a basic level."[17] Our culture is "corporate" and is homogenized by corporate design. Corporations, for reasons of standardization, seek to brainwash people all around the world into becoming a sort of robotic global consumer, who mindlessly shuffles along in his Nikes and Manchester United or Los Angeles Lakers jersey from McDonald's to Wal-Mart to the corporate multiplex cinema in an orgy of pointless, brand-conscious consumption. The world becomes a dreary, uniform place where Atlanta looks like Osaka, Osaka looks like Mexico City, Mexico City looks like Moscow, and Moscow is simply Atlanta with domed churches and long winters. The food is the same, the music is the same, and (most ominously) the news is the same, the product of the soulless corporate (or corporate-controlled) journalists at CNN, The New York Times, and the other outlets of Big Media.

A third tacit belief of the ACM is a preference for *collectivity* in thinking about corporations and the world they inhabit. By "collectivity" I mean the habit of making groups of individuals rather than individuals themselves the fundamental unit of analysis. All the world's corporations in particular are a collective entity that have a single, common interest and that decides collectively how to pursue that interest. In this pursuit, they disrupt "communities," "workers," and other collectives. Even financial markets are seen (in contrast to most theories of such markets) as a unitary actor, with a unitary set of objectives, whether the markets go up or down, whether they favor some industries or others. The prices for stocks, bonds, and currencies are not driven by global flows of capital aggregating the beliefs of millions of atomistic traders, but a single tool in the hands of a monolithic corporate sector. Traders don't buy or sell, "the market" does. "The market" forces governments to change economic policies when their currencies collapse or their stock markets feverishly fall. But a different way of thinking about corporations and the markets in which they trade is in terms of individuals—the individuals (often with conflicting interests) who work for corporations, the individuals who buy their products, the individuals who buy and sell their shares, and so on. Such an approach will ultimately be more fruitful in understanding how corporations add to (and, occasionally, subtract from) society. That corporations and free commerce more generally might actually liberate *individuals* in historically unprecedented ways is another important claim of this book.

The movement also asserts that there is a broad, universal, obvious yet never explicitly deduced or verified outcome known as the *"public good,"* against which is placed the private, selfish interest of corporations. In the modern world, the natural tendency of any human collective, whether it is the local community seeking self-reliance, or a nation-state seeking to govern itself, to pursue the public good, is frustrated by corporate power. The early Hobbesian conception of man against man, or the idea found in the Federalist Papers that individuals of similar interests form *many* factions that can subvert freedom through factional warfare or capture of the state, is not to be found in anti-corporatism. Instead, the conflict between the private interests that are corporations and the broader public interest made famous by Jean-Jacques Rousseau in *The Social Contract* is critical in the anti-corporate understanding of the world. The movement places great stock in particular in democracy as the means of ascertaining the universally acknowledged public good, and so democracy's alleged subversion by corporations becomes a profound crime. The controversy over the government as servant of the public will versus referee among private interests is a long one in Western political philosophy. While both approaches have value, the ACM comes down squarely on the side of the former belief.

This is in part due to the influence in the newer wings of the ACM of what is known as systems theory and complexity. The practitioners of such fields describe its virtue as its ability to analyze a collection of seemingly independent units–e.g., disparate organs in the case of the human body—as a whole. Rather than focusing on the individual as the unit of analysis, these branches of knowledge claim to be able to diagnose the overall way in which the entire system functions based on the behavior of its components. Humans, for example, are often depicted in anti-corporatist literature as members of an ecosystem, whose entire flow must be depicted for corporations and their effects to be properly understood. The irony is that mainstream economics, which anti-corporatism often views contemptuously, also claims to be able to describe results for an entire population—a nation, for example. The difference is that orthodox economics tends to reduce collectives, often by mathematical modeling that anti-corporatists reject as excessively simplistic, to the individual, which is the smallest possible unit for formal, rigorous analysis. In particular, economic modeling generally tries to diagnose how well off each individual can possibly be given the set of technological, ecological, resource, and other constraints he faces. The value of a particular form of social organization is explicitly derived from how well each individual fares under it and under the assumption that individual choice, which is explicitly described, determines the "system's" outcome. In systems theory, the most basic element that can be analyzed is some aggregation above the individual—corporations, workers, and communities, rich and poor nations, or a series of disjoint "cultures" whose integrity is threatened by multinational commerce. A description of how these components interact is assumed to be sufficient to describe the welfare properties of the entire system, with little attention paid to how flesh-and-blood individuals, with different goals, beliefs, and means, would fare if the world were changed in the way the ACM desires. The "system" either functions well or does not, and if it does not, it is because of the misbehavior of one of its abstract components—corporations in this case.

Alas, the trouble with "systems" is that they are often too complex to reengineer, so that tinkering with them causes consequences the tinkerer didn't expect. As Virginia Postrel notes in her 1998 book *The Future and Its Enemies,* "A city, an economy, or a culture is, despite the best efforts of stasists, fundamentally a 'natural' system. As a whole, it is beyond anyone's control."[18] Systems surprise us. Our efforts to regulate them from on high mean that we face a future with unexpected, unpredictable costs and invisible but often substantial foregone benefits. In the concluding chapter, I will try to speculate on what some of those might be if the ACM gets much of what it wants.

These broad anti-corporate themes are moral and philosophical at least as much as empirical. They are also the sorts of things about which reasonable people can surely differ. A final tacit belief that is somewhat more disturbing is the way the movement thinks about how people choose, an assumption of *human passivity.* Anti-corporatists often believe that individuals' opinions, dreams, desires, and choices are soft and very subject to manipulation by others, particularly slick corporate marketers. People (anti-corporate activists conspicuously excepted) are passive recipients of whatever toxic advertising and branding trickery corporations choose to pour into them. Even reporters who work for "corporate media" or researchers tainted by "corporate funding" unavoidably do corporate bidding. (Whether due to corruption or fear is seldom specified.) Rather than carefully assessing moral trade-offs or evidence necessary to make choices, people are susceptible to tactics designed to make them see things as corporations want them to be seen. In doing so, the movement largely rejects the model of human cognition most widely used in economics and political science, that of rationality—the ability of individuals to rank choices in accordance with their preferences and to make the choices that for them are best. If people are rational and corporations meaningfully compete (and anti-corporatism disputes both claims), then corporations over the long run cannot continue to deceive them into making choices that, absent such trickery, they would not make. To anti-corporatists, this rationality is vulnerable on two counts— because human cognition is empirically not perfectly rational (a true but limited claim) and because the movement (erroneously) equates rational pursuit of one's self-interest with greed, which is actually something quite different. However, in criticizing that model of decision-making, the movement unknowingly adopts a far more dismal one—one where the individual and his dreams are nowhere to be found.

These hidden beliefs of anti-corporatists decisively shape how the movement has come to think about corporations. At the leading edge of the movement, the world is the way it is because of the results of a plan orchestrated by a relatively small number of people who staff or own the world's largest corporations. Such views are contrast to the kind of thinking, best exemplified by Charles Darwin in biology and the Nobel laureate Friedrich von Hayek in economics, that the future unfolds the way it does because of huge numbers of reactions by the atoms of society to their changing and complex circumstances. Those atoms—species or genes in biology, citizens (as buyers and sellers) here—constantly experiment, and experiments well-suited to the surrounding environment succeed while others fail. What we observe in the world around us is thus the result of a sequence of unimaginably large numbers of these experiments. Corporations, like many other social institutions, are an example of such an adaptation. This assertion of corporations as evolutionary best response is known to the movement, which adamantly rejects it, and so part of the task of the final chapter is to summarize why we have corporations and then to tie the book's findings together in order to predict the likely future of anti-corporate thinking, explore its internal coherence, and how the world may change if enough people believe in it.

NEITHER DEVILS NOR ANGELS

Finally, it is best to be explicit that I do not depict corporations as angels. While, as will be seen, there are many compellingly beneficial tasks that corporations can achieve better than other forms of social organization, corporations are fundamentally the same as other groups. They—or, more properly, the individuals whose actions and choices determine how they behave—can and do perform acts in their own self-interest that are also of tremendous value to the rest of society, and they also engage in behavior that merits the condemnation it receives when the ACM points it out. Corporations certainly do not seek to increase people's control over their own lives, to help remove hundreds of millions from poverty, to lessen ethnic conflict. Nor, despite their public-relations releases, do they always seek to be "socially responsible." What they usually seek to do is to maximize their profits. But it turns out that many of these beneficial results are achieved as a result of this pursuit of money, even as the ACM adopts a singularly dismal model of the corporation that does not in the end withstand scrutiny. And so the goal in evaluating the movement's claims is to suggest alternative ways of thinking about corporations that see them as they are, for good and for ill.

It is finally also necessary to place the movement I describe in proper context. The story told here is not about populism, the American belief that a set of *individuals*—rapacious plutocrats and their corrupt lackeys in government—run the government for their own purposes. Because, as suggested above, this is a recurring theme in American political contests, there is nothing historically distinct about politicians or public intellectuals inveighing against the "powerful." Nor is it an evaluation of the prevailing distribution of income and wealth in the United States or the world—an argument that it should or should not be more equal. Instead, the study's objective is to describe and evaluate anti-corporatism as a distinct and increasingly important American and global social movement.

Chapter 2

A Brief History of the Corporation

The corporation—large or small—is without question the dominant business form in the most globalized and modern societies. The law that governs it differs from country to country but has many fundamental components that are the same everywhere. The size and economic importance of some corporations are great, although less, relative to other social institutions, than the ACM asserts. Where did this innovative, immensely successful (in its ability to replicate) institution come from? The ACM has an accepted history of the corporation, whose details differ depending on the telling. Its members note, accurately, that corporations were for much of their history a pure creature of the state, with charters that were either granted for fixed terms or could be repealed at any time. A corollary belief is that corporations often did lose their charters when they acted against the public interest. The creation of the modern, unaccountable corporation allegedly took place in the 1800s, largely as a result of corrupt shenanigans involving rich businessmen and governments. Corporations during this period were redesigned to be accountable only to shareholders. In this narrative, this redesign led to catastrophic incentives and, in conjunction with corporate takeover of governments, disproportionate corporate influence in and even control of the world, particularly the advanced democratic societies that might be expected to confront this new power. And thus the task at hand is to restore the corporation to its proper place by placing it back under the control of society.

As will be seen, this is a tale that is deficient in several respects. The full development of anti-corporate thought is presented in the next chapter; this one is devoted to a brief history of the modern corporation.[1] It is best to be clear about what the "modern corporation" is. I will identify, largely in agreement with the ACM, three main characteristics. The first is *share-holding*—firms are owned by stockholders, who have the authority to make decisions about how to operate the company (which they may delegate to managers) and are compensated from corporate revenues in the form of dividends. A related aspect of many modern corporations is that ownership shares are widely dispersed. Huge numbers of them are created, and they are often held in very small fractions by thousands or even millions of individuals. The second characteristic is *limited liability*—shareholders are responsible for corporate debts only to the extent of share ownership, and their personal property cannot be attached for judgments against the firm. The third feature, *personhood,* means that the corporation possesses many of the rights that individuals do—the right to contract, most importantly. But corporate personhood departs from its literal equivalent in that the corporation can have permanence—i.e., it may outlive those who originally create it or who compose its current governing authorities. The corporation, in principle, can live forever. (Both personhood and limited liability may be employed without issuance of shares by corporations as small as a single individual—an accountant or other small-business owner, for example.)

The idea of dividing up initial investment capital among shareholders in exchange for shares of the profits is the most straightforward of the three features, and so unsurprisingly it is the oldest. There is nothing particularly Western or modern about such arrangements; many premodern civilizations developed them. Assyrian documents from the second millennium B.C. show a partnership arrangement in which shareholders floated money to be invested by a single manager, and the Roman Republic had its *societate, collegia licita,* and *publicani,* which involved various combinations of state chartering and personhood, including permanence. These were used for civic, religious, and public-contracting purposes. (Roman merchants and artisans formed groups sometimes called *corpora,* with the Latin term for "body" forming the root of the modern term. These bodies, licensed by the state, were more akin to medieval guilds or modern professional associations, having the effect of restricting rather than promoting competition.) The Arabs had their *muqarada,* which allowed for ventures to be funded through profit sharing in order to avoid the Islamic prohibition on interest. (The term is still used today to refer to an arrangement giving the investor the right to a share of profits, exposure to risk of loss, and no voting power in firm governance.) The Société des Moulins du Bazacle (Bazacle Mills Co.) in France issued shares in a watermill c.1200, which traded under a variety of names for centuries until the French government nationalized the mill shortly after World War II. While centralized locations for trading debt securities such as those of city-states in Italy already existed, the first exchange for trading stock shares is variously credited to Lyon (c. 1540), Antwerp (in the mid-1400s), and Amsterdam (in the early 1600s). In the 1500s and 1600s, some expeditions from the maritime Italian city-states were financed by shareholding partnerships.

Note too that in the original Roman and later European meaning, "corporations" could be any collection of people wishing to organize for a particular purpose over a period of time; a charter did not have to involve commercial activity. Among the earliest recipients of corporate charters was the University of Cambridge shortly after its founding in the early thirteenth century. The Royal Society, Britain's long-standing organization devoted to the advancement of scientific knowledge, received its initial charter in 1661. Most of the early American colonies were founded as chartered corporations of a sort. Even now, some American states employ the term "corporation" in lieu of "city" in their laws. Corporations, thus, were never (and are not now) exclusively about profit-seeking. Rather, the corporate charter is a way to enable people to pursue their shared interests, of which the pursuit of profit is merely an example.

But, critically, surviving records suggest that at least in Europe for-profit corporations were arrangements that, like most large-scale commercial activity over these centuries, required explicit permission of the sovereign and were state-granted monopolies. Under Henry III, England gave such a charter to the Staple of London to control that country's wool trade; ultimately future monarchs would call on the Staple for loans in exchange for the continuation of the privilege. Such charters were granted to many of the seagoing voyages during the Age of Exploration, and shares of these ventures were publicly traded. And it was such chartering that launched the first giant multinational corporations, the Dutch and British EICs (East India Companies), which forever changed the scale of what could be achieved in a commercial enterprise.

THE RISE OF SPECIAL-PRIVILEGE CORPORATIONS

The DEIC (Dutch East India Company) was founded in 1602 on the basis of a monopoly granted (at that time for a temporary period, although it was continuously renewed until the company's demise almost two centuries later) by the Dutch Parliament for trade in Asia. Like many corporations today, it manufactured little but nonetheless performed the critical economic function of matching buyers in one location and sellers in another. Much of its trade involved transporting precious metals from Spanish colonial mines to India and China, which were traded for textiles from India and China, which were either brought back to Europe, sold elsewhere, or traded for spices in Asia. It for many years maintained the trading center near Nagasaki, which was the only outpost for Europeans during the centuries in which the Tokugawa regime forcibly imposed isolation on its Japanese subjects. It was also responsible for exposing residents of several of its Asian outposts to European culture and technology. Although it would never have occurred to anyone to make such a criticism then, such practices resembled the cultural exposure brought by modern multinationals based in advanced countries and operating in developing ones, exposure that as we will see is sometimes characterized as cultural imperialism. The DEIC also introduced the innovation of issuing company shares that were not only tradeable but that paid dividends at fixed intervals based on all its combined activity. The joint-stock company (i.e., a company that issued tradeable shares) did not yet possess limited liability, but it did possess the other two features of the modern corporation. It ultimately established trading outposts in what are now Iran, India, Malaysia, Indonesia, China, and (most famously) Manhattan.

The BEIC (British East India Company) was built from similar motivations upon its founding in 1600, as the potential profits from the trade in silver, cotton, and spices among the Spanish New World, India, and what is now Indonesia motivated its founders to ask for and get approval from Queen Elizabeth I to monopolistically set up trade in the islands surrounding India. (The company ultimately diversified into, among other things, the opium trade in China and the east-moving slave traffic from Madagascar to India, demonstrating that corporations provide whatever is valued very efficiently. Trade that is valuable to some buyer can still be trade that is immoral.) Like its Dutch counterpart, the BEIC engaged in activities of tremendous risk and incurred occasional unexpected and disastrous costs—e.g., ships were lost to storms and cargoes to pirates and significant numbers of their crews died at sea. (One of their customers, the Sultan of Achin, is said to have demanded an English woman for his harem, which the Company found for him only to have King James I forbid the transfer.) Unlike the Dutch company, which had the already sophisticated financial markets of Amsterdam at its disposal, the BEIC had to issue shares in each voyage.

The two EICs collectively changed the face of the joint-stock company, despite their ignominious end. (The DEIC could not meet its obligations when the Dutch government fell into financial crisis after the outbreak of the 1780 war with Britain. Its payments were ultimately guaranteed by the Dutch government, but it was shut down in 1796 after losing most of its Asian territories to the British with the eruption of yet another war against them in 1795 and the conquest of The Netherlands by Napoleon. The BEIC lost its monopoly power in 1813 by an Act of Parliament but continued to rule parts of India until it lost first this right and then its remaining properties following the Sepoy Rebellion of 1857.) Their first achievement was the demonstration of the feasibility of coordinating economic activity all over the planet via a single organization. The second was the funding of such a large enterprise through the issuance of shares.

While there was much yet to be done to achieve the modern corporation, a big part of the basic form was now in place. Such joint-stock companies did not yet generally have limited liability, but they were already an important economic phenomenon.

And yet the era of the two EICs was darker, as they wielded authority that even much of the modern ACM does not (yet) attribute to modern corporations. By 1670, the BEIC having established trading posts on the Indian mainland after agreements negotiated with the Moghul emperor in 1615, it then received the right from King Charles II to maintain and use military forces and govern territory. During the next several decades, it acquired territory in India, and its troops fought the French there during the Seven Years' War. Dutch and British troops fought over spice concessions in what is now Indonesia, culminating in the Amboyna Massacre in which Dutch soldiers tortured and killed survivors of their attack on a BEIC factory there, poisoning Dutch and British relations for years. After the Battle of Plassey in 1757, the BEIC in essence was the privatized government of much of India, as Britain's victory in that faraway little war left the company in a dominant position on the continent with respect to other European armies. It drew up laws and set up a court system to administer them; it levied taxes and raised military forces. It was not until a series of ever more restrictive laws enacted from 1773 to 1833 that the British crown obtained full sovereignty over the subcontinent. (Recall the famous saying by the British historian Sir John Robert Seeley that the British Empire was built in a fit of absent-mindedness.) These laws brought to an end a period of almost a century in which an entire civil and criminal code had been created and administered by a private company.[2]

The DEIC had an analogous if less dramatic experience as it built its mercantile empire in Java. Indigenous political turmoil and internecine warfare in Java caused the firm to hire military forces, partly for its own defense and partly for conquest, which came to the aid of the crown prince of the Javanese region of Banten during one such struggle in 1684, resulting in the de facto establishment of company sovereignty. This sovereignty, which extended to the freedom to establish garrisons and the exaction of tribute from various Javanese rulers, was expanded until it covered most of the island by 1753. The company's officials proceeded to overtax the country's soil and other resources, and after French forces took over the Netherlands, the company's charter was allowed to lapse.

Clearly, if ever there was a case of corporate "power," it was supplied by the example of the two EICs. And while they were amassing their empires, two episodes of another sort of abuse arose elsewhere, one of which prompted the British government to misdiagnose the disease and hence prescribe the wrong medicine. Both involved stock-market bubbles and financial double-dealing by the managers of large joint-stock companies. The first centered around France's Mississippi Company. The Scottish financier John Law had persuaded his friend, King Louis XV, to allow him to set up a French national bank in 1715 to issue paper currency, before then unknown in France. The French government in effect subsidized this act by requiring that taxes be paid in the new notes. Law's control of French paper currency led him to acquire French government bonds and to use these in turn to buy the Compagnie d'Occident, which he renamed the Mississippi Company. That company was granted a monopoly in trade with French North America and quickly acquired other monopoly trading companies, thus in a matter of a few years gaining control over almost the entire French colonial trade. (The currently fashionable claim that only with the invention of the Internet has the world become "fast" should perhaps be reevaluated in light of how quickly Law achieved his dominance.) Law knew an opportunity when he saw it and began to issue more company shares to pay out large dividends and to issue stock options, creating speculative mania in the company's shares across much of Western Europe, even as its acquisitions slowed down. But Ponzi's relentless arithmetic soon asserted itself, and the bubble collapsed in late 1720.

The more famous South Sea Company story differs in some particulars, but the basic ingredients—a trading company with monopoly privileges (with Spanish America, in this case), the issuance of company shares to be exchanged for sovereign debt, public "pumping" of the stock's value by its leaders, a vast inflation of shares and then the sudden burst of the bubble—were the same. As share prices were beginning to fall, Parliament passed the Bubble Act in 1720, which practically outlawed the creation of new joint-stock companies, requiring that they possess an explicit charter. (At least one work contends that the Act was actually corruptly motivated by a desire to keep the bubble going by preventing new firms from competing for investment funds.[3]) That getting such a charter was so costly and risky largely eliminated the incentive to create such shareholding companies. The Act would ultimately be repealed in 1825, and its repeal will turn out to be an informative development.

Corporations serving as explicit governments, manufactured demand for ultimately worthless shares, corporate abuses of basic human rights (some chartered corporations engaged in the slave trade and other abuses in the colonies, which reached their nadir with the monstrous behavior of King Leopold II's private holding company in the Belgian Congo in the 1880s)—the litany of abuses sounds like something that could have been rolled out in an anti-corporate press release today. And yet the corporations of this era were different in a single, critical way from those that we know today—they were what I will call special-privilege corporations. Their entry into a line of business required permission from a national government, which they obtained typically in exchange for income from the resulting venture. Such revenue would, of course, be much greater if the firm had a monopoly in a particular region or activity, which the government was all too eager to grant. Such corruption would be familiar to anyone who must deal with modern shakedowns by officials in today's more flagrantly corrupt countries. In essence, these corporations were built on bribes paid to important government officials (often heads of state themselves) in order to get in on a lucrative business. These firms needed a critical input beyond labor, ships, fuel, etc. that only the sovereign possessed—a piece of paper, in the form of the charter, that entrepreneurs were required to purchase to obtain permission to engage in the business in the first place, a tradition the new United States would inherit from the British.[4]

Such events—bribes paid in exchange for special privileges in the form of monopoly charters—were common, and the extortion inherent in the special-privilege corporation is a classic case of what economists call rent-seeking. This is a term that has achieved such condemnatory power that economically literate people now affix it to any activities they dislike, but when coined it referred exclusively to the devotion of resources to obtaining special government favors.[5] The rent-seeking problem derives from the fact that government officials uniquely possess the power of coercion, the ability to impose fines or imprisonment (or worse) if their rules are not followed. Officials who possess the power to restrict or ban trading opportunities are thus in possession of a key resource—their permission. Just as we would expect workers to auction their labor to the highest-paying employer and investors to auction their funds to the projects perceived to have the highest return, so government officials who have the power to distribute special privileges all too frequently auction them off to the highest-bidding supplicant. Indeed, whereas a laborer's power to sell more of his time is constrained by his need to eat, sleep, etc., the ability of government officials to create special privileges and permission requirements is practically limitless, which is what makes the heavily interventionist state so dangerous. Having discovered that they may exact bribes by requiring, for example, that businesses that wish to import a particular item obtain an import license from a government official, they may then extend those licensing requirements to many other imports and indeed to many activities that do not even require imports. Unsurprisingly, governments that intervene more heavily in the economy are well-known to be more corrupt.[6]

And so in the age of special-privilege corporate charters, it was common for government officials to demand significant portions of the monopoly profits. We saw above that the Staple of London was used to obtain loans for the English king from the charter holders. The chief minister of Louis IV and architect of the modern French bureaucracy Jean-Baptiste Colbert extracted tribute on the king's behalf in exchange for the charter to the French East India Company. Such rent-seeking has nothing to do with any autocratic nature of the governments seeking the rents per se but is intrinsic to any process whereby government officials use their unique powers to hand out special privileges. (Such democratic societies as Brazil and India and, in the form of campaign-finance shakedowns, the United States are afflicted with corruption problems just as surely as more autocratic ones such as China.) The monopoly grants of the special-privilege era frustrated free commerce and generated artificially high rates of return for both those businesses that held the privileges and those government officials who dispensed them, which in turn raised the incentive for kings and ministers to seek yet more rents. The Bubble Act, by making it *harder* to compete with existing charter holders (including the South Sea Company) via the establishment of new joint-stock companies, was actually a step backward. The demise of the special-privilege corporation is a key episode in the history of the corporation, a development never noted by the ACM when it recounts these older abuses.

THE CONSTRUCTION OF THE OPEN-ACCESS CORPORATION IN AMERICA, BRITAIN, AND BEYOND

In the early days of the American republic, the special-privilege model was the only one that existed. To the anti-corporate romanticists, this was an era when the corporate charter was a tool to be mobilized for achieving some great public purpose such as a canal or road network and was revocable at the whim of democratically elected legislatures in the pursuit of the public interest.[7] But, in fact, the ability of legislators to extract bribes in exchange for doling out special-privilege charters to those who sought them was immensely costly. As the economic historian David A. Moss describes it:

> [C]itizens wishing to incorporate had to make special appeals to the legislature. Lawmakers enjoyed complete discretion over the process, often wielding their authority with all the subtlety of a sledgehammer. Special favors, connections, and payoffs frequently made the difference in a rough-and-tumble political system where successful appeals were more the exception than the rule.[8]

And so the special-privilege corporation gave the chartered firm the ability to issue shares and to contract as a single entity in the manner of a person—but only at tremendous cost because of government corruption and the creation of artificial monopolies sheltered from entrepreneurial competition.

But in the early 1800s, the governments of the United Sates and the various states were also trying to devise ways to promote industrialization for purposes of countering British power and expanding the national territory and strength (as the Germans would do under Bismarck in the face of French power later in the century). A manufacturing base was seen as critical to economic vitality, and states sought all kinds of tools to promote one. Some of these measures involved direct subsidies to manufacturers, especially in New York and Massachusetts. In some sense, these states were carrying out primitive versions of what is now called industrial policy, but the mix of politics and risky investment was no more likely to succeed then than now, both because of the aforementioned corruption and because of the carelessness that naturally comes with spending other people's money (a problem that also afflicts modern corporations to some extent, as will be seen in Chapter 4).

But a number of more permanent legal innovations also occurred during this pursuit of economic development, some of which concerned the terms under which citizens could form corporations. In 1811, the New York legislature enacted a law of general incorporation, which meant that those wishing to incorporate—to create a legal "person" entitled to issue shares—did not need a special charter from the legislature but merely had to file pro forma paperwork with the state. Over a hundred manufacturing firms incorporated there over the next four years, vastly outstripping the pace before the law's enactment.

It is hard to overstate the magnitude of this change. With the establishment of a primitive form of open-access law (initially only available to some types of manufacturers but subsequently expanded), the registration of a joint-stock company by an ambitious entrepreneur no longer required him to navigate various political shakedowns. He could instead through stock issuance pursue any business idea that occurred to him. This was the key to ending the undeniable corporate abuses of the last two centuries. In all of its indictments of older corporations and criticisms of the ability of modern ones to function without continuously answering to the government, the ACM has completely missed the importance of being able to associate in an organized way for pursuit of profit without having to face kings demanding favors. This was the key to ending the undeniable corporate abuses of the era. (The ultimate reason, for example, that the Boston Tea Party was launched in objection to the chartered BEIC's monopoly on tea sales in North America was not, as the ACM contends, that it had a corporate charter but that it was a special-privilege monopoly.[9]) By eliminating the prospect of such state-chartered monopolies, open-access incorporation completely changed the relation between risk-taking businessmen and the state. It transformed the special privilege of the few—access to the opportunity to pursue wealth—to a general right accessible to all. From this period on, anyone with the proper legal structure could start a corporation, no matter her last name, his race, or her goals. The development of open-access incorporation proved to be a powerful tool for individual liberation. And unsurprisingly, given their immediate and obvious payoffs in terms of the number of entrepreneurial ventures registered in the states that adopted open-access laws the earliest, such laws were widely duplicated.

But the firm was still vulnerable even if opening the business was easy, as long as renewing its charter was not. The New York law continued to make charters temporary, renewable every twenty years, and subject to revocation at any time in the interim. If such renewal is a formality and revocation unlikely absent clear corporate misconduct, this is obviously a nonissue, but what if it is not? What if, in contrast, the state chooses to arbitrarily revoke a charter for its own political and especially corrupt reasons? This dramatically raises the risk of incorporation, because the durability of the charter under which stakeholders make their various investments is only as good as the last election, the last political contribution, or the last mood swing of the monarch.

Given the risk that charter holders faced from arbitrary diktats from the state, the issue was inevitably litigated before the U.S. Supreme Court in an important case in the history of American corporate law, *Trustees of Dartmouth College v. Woodward.*[10] Dartmouth had been founded in 1769 by the Rev. Eleazar Wheelock to educate the children of American Indians in both the three Rs and Christianity. In order to enable his creation to accomplish these tasks, he saw, according to the charter ultimately granted by the colonial governor of New Hampshire under the ultimate authority of George III, "a necessity of a legal Incorporation in order to the safety and well being of Said Seminary, and its being capable of the tenure & disposal of Lands & bequests for the use of the same." The state of New Hampshire wished to alter the charter by changing the school's governance mechanisms in ways that essentially placed it under state control. The Dartmouth trustees sued and argued that this was a breach of contract, plain and simple. The controlling opinion authored by Chief Justice John Marshall noted that earlier cases had established that the state may not foist a new charter on an established corporation and reasoned thus that nor may it alter the existing one:

> It is probable that no man ever was, and that no man ever will be, the founder of a college, believing at the time that an act of incorporation constitutes no security for the institution, believing that it is immediately to be deemed a public institution, whose funds are to be governed and applied not by the will of the donor, but by the will of the legislature. All such gifts are made in the pleasing, perhaps, delusive, hope that the charity will flow forever in the channel which the givers have marked out for it. If every man finds in his own bosom strong evidence of the universality of this sentiment, there can be but little reason to imagine that the framers of our Constitution were strangers to it, and that, feeling the necessity

and policy of giving permanence and security to contracts, of withdrawing them from the influence of legislative bodies, whose fluctuating policy, and repeated interferences, produced the most perplexing and injurious embarrassments, they still deemed it necessary to leave these contracts subject to those interferences.[11]

In other words, the state, having agreed to authorize a right to transact as a corporation on certain terms, could not then change the rules midstream. The opinion also noted that had the government wished to exercise control over the activities carried out by Dartmouth, it could have established a public organization for this purpose but chose instead to issue a specific charter to Wheelock. Having promulgated an agreement with a private group instead, it had therefore made explicit promises, and those promises continued to be binding for as long as the corporation would exist. Holding the government to its word meant that trustees (or, later, directors and shareholders in for-profit corporations) could plan in greater confidence.

In the business context, the damage caused by allowing the state to pivot on a whim is obvious; the ability to trust the promises of the state, and hence the willingness to transact under its protection, would erode to almost nothing. Why would anyone in a remotely risky activity (and new business ventures are often already extraordinarily risky) take on that risk knowing that he was also incurring the extra risk of revocation of his ability to keep most of the profits if the idea succeeded? The extensive costs in poor countries when economic actors must trade without being able to draw on state protection of property and contract rights and thus to constantly be in danger of predatory behavior from government officials, i.e., when they must transact in the "informal economy," is an example of this phenomenon.[12] To make corporations temporary and subject to government interference in their basic operations, especially given the history of politicians doing precisely that for corrupt purposes, is a cure far worse than whatever disease exists. A major defect in anti-corporate thinking is its ignorance of public corruption and its corresponding equating of any legislative decision with the "public interest," a topic explored further in Chapter 5.[13]

The danger of believing that any change of the terms of a corporate charter must be something done in the public interest can be found in the very facts that led to the suit. New Hampshire had authorized the expansion of the number of trustees and given the power to appoint them to the governor, as well as placed the trustees themselves under a state-appointed board of overseers, motivating the trustees to sue. Had *Dartmouth* gone the other way, in other words, *it would have authorized the state takeover of a private university*. The risks of giving the state such authority are readily apparent, and that anti-corporate thinkers so bemoan this case in light of these facts is indicative of its limited understanding of how governments behave.

Dartmouth thus contributed to a common-law evolution that granted corporations some rights to be free from arbitrary treatment. In conjunction with the open-access laws rapidly spreading through the United States and elsewhere, it marked a complete democratization of access to the corporate form. And so in the United States, the open-access model gradually spread from state to state, even as the laws themselves were expanded to cover more and more (and eventually all legal) businesses. The rights of corporations were further cemented in *Santa Clara County v. Southern Pacific Railroad Co.*[14] The case itself hinged on an arcane tax matter, but the U.S. Supreme Court took the ability of the corporation to be treated as a person for granted, and subsequent U.S. jurisprudence has cited the case as affirming that corporations have the rights individuals do. The ACM routinely overstates this case's importance, in that the notion of a group of individuals functioning as a collective has precedents dating back centuries; its nature as a collective, transacting as an individual and capable of functioning (subject to revocation by the sovereign) beyond the life or investment of the individuals who founded it, was already known to Blackstone in his *Commentaries on the Laws of England,* published in the 1760s. In fact, contrary to the claims of the ACM, for which repeal of corporate personhood is a major goal (because allowing corporations to assert "rights" strengthens their position at law), this right is neither new nor limited to for-profit corporations. Blackstone defined personhood as dating to Roman times, and a corporation was, by the time of his writing, defined in English law very broadly as "a franchise for a number of persons to be incorporated and exist as a body politic, with a power to maintain perpetual succession, and to do corporate act, and each individual of such corporation is also said to have a franchise, or freedom."[15] The only possible innovation in *Santa Clara* is the extension of rights that were themselves novelties in American as opposed to English law (e.g., a formal constitutional guarantee of free speech) to these collectives.

Overseas, Britain (then the most advanced economy in the world) gradually whittled away at the legacy of the Bubble Act, repealing it in 1825, and loosened restrictions on joint-stock companies until, motivated significantly by the massive need of railroads for capital, the Joint Stock Companies Act of 1844 adopted an open-access approach. France began to achieve open access with a law enacted in 1807 that authorized the creation of classes of firms that still exist in French law. *Sociétés en commandite* were akin to limited partnerships in that they could simply be registered with the state and have governing partners liable for all corporate debts and passive partners who could contribute great amounts of money without such unlimited liability. But it was not until 1867 that the joint-stock firm with limited liability and tradeable, widespread shares, the *société anonyme,* was available on an open-access basis. In Japan, incorporation occurred even without formal authorization by the weak government of Japan in the years immediately following the overthrow of the Tokugawa shogunate. Believing them to be one of the ingredients in Western economic power, the Meiji government authorized general incorporation in the commercial code enacted in the early 1890s. Western commercial law, with modifications for distinct local conditions, spread around the world in stages throughout the colonial, postcolonial, and post–Cold War period. The worldwide spread of open-access incorporation is clearly a story of evolutionary competition among legislative entities in both United States and European countries. Like biological evolution, social and political evolution is a trial-and-error process. That Britain first banned joint-stock companies in 1720 only to revoke the ban after successful experiments in the United States suggests that the costs of such a ban became apparent. If Britain were alone in the world, the Bubble Act might have lasted even longer than it did, but, in any event, what Britain had to forgo in terms of pent-up entrepreneurial creativity eventually became too much to bear.

This worldwide spread is important, because anti-corporate thinking has no choice but to treat it not as an evolutionary response but as an exercise in corporate power—corporations shaping the law to their liking everywhere. This requires that corporate money has been calling the tune all over the world for over two centuries, a story that is a tough sell. Far more likely is that the open-access corporation was so powerful in unleashing creative forces and in democratizing access to capital that governments were forced to adopt it despite the constant opportunities for corruption the special-privilege system offered. Indeed, it is very plausible that small states like Delaware (like small banking-haven nations such as Luxemburg or Monaco) may have an advantage in writing efficient corporate-chartering law because the firms incorporating there do little business in these locations and thus interact very little with pressure groups found there. The governments of these jurisdictions will thus emphasize the revenues from chartering rather than the political pressure from local interest groups to channel corporate income their way. In California or New York, for example, organized labor might be sufficiently powerful to lobby successfully for veto rights over corporate decisions to close the significant number of factories located there. In Delaware, with little business done there by these corporations, such pressures are absent. Such small jurisdictions can write laws with fewer concerns about such factional pressures.[16] The wealth generated by more efficient chartering—not the fees generated by incorporation as much as the increased economic activity and hence tax revenue from unleashed entrepreneurship—thus compels other states to water down the rent-seeking payoffs in their own chartering laws. In that sense, it is understandable why anti-corporate pressure groups have from time to time advocated a federal incorporation law, which would magnify their influence relative to what it is in a state like Delaware. Such centralization of corporate chartering limits jurisdictional competition and thus moves the United States closer to a conditional, privilege-based approach to incorporation.

Anti-corporate scholarship and activism typically asserts that this is not competition but a "race to the bottom," in which socially valuable legislation is jettisoned by states desperate for corporate charters.[17] But that explanation fails to indicate (except with the implied premise of political payoffs to legislators by corporations) why, if the special-privilege model is so valuable, politicians will abandon it. But it turns out that states that were late in adding open-access incorporation were also those that held on to other provisions that protected in-state businesses from outside competition the longest. This is again consistent not with a race to the corporate-corrupted bottom but with an argument that states differ in their vulnerability to local pressure groups who resist measures that hurt them but benefit the broader population; the gradual spread of the open-access model was the result of overcoming these pressures.[18]

General incorporation for profit-making businesses was also not created out of whole cloth but extended a practice already allowed in many states since the late 1700s to religious and civic groups, such as fire companies and societies devoted to scholarly activity. (Dartmouth, recall, was a nonprofit entity when it sued the state of New Hampshire.) From 1837 to 1858, a dozen states thought general incorporation so important that they wrote provisions enabling it not just into state law but state constitutions, with many of those constitutions outlawing the special-privilege corporation.[19] Indeed, it was American federalism and the autonomy that it gave to U.S. states to develop their own incorporation rules without permission from Congress that probably explains why general incorporation was developed and refined in the United States first.[20] The New York laws actually replaced a means of control simultaneously more purely "democratic" and yet less effective, direct investment by the legislature of that state in manufacturing corporations. Legal tinkering typically did not end with the adoption of the first open-access statute, because often states limited it to particular kinds of firms. (New York's 1811 law, for example, applied only to manufacturers.) Arrival at the modern legal presumption of freely available incorporation to all comers, profit or nonprofit, required a process of trial and error that for some states was not completed until the 1880s. This is a story of evolving public policy, not corporate pressure.

LIMITED LIABILITY

The development of limited liability also bears the hallmarks of such an evolutionary process. Modern corporate law allows firms to incorporate under terms such that shareholders' personal assets cannot be used to settle corporate debts. Prior to that time, to invest in a business was essentially to lend money to it. The business owner could hope that he would generate enough revenue to pay the debts back, but if not the creditor could go after his wealth, home, and everything in it, just as is true to varying degrees (depending on the state) in American bankruptcy law today. Indeed, given the existence then of debtors' prison, the would-be entrepreneur risked a far worse fate than mere loss of personal property.

Note that limited liability, like the issuance of stock, is not a requirement in corporate law but an option. In other words, it is possible to form partnerships or even issue shares with the understanding that shareholders *will* be liable. The various laws merely allowing limited liability served as a legislative modification to common-law liability principles, which had to be annulled by such measures. The deterrent effects of unlimited liability on risk-taking behavior are obvious, and the desire to encourage risk-taking by businesses was a big part of the motivation for such laws. Like the issuance of shares, limited liability did not emerge from nowhere as the result of corporate thuggery. It was found in isolated instances throughout history before the wave of reform in the 1800s. Some examples of limited-liability ventures have been found in Byzantine law in the eighth and ninth centuries A.D. and beginning in the eleventh century A.D. in Italy.[21] The charter granted to the DEIC provided it to shareholders.

But this great historical revolution again involved a competitive process among American states. The 1811 New York law provided limited liability, although this provision was weakened, with the Supreme Court of New York in 1826 imposing, somewhat bizarrely, liability that encroached on personal wealth but not to an unlimited extent, with total liability arbitrarily set at the value of shares owned plus an equal amount from personal assets. By the end of that decade, New Hampshire, Connecticut, and Vermont were including limited liability in their special-privilege corporate charters, and Maine included it in its open-access law in 1823. This led to pressure on Massachusetts, which was then one of the economically most advanced and sophisticated states. At the time, it remarkably had an extreme rule of joint and several liability, which meant that any single shareholder could be held fully liable for all of the debts of the firm, and also allowed shareholders to be pursued even if they no longer held stock. After considering (and rejecting, as New York had in the late 1700s) a rule that shareholders were liable in proportion to their ownership shares in the corporation, limited liability for newly incorporated manufacturing firms was adopted in 1830. Again, the evolutionary pattern—one state adopting a rule, another state observing and perhaps modifying it—is visible. If anything limited liability is *still* evolving. As the country expanded, so did limited liability, with California being the last to adopt it in 1931. Four states (New Hampshire, Michigan, Wisconsin, and Pennsylvania) actually achieved at various points the anti-corporate dream of repeal of limited liability only to reintroduce it soon after. It was extended to services (law, medicine, accounting, etc.) in many states in the 1960s and 1970s, and hybrid forms involving the limited liability of corporations combined with some governance features more characteristic of partnerships have been adopted in recent years.

Overseas, the French corporate code enacted under Napoleon in 1807 provided limited liability for the narrow class of firms that could incorporate under its provisions, which were extended to all when access to incorporation was expanded in 1867. The 1807 code was influential in both Latin America and French colonial Africa. As part of the more general liberalizing of commerce that occurred in the early and mid-1800s, Britain enacted the Limited Liability Act in 1855, which granted the right to incorporate under limited liability to firms that met certain financing requirements. The next year, this right was extended to most corporations. As with open-access provisions on the issuance of stock and the establishment of a single corporate legal identity, the British took somewhat more slowly to limited liability than Americans did, perhaps hampered by the high degree of centralization in political decision-making. There was also fear that limited liability would allow wealthy investors to swindle the general public. *The Times* declared on May 25, 1824, that

> Nothing can be so unjust as for a few persons abounding in wealth to offer a portion of their excess for the information of a company, to play with that excess—to lend the importance of their whole name and credit to the society, and then should the funds prove insufficient to answer all demands, to retire into the security of their unhazarded fortune, and leave the bait to be devoured by the poor deceived fish.[22]

But in the end, like American states, once other countries took to limited liability, they never went back. Perhaps the best example of the evolutionary fitness of limited liability as an option for entrepreneurs comes from Japan, which has the advantage of not having a Western legal tradition that would have otherwise prohibited it. (The Japanese legal code had to be completely written from scratch after the fall of the Tokugawa regime.) As noted in the previous section, within a few years after the country opened up to the world, businesses began creating limited-liability arrangements for their shares absent both legal prohibition and explicit authorization. In the revolutionary Commercial Code of 1893, the government included limited liability as part of a package of Western-oriented legal reforms, even as the particulars of Japanese corporate law would ultimately evolve in different directions.[23]

With the establishment of limited liability, the modern corporate form was complete. From then on, the growth of corporations was constrained only by the ingenuity of those who might found them. The establishment in law of the framework of the corporation invariably led to a surge in activity. Recall that the introduction of the 1811 open-access law in New York generated a dramatic increase in new manufacturing ventures. Hard numbers for the entire country are unavailable before approximately 1850, but from 1850 to 1870, the growth of the number of corporations initially left them still vastly outnumbered by partnerships, which counted for nearly nine in ten of non–sole-proprietor businesses. The percentage of such multiowner firms that were corporations rose to 29 percent by 1900 and well over half by 1920. [24] To be sure, many of these firms were unable to exploit whatever "power" their status gave them and folded in short order when they could not deliver the greatest value at the lowest cost. (This turnover is illustrative in itself, as will be seen.) But it was a series of technological transformations, especially the rise of mass production combined with the enabling power of the new legal structure, that created the corporation as the modern era now conceives it.

THE RISE OF THE GIANT GLOBAL CORPORATION

The introduction of modern corporate law was a critical feature, though far from the only one, in the radical transformation of society that was the Industrial Revolution. Over the course of this revolution and its aftermath, village life was uprooted, global commercial ties dramatically thickened, and living standards rose again and again. And another change was the introduction of a new form of social organization unlike the church, the nobility, guilds, family-based larger businesses, traditional commercial organizations, or anything else seen before it—the giant corporation. The rise of such firms was both a product of the industrialization process and a way of remaking the economic fabric of society.

Many who write about the great industrial transformation divide it into several stages. The first involved the construction of railroads, a revolutionary device based on applying the huge amount of mechanical power made available with the invention of the steam engine to transport, liberating humanity forever from both the speed and the load restraints of human or animal transportation power. An engineer from Cornwall named Richard Trevithick first mastered the application of steam power to mechanized transport in 1801, and another named George Stephenson oversaw the construction of the first rail line between Liverpool and Manchester. The world was never the same again.[25] Ultimately the tracks would crisscross first Britain (the first version of the English network, completed by 1840, was constructed entirely by stock-issuing corporations), then Europe and North America and elsewhere. Their construction often became patriotic national projects (think of the celebration attending the completion of the trans-American line at Promontory Point, Utah), and societies confronting the modernized West, such as Japan, immediately turned their attention to constructing rail networks.

But constructing these lines and building and maintaining the cars were expensive. The railroads needed huge amounts of capital, and the obvious benefits from linking previously dispersed people into a network for transporting both themselves and merchandise at much greater speeds and in much greater quantities motivated rail entrepreneurs to seek, and governments to grant, many reforms, including open-access incorporation and limited liability. The benefits for the railroad entrepreneurs were monetary, as many of them became fabulously wealthy. The benefits for the public were in their ability to move about and to trade much more easily, which is in fact what generated the monetary rewards for the entrepreneurs to begin with. And gradually the number of railroad companies declined on both sides of the Atlantic as bigger companies bought out smaller ones, with owners of contending companies often warring ferociously in the United States, in particular, over the takeover of other lines.

After the railroads had been built, it was the age of the things they would carry. Giant businesses such as U.S. Steel and Standard Oil appeared in heavy manufacturing. And there thus also arose giant firms to find markets for manufactured goods and then to knit together the places things were made and the places things were wanted. This was the story of the rise of first the Montgomery Ward company, which would ultimately be shoved aside by Sears, Roebuck, which would in turn be displaced in recent years by Wal-Mart. Each firm adopted a business model that improved on what came before it, and each model in turn seemed more giant and influential than the one prior.

This dynamic toward ever-greater size happened primarily because of economies of scale. Many (though far from all) kinds of economic activity are characterized by very high initial costs. (Mastering how to produce a good properly, or the knowledge of where suppliers and demanders are, is often a very important up front cost.) In a new industry, firms that rise to dominance early on based on a superior product, better marketing, etc. find that dominance reinforced by the effects of rapidly growing size. This allows them to invest in more expensive mechanization, which may increase their cost advantage further. And so in both retail and heavy industry, as with the railroads before them, a relatively small number of giant firms came to (temporarily) dominate. The lack of precedent for organizations with more manpower than some nation-states, and yet not governed as nation-states were, proved deeply disquieting, as will be seen in the next chapter.

Above all, the giant firm was perfected in America, where the likes of Rockefeller and Carnegie in manufacturing, Morgan in finance, and Vanderbilt in rail transport became in their wealth and brutal business tactics (including their willingness to throw their financial weight around in dealing with politicians) the symbols of a new era of gigantism. In hindsight, it is astonishing how small was the interval between the legal reforms of the first half of the nineteenth century and the rise of these colossuses. By 1930, the nation's 200 largest nonbanking corporations were estimated to earn about 43 percent of the income earned by all such corporations.[26] However, that some firms were gigantic in no sense made them economically dominant; it was also true that the thousands of corporations with assets under one million dollars held over a third of the national corporate income. Indeed, controlling a disproportionate share of the income is the very meaning of "big," and so appeals to the percentage of assets owned or income accruing to the largest corporations are never as informative as anti-corporate advocates allege. By way of comparison, according to the U.S. Bureau of the Census, the four most populous countries in the world had 45.4 percent of the global population, and yet a casual glance at the newspapers indicates that the power of these nations to bend others to their will is extremely limited. The world still possesses an immense variety of cultures (as will be demonstrated in Chapter 7) and societies that pursue policies and behave in ways substantially independent of dictation by China, India, the United States, and Indonesia. So too five minutes with an overstressed executive of a giant corporation is sufficient to persuade the listener of the competitive stresses his firm faces. (This will be explored further in Chapter 5.) And so size is not necessarily power. But clearly the rise of these gigantic, seemingly omnipresent and omnipotent organizations without any clear historical precedent was unsettling.

This rise also is argued to have generated a new species of economic man, the corporate manager.[27] In the United States, in particular, the story of company founding fathers being elbowed aside in favor of trained business professionals once the company passes from dynamic startup to mature giant is a common one. Typically, the founding genius would find that his empire had outgrown his ability to monitor it and would have to hire divisional managers, regional managers, etc. Upon the founder's death or (sometimes forced) retirement, the managers would often take more control as the vision of the founder, so appropriate for a small company trying to rise to dominance, proved inadequate to running a stable firm that had to engage in long-term planning, worry about the financial markets as much as the details of product design, and the like. Ultimately, skills in marketing, accounting, or finance would prove as important as a background in engineering or product design in determining who rose to the top of suddenly very tall corporate ladders. Indeed the triumph of such professional managers far removed from any contact with consumers who bought the firm's product would be a major source of criticism as American firms struggled with global competition from the 1980s on.

CORPORATIONS GO GLOBAL

The corporation was such an obvious force for accelerating industrialization and modernization that societies around the world took to it enthusiastically. The particulars differed from country to country, depending on the cultural and historical circumstances of each. In Britain, the presence of sheltered colonial markets, a lack of Yankee enthusiasm for commerce as a virtuous activity in its own right, and the inability to rely on economies of scale in a huge domestic market meant that British corporations, while they grew very important there, would not stride the global stage quite the way American firms did. In France, with its long history of political centralization and economic *dirigisme,* corporations came to be as much directed by or at least symbiotic with the state as antagonistic to it, particularly after World War II. In Japan, during the industrialization process before the militarist era (when they came to be known as *zaibatsu*) and again after World War II, large corporations evolved from small firms but were governed at the highest levels by the founding families. This was until recently a significant contrast to the United States, distinctly marked first by the gentler dislodging of founding entrepreneurs by professional managers and later the bare-knuckle attacks on those same professional managers by takeover artists, who used the free trading of shares to attempt to reorganize these giant firms.

Perhaps the most anomalous case among the major extensive trading nations during the later 1800s was Germany. That company's corporate law was developed as part of the great Bismarck project of constructing a powerful nation, which in his view required a society with a place for everyone and everyone in his place. After he oversaw the unification of the country after the Franco-Prussian war, his desire to outflank German socialists led him to oversee the creation of health insurance, pensions, and accident and disability insurance, with German businesses paying for a portion of the cost for their employees. Job security too was assumed to be part of the patriotic corporation's duty. These beliefs became ensconced in the inaugural German commercial code of 1897, and German legal traditions now require that management and labor cooperate for the broader benefit of the firm and include the codetermination system, in which workers are guaranteed some representation in corporate governance. The corporation has thus been absorbed into the achievement of what the German government defines as the public purpose, and the freedom of shareholders is restrained. Germany, in some sense, is an incomplete triumph for anti-corporate beliefs. To the optimist, this makes the German firm more representative of all constituencies, but such cultural comfort with the corporation being appropriated for the government's purposes made it seem more reasonable for fascist governments to co-opt large firms in the 1930s, not just there but in Italy and Japan, whose corporate law was also heavily influenced by Germany.[28]

The early postwar period was marked most compellingly by the rise of the American multinational firm, a form not seen since the days of the EICs. Like those firms, it produced and sold in countries all over the world, although unlike them it answered only to shareholders (and therefore to customers) rather than to king. The late 1960s saw great skepticism of American multinationals in Europe and in developing countries as almost an invading army, but ultimately European countries and Japan developed firms with global reach and recognition. In recent years, countries such as India and China have made the establishment or modernization of commercial codes part of their arsenal in their modernization. India's laws broadly parallel those of Britain, although they have been modernized since economic reform began there in 1991. After the communist revolution, China of course had repealed the corporate law it inherited from the Republic of China but saw a need to reintroduce it, one baby step at a time, after economic reform began in 1979. Limited liability was granted to joint ventures between foreign and (state-owned, there then being no other kind) Chinese firms in that year. Other joint ventures were authorized soon after, and China introduced a full commercial code enabling joint-stock companies with limited liability in 1994. The law has been tinkered with continuously since, as in almost any society serious about global engagement. In Russia, with its ongoing struggle among an increasingly authoritarian state, a nascent entrepreneurial culture, and a series of essentially special-privilege corporations such as the fossil-fuels giant Gazprom, the jury on legal transformation is still very much out.

A spreading of corporate wings into the broader world is now taking place in the Middle East and Latin America too. By 2006, *Fortune* magazine's list of the 500 biggest companies in the world (most but not all of which are private corporations) had entries from 32 countries, 13 of which (accounting for 128 firms) were located outside of Europe and its offshoots (Australia, Canada, New Zealand, and the United States). In terms of representation, the set of successful global corporations is itself now more ethnically diverse than any political assembly ever constructed. The ability of, for example, Indian information-technology firms to start from nothing and, thanks to their founders' ingenuity, developments in global communications technology, and corporate law, become global giants in just a few years is a striking sign of the democratic nature of globalization, of markets, and of the corporation itself.

CONCLUSION

The introduction of open-access incorporation and limited liability contributed substantially to the Industrial Revolution. Their absence would have slowed down economic growth and the rate of transformation substantially, although it is impossible to say by how much. It is certainly true that other factors, forming a list almost too long to contemplate and compiled by scholars over centuries, are plausible contributors to the economic changes that began in England and Holland in the 1600s and changed the world. For example, the practical mastery of technology such as steam power made rail transport possible in an engineering sense. But that raises the subsequent question of how society was in a position to capitalize on such breakthroughs. Many tales can be told of technological advances in other societies that came to naught because they were not made widely available through commerce. (The Chinese, for example, are said to have learned how to effectively produce steel centuries before Europeans, but it was only in the 1800s that Europeans commercialized it as mass manufacturing.) And this is a key historical role of the corporation—to make risky ventures for unsecured entrepreneurs possible by enabling fund-raising from strangers and limiting the potentially disastrous risk of unlimited liability. The absence of corporate law would not have prevented the Industrial Revolution (which in fact began before the enactment of open-access measures), but it would have slowed it down and made it less dramatic.

Chapter 3

A Brief History of the Anti-Corporate Movement

Truth be told, compared to the two other grand branches of knowledge, there are not that many truly revolutionary ideas—ideas that cause much existing thinking to be discarded—in the social sciences. This is a marked difference from the hard sciences, which have flourished for centuries on revolutionary ways of thinking about the physical world, and the humanities, which interpret humanity's history and achievements and are constantly incorporating new interpretations. But the social sciences are an uneasy marriage between the expressive investigation of the human condition that has long been the province of history and the arts on the one hand, and the use of the experimental method as the arbiter of what is and is not true that is the essence of the hard sciences. Much of the heavy lifting in economic theory, for example, was done over a century ago. Like most social sciences, it seldom suffers a revolution of the magnitude of, say, relativity or before that Newtonian mechanics. Instead ideas are tinkered with, and they adjust and evolve, and are all too often tailored (and sometimes overstretched) to suit the political purposes of their current users. In economics, for example, the development of information economics in the 1970s did not so much overturn as modify orthodox economic theory; how important it is, particularly with respect to questions of the appropriate boundary between the market and the state, depends on the politics of the speaker in question. More than the other branches of knowledge, the social sciences are evolutionary rather than revolutionary, and theory can be tailored to support the speaker's politics. Being the study of humans and human society, the social sciences are conscripted into the service of political ends.

And this probably makes it easier for bad ideas to live on, the Darwinian scientific processes being less cruel in the relatively forgiving social-science environment. And so the roots of many of the beliefs underlying the modern ACM can be clearly found in older ideologies involving commerce, capitalism, and the pursuit of wealth. The modern ACM has sometimes unknowingly knit some of these claims into a new set of unifying beliefs and principles. That the laws governing corporations and their incorporation in particular have become the movement's primary villain is a somewhat curious development, but one whose influence has created an ideology and global movement all its own. Ideas, including old and bad ones, have consequences often deeper than we appreciate.

ANTI-CORPORATISM V.0: THE RAW MATERIALS

We know from the previous chapter that the term "corporation" has meant different things at different times. The abuses associated with special-privilege monopolies (many of which were committed by ravenous state officials as much as business leaders) have by now faded away into insignificance. The modern ACM now focuses on several key aspects of modern open-access corporations, even though much of its supporting evidence comes from the special-privilege era. It is critical of all three characteristics of the modern corporation outlined in the previous chapter—limited liability, the primacy of shareholder interests, and corporate personhood. But this thinking has its roots in an older time, and it is worth tracing that route.

Skepticism of commerce, which reaches its greatest heights when applied to big business, is nothing new. The Tenth Commandment implicitly cautions against acquisitiveness by forbidding the believer from coveting that which is his neighbor's, and Christ expelled the money changers from the Temple. (At least one work has in recent years extended this historical Judeo-Christian skepticism of commerce by arguing that business not only operates against the commandments of the Gospels but also has actually corrupted modern Christianity.[1]) Plato's ideal Republic abolished private property and left all the productive labor to the slave class (itself nearly subhuman and assumed to be born to such degrading activity), and Aristotle also often took a dim view of commerce. The arts too have provided much grist for anti-business sentiment, from the abolition of money and/or property in such Utopian fiction as Tommaso Campanella's *The City of the Sun* to Shakespeare's Shylock to the meat-packing overlords of Upton Sinclair's *The Jungle* to the spiritual emptiness of Sinclair Lewis' Babbitt. That business, especially big business, must battle this long-standing suspicion (sometimes countered in the United States, to be fair, by admiration for the heroic entrepreneur) means that the ACM is to some extent shooting from the high ground in the battlefield of ideas.

The greedy or hollow businessman being such a common cultural/literary archetype, that it might influence social thought is unsurprising. The giant corporation, as we saw in the previous chapter, is a product of the modern era, and anti-modernism is also a key compound in the soil that generated the modern ACM. The revolution in thought that occurred during the Enlightenment, particularly in its more violent French (as opposed to Scotch/English) incarnation, generated a profound counterreaction—European suspicion of modernity and of radical social transformation. From Edmund Burke's startlingly prescient criticisms of the way the French Revolution, by overturning centuries of tradition and all the invisible social knowledge contained within it, would inevitably end disastrously to the artistic innovation in the Romantic period that turned artists into critics of conventional bourgeois behavior and of the submerging of the full tapestry of humanity to mere commerce and technology, the arrival of the corporation occurred when there was much raw material to work with with respect to broader skepticism of commerce and dynamic business competition. The business corporation, as a creation of law fundamentally driven by utilitarian calculation, is (perhaps uniquely) toxic in all of these senses—a potential agent of radical social change, and one driven by grubby, uncultured, selfish businessmen at that. And yet even before large modern corporations became so common, some of the themes that now dominate the ACM began to emerge, both because of the abuses of special-privilege corporations and because of other intellectual developments.

ANTI-CORPORATISM V.1: FROM SPECIAL-PRIVILEGE CORPORATE ABUSES TO MARXISM AND BEYOND

Anti-corporate thinkers are fond of noting that classical economists and many of the American Founders were skeptical of corporations, and those thinkers are right. We saw in the introduction that Jefferson was skeptical of the moneyed interests he saw as a threat to his agrarian republic, and corporations in particular drew his concern. In a fragment from his unpublished autobiography dated 1821, he lists "the shackles on Commerce by monopolies; on Industry by gilds & corporations" as two of a long list of "monstrous abuses of power" that the French suffered just before their Revolution.[2] In a passage from *The Wealth of Nations* that, given his credentials as a general advocate of free commerce, unsurprisingly finds its way into the anti-corporate literature, Adam Smith writes that

The directors of such companies, however, being the managers rather of other people's money than of their own, it cannot well be expected that they should watch over it with the same anxious vigilance with which the partners in a private copartnery frequently watch over their own. Like the stewards of a rich man, they are apt to consider attention to small matters as not for their master's honour, and very easily give themselves a dispensation from having it. Negligence and profusion, therefore, must always prevail, more or less, in the management of the affairs of such a company. It is upon this account that joint stock companies for foreign trade have seldom been able to maintain the competition against private adventurers. They have, accordingly, very seldom succeeded without an exclusive privilege, and frequently have not succeeded with one. Without an exclusive privilege they have commonly mismanaged the trade. With an exclusive privilege they have both mismanaged and confined it.[3]

There was skepticism of corporations in many of the early American states, which restricted their operations. Britain of course enacted the Bubble Act, banning stock-issuing companies without special royal charters, in 1720. But of course these were all objections to special-privilege corporations, the open-access corporation not yet existing. It was generally assumed (for good reason) that the arrival of open-access chartering would change for the better the social value of incorporation, but ultimately anti-corporatism would return even in the open-access era.

Marx's "most revolutionary role"

But even in the early open-access period, corporations began to be feared and reviled, although often as part of greater hostility to mass commerce. The opposition at first was generally not because they were corporations per se but because of their reach and influence. One important development that would ultimately help turn the anger toward corporations in particular occurred in the work of a young philosopher who, after his dissertation had been approved at the University of Jena, turned his attention to questions of human society and how it was shaped by the surrounding economic environment. Before and after coauthoring *The Communist Manifesto*, Karl Marx developed ideas that both directly and indirectly influenced anti-corporate thinking. Indeed, one of the primary achievements, even if inadvertent and unknowing, of later anti-corporate thinkers was their ability to make Marx's own densely presented ideas tractable for the broader educated public.

Two themes are of interest. The first appears in the first chapter of Marx's magnum opus, *Kapital*. It is the notion of "commodity fetishization," which holds that the development of modern, sophisticated commercial economies disrupts social relations by making commodities (including human labor) rather than more traditional obligations the central organizing principle of society. The impersonal trading relations that capitalist society spawns, necessitated by the continuing need to exchange commodities even after a highly refined division of labor has developed, replace the social fabric that would otherwise bond us together. There are no more nobles, guilds, serfs, lords, or burghers—there is only mass commerce with strangers, whose spread is itself a key theme of Marx. While *Kapital* was essentially an academic work, designed to be read and assessed by other scholars, in the polemic *The Manifesto of the Communist Party*, Marx and Friedrich Engels similarly noted:

> The bourgeoisie, wherever it has got the upper hand, has put an end to all feudal, patriarchal, idyllic relations. It has pitilessly torn asunder the motley feudal ties that bound man to his "natural superiors," and has left no other nexus between people than naked self-interest, than callous "cash payment." It has drowned out the most heavenly ecstacies of religious fervor, of chivalrous enthusiasm, of philistine sentimentalism, in the icy water of egotistical calculation. It has resolved personal worth into exchange value, and in place of the numberless indefeasible chartered freedoms, has set up that single, unconscionable freedom—Free Trade. In one word, for exploitation, veiled by religious and political illusions, it has substituted naked, shameless, direct, brutal exploitation.[4]

That this commodity-dominated system also facilitates the exploitatively hierarchical nature of society—the greedy at the top pitilessly extracting the last dime of what Marx termed "surplus value" from the masses below—makes it all the more objectionable. The fetishism notion was further bound up with individual alienation from the broader society, itself a focus of some of Marx's earlier work. Sophisticated division of labor and vast, complex commercial markets separate people from the results of their work and hence divorce them from their fellow humans. Whereas the small farmer or the craftsman sees the social value his labor generates, to the anonymous factory worker his work has no meaning. Traditional social cohesion is torn asunder by the market, replaced by subservience to the needs of mass commerce. These arguments are the antecedents to the modern anti-corporate themes of virtuous local self-reliance versus standardized global commerce, as well as the purported attack on the broader public interest by corporate profit-chasers.

Marx's second major legacy to anti-corporate thought is his belief in historical materialism, which contends that economic conditions almost exclusively determine larger political and social trends. While taken to grotesque extremes in the ideology of Communist states, where all historical events were interpreted in terms of economic or "material" forces—so that art or science could be rejected as "bourgeois"—this is an idea that in more anodyne forms has become hugely influential in modern economics, in ways that Marx himself could not have envisioned. Scholars argue, for example, that such broad forces as technological progress or globalization almost mechanistically create better governance or that democracy in the most advanced economies deterministically leads to national decline.[5] And in the Marxist conception of historical inevitability—in the end, we will all be communists—the system of commodity fetishism, for all its faults, was an unavoidable step on the road from feudalism to the workers' paradise. (Marx should be credited for boldness in his willingness to make predictions about the future, even if most of the predictions were ultimately found, after horrendous consequences, to be false.)

And here modern anti-corporatism departs from the Marxist portion of its roots in rejecting such determinism. As well shall see, the ACM accepts that corporations (rather than Marx's capitalists) have come to dominate the world but rejects the inevitable fading of their dominance. Corporations will be dominant yet only have the potential to be displaced through the old-fashioned political toil required in democratic processes. But Marx's work was critical in setting the stage for the merging of the idea of business as evermore powerful, driven by the imperatives of history, with other fears of the great upheavals brought about by modernization to create the seeds of the modern ACM. While Marx's devotees in later years—both scholars and eminently practical tyrants such as Lenin—would continue to deal in the abstractions of class conflict and "monopoly capital," with corporations being simply a manifestation of these broader forces, the framework into which modern anti-corporatism in particular would be fit was aided considerably by Marx's analysis. Like other ideas that have since evolved and yet whose Marxist origins are still recognizable (e.g., the notion of unequal power distributed by "race, gender and class" and the very notion of transformation from preindustrial to "modern" society), Marx's contribution to the modern theory of corporate power is profound.[6]

The Rising Fear of Big Business

Meanwhile, the foundation of anti-corporate thinking in the United States was becoming more recognizable, thanks largely to increased public resentment over the perceived abuses of swaggering American industrialists as the country passed through the Industrial Revolution. The transformation of corporations from wards of the state to the open-access model, combined with the growth of the giant railroad corporations, led to companies issuing huge numbers of shares, which were in turn dispersed among many owners. This prompted the rise of an accusation that was familiar to Adam Smith, that shareholders had no meaningful control over managers and executives, who were then free to run firms for their own private interests, often at great social cost. This charge will be assessed in the next chapter. For now, it is sufficient to note that this problem loomed large in political criticism of the corporate form from after the Civil War through the end of the Great Depression. For example, in his 1871 inaugural address upon taking office as governor of California, Lewis Booth bemoaned (along with crooked corporate influence on politicians and the large number of shares that corporations owned in one another) the fact that dispersed ownership kept effective control in the hands of supershareholders who could manipulate the firm to their purposes, which meant that "between majorities and minorities, directors and stockholders, cases of the grossest injustice are constantly arising."

Symbolic of the manipulations that so concerned the public was the epic struggle over the Erie Railroad company between the magnate Cornelius Vanderbilt and the very archetype of a managerial insider, the Erie treasurer Daniel Drew. In the course of amassing colossal wealth, Vanderbilt had taken over one railroad after another in the 1860s, sometimes at Drew's expense. When Vanderbilt set his sights on the Erie, Drew oversaw a process in which tens of thousands of new shares were created, diluting the voting power of existing ones.[7] After Vanderbilt had bought enough of them, he realized that, thanks to Drew's shenanigans, their ultimate voting power would be minimal. In a battle involving competitive bribery of judges and legislators amid the astonishingly corrupt backdrop of contemporary New York and New Jersey, amounting to what one scholar has called "regulatory arbitrage,"[8] Drew ultimately prevailed. Much of the public was convinced by the episode both that corporate excesses were the norm and that Vanderbilt in particular was a threat to democracy. (The latter's robber-baron image is somewhat ironic in that upon gaining control of railroads, he generally upgraded the quality of the lines, extended service to other cities, and provided large numbers of jobs.)

Also important in generating such resentments were the corporate mergers that were motivated in part by the Sherman Antitrust Act's prohibitions against cooperative cartel behavior by separate firms, an episode that itself demonstrates the folly of the unintended consequences corporate regulations so often create. These giants without any historical precedent, such as Rockefeller's Standard Oil and what ultimately became U.S. Steel, undoubtedly combined with the radical social transformations taking place in the Gilded Age—mass immigration, the uprooting of agricultural life, the rise of giant cities with vast slums—to generate widespread disquiet over a society rapidly being remade from the familiarity of small farmers and merchants to something new, mysterious, and unsettling. The rising outrage over corporate "monopolies" was hardly limited to their anti-competitive effects, with the abuses of management-hired private security forces employed against striking workers and the impact of recurring financial crashes interwoven into a broad fear that society was rapidly changing (as, of course, it was). This led to broad (if not necessarily majority) hostility to the mighty business empires being constructed and recombined. President Rutherford B. Hayes bemoaned in his diary that "[t]his is a government of the people, by the people, and for the people no longer. It is a government of corporations, by corporations, and for corporations.—How is this?" (It should be noted that while often used by anti-corporate authors as a criticism purely of corporations, these words are actually a portion of a much larger concern about the corrupting effects of great individual wealth.[9])

Amid this disquiet over the large fortunes being created, there emerged for the first time two notable intellectual attacks on the modern corporate form in particular. The first was a series of essays by the brothers Charles Francis Adams, Jr., and Henry Adams (both grandsons of President John Quincy Adams) on the struggles over Erie Rail, which depicted the corporation in particular as a creation of the state and as now evolving beyond democratic control, a critical theme of the modern ACM. The second was a series of articles in *Harper's* magazine by the socialist economist Richard T. Ely, a founding father of the American Economics Association (which still holds an annual lecture in his honor to this day). In a more subtle and remarkably prescient series of articles with respect to future thinking both pro- and anti-corporate, Ely, on the one hand, acknowledged the power of corporations to give the general public access to the wealth they generated via share ownership (forecasting the "ownership society" concept popularized by British Prime Minister Margaret Thatcher in the 1980s and later by U.S. President George W. Bush) and, on the other, both flagged the danger of their tendency to become monopolies and insisted on the ultimate accountability of corporations to democracy. Ely's work was flush with the new language of Marx, with its references to labor and capital, and viewed the corporation as a tool whose gigantism was in fact essential to the welfare of society but whose power meant that it must be subservient to democratic devices; indeed, ultimately, he foresaw (less presciently) that corporations would be forced by the state to become something indistinguishable from quasi-socialist cooperatives.[10]

Despite the relative rarity to this point of focused attacks on corporate law and its devil spawn in particular, the notion of something beyond mere suspicion of big business—namely out-and-out big-business control of the nation's economy and even the broader society—nonetheless was planted during this period.[11] The U.S. Interstate Commerce Commission was formed in 1887 to regulate the monopoly pricing power of the transportation corporations. (It was quickly captured by those very same companies, which ultimately turned its authority designed to protect consumers from prices that were too high into regulations setting *minimum*

prices nominally in the interest of stability but having the effect of thwart-
ing competition. Unintended consequences again.[12]) Presidents Theodore
Roosevelt and William Howard Taft actively used the Sherman Antitrust
Act to prosecute many large corporations. One of the most important
events in this combined campaign against corporations in particular and
big business more generally was an assume-the-conclusion investigation
by a Congressional committee headed by the Louisiana Congressman
Arsène Paulin Pujo into the "money trust," a nexus of financiers who, it
was thought, controlled the nation's money supply in an era before
national central banking. The mighty financier J. P. Morgan himself was
called before the committee and grilled by its counsel, Samuel Unter-
meyer, an event far more dramatic (because of Morgan's perceived power)
in its day than, say, the various testimonies of Bill Gates during Microsoft's
antitrust battles in the 1990s. The alleged money trust and its abuses
loomed large in the 1912 presidential campaign of Woodrow Wilson, and
the Pujo committee ultimately found in 1913 that the trust did in fact exist
and that its costs to the nation were dramatic. Indeed, in a book based on
his campaign speeches from 1912, Wilson anticipated a major tenet of
modern anti-corporatism. While he did not address corporate dominance
of the state, he did argue that corporations inevitably became very large
and that they were uniquely pernicious in that they were unaccountable
and omnipotent:

> We have come upon a very different age from any that preceded
> us. We have come upon an age when we do not do business in the
> way in which we used to do business—when we do not carry
> on any of the operations of manufacture, sale, transportation, or
> communication as men used to carry them on. There is a sense in
> which in our day the individual has been submerged. In most parts
> of our country men work, not for themselves, not as partners in the
> old way in which they used to work, but generally as employees—
> in a higher or lower grade—of great corporations. There was a time
> when corporations played a very minor part in our business affairs,
> but now they play the chief part, and most men are the servants of
> corporations.
>   You know what happens when you are the servant of a corpora-
> tion. You have in no instance access to the men who are really
> determining the policy of the corporation. If the corporation is
> doing the things that it ought not to do, you really have no voice
> in the matter and must obey the orders, and you have oftentimes
> with deep mortification to co-operate in the doing of things
> which you know are against the public interest. Your individuality
> is swallowed up in the individuality and purpose of a great organi-
> zation.

It is true that, while most men are thus submerged in the corporation, a few, a very few, are exalted to a power which as individuals they could never have wielded. Through the great organizations of which they are the heads, a few are enabled to play a part unprecedented by anything in history in the control of the business operations of the country and in the determination of the happiness of great numbers of people.[13]

These findings and beliefs quickly contributed to the establishment of the Federal Reserve in 1913 and the passage of the Clayton Antitrust Act, which remedied some of the perceived weaknesses in the Sherman Act, in 1914. Meanwhile, the corporation itself continued to come into focus as a problem in its own right, distinct from individual personalities like Rockefeller or Morgan, because of the way in which its exclusive pursuit of profit was a danger. From the world of ideas, several noted scholars began at least in part to pick up Ely's torch by identifying corporations as particularly problematic because of their essential nature—power combined with a lack of representation of the public in their decision-making. In *The Promise of American Life*, Herbert David Croly argued that corporations above a certain size must be brought under the aegis of federal law not just via antitrust law, which was simply designed to insure competition, but through democratic participation in their governance.[14] "Industrial democracy" with "scientific management" would insure that corporations behaved more efficiently by better motivation of workers and through other channels.

In 1923, the brilliant and eccentric economist Thorstein Veblen devoted a chapter of his *Absentee Enterprise: The Case of America* to "The Rise of the Corporation."[15] One of its most important contributions was the idea that corporations did not respond to consumer desires but manufactured them, primarily through advertising (foreshadowing the human passivity theme from Chapter 1). Admittedly, some of his claims actually strike the modern reader as odd. For example, he argued that when corporations issue stock, the wealth used to purchase it increases the "credit" in the economy (what we would now call the money supply), causing a "general inflation" in prices in combination with no increase in the supply of real production. Stock issuance, in other words, is inflationary. Indeed, at one point, he argued that it is against the corporate interest to increase production of actual goods, because of the liquidation of inventory that would have to follow. All of this is a consequence of the fact that production is carried out through corporations run by financiers rather than, as he thought best, scientists and engineers. This stock-propelled credit expansion in turn causes an acceleration of the business cycle, with expanded booms and then more dramatic busts than would occur in the absence of large stock-issuing firms.

This argument surely sounded more reasonable in the wake of the 1929 stock-market crash, when skepticism of the wealthy and the large corporations whose financial excesses during the Roaring Twenties allegedly brought it all about crested.[16] Further, in 1932, two economists released (or, more accurately, two authors wrote and the corporate publisher McMillan released and distributed) a landmark work entitled *The Modern Corporation and Private Property*.[17] In many respects, they were able at the depths of the Depression to provide a framework for the public conversation about corporations that persists even to this day. Their work documented what they saw as the raw economic power of the largest corporations—in particular, the high degree of concentration of asset ownership among a small number of large firms. It also explained for a mass audience the problem, explored in Chapter 4, of managers exploiting corporate wealth for their own ends rather than those of a widely dispersed ownership incapable of monitoring their behavior. Both concerns still loom large in both academic and broader political discussion of the role of corporation in society.

In light of the influence of these ideas, antitrust laws were now not enough. The Securities and Exchange Commission was established in 1934 largely to look after the interests of the small shareholder threatened by the intrinsic temptations that corporate management faced. By the time of his second acceptance speech as the presidential nominee of the Democratic Party in 1936, Franklin Roosevelt could place into the historical record his rather extreme (to modern ears) statement of the raw power that corporations in his judgment held not just over the economy but over the state and society themselves:

> For out of this modern civilization economic royalists carved new dynasties. New kingdoms were built upon concentration of control over material things. Through new uses of corporations, banks and securities, new machinery of industry and agriculture, of labor and capital—all undreamed of by the Fathers—the whole structure of modern life was impressed into this service.
>
> There was no place among this royalty for our many thousands of small businessmen and merchants who sought to make a worthy use of the American system of initiative and profit. They were no more free than the worker or the farmer. Even honest and progressive-minded men of wealth, aware of their obligation to their generation, could never know just where they fitted into this dynastic scheme of things.
>
> It was natural and perhaps human that the privileged princes of those new economic dynasties, thirsting for power, reached out for control over government itself. They created a new despotism

and wrapped it in the robes of legal sanction. In its service new mercenaries sought to regiment the people, their labor, and their property. And as a result the average man once more confronts the problem that faced the Minute Man.

. . .

For too many of us the political equality we once had won was meaningless in the face of economic inequality. A small group had concentrated into their own hands an almost complete control over other people's property, other people's labor— other people's lives. For too many of us life was no longer free; liberty no longer real; men could no longer follow the pursuit of happiness.

This notion of "power" and control is so important that it will be extensively investigated in Chapter 5. It is important to note in fairness that Roosevelt was by the temper of the times, and especially compared to the out-and-out warfare among fascists and communists going on in the streets of places like 1920s Germany and 1930s Spain, no radical. He was rather speaking the language of a politician seeking to fire up the troops at a very difficult time in U.S. history, and this language was part of the bitter conflicts in American society over the New Deal. Despite his red-meat rhetoric, Roosevelt was no socialist, although it was probably true that many in his administration desired to bring corporations substantially under not just the regulatory guidance but the outright control of the state. But that he would choose such a prominent platform to equate large corporations to British colonial rule, which of course culminated in violent revolution, is telling.

Through the compromises of politics, most notably the acquiescence of the Supreme Court in the late 1930s to much of the New Deal following the Roosevelt court-packing episode, the state achieved a *modus vivendi* with corporations that allowed them to operate subject only to basic restraints on size and fraud. Yet Roosevelt's achievements during the 1930s set the stage for much of the ambitious postwar thinking of the American left, and the skeptical attitudes toward corporations in that thinking would remain after the war, not least because corporations' size and economic importance would seem to be even greater than before, despite the half-measures of the New Deal. And a key plank of anti-corporate thinking was now permanently established in the open-access era: the distinction between private corporate interest and broader public interest. Large corporations—not just plutocrats—were, while not sufficiently toxic to society that they should be eliminated, powerful enough that they should be brought to heel and made to bow to the universally acknowledged general welfare of society.

ANTI-CORPORATISM V.2: RETREAT AND REBIRTH IN THE AGE OF THE MANAGERIAL STATE

While it is far from obvious (despite generations of lessons by well-intentioned high-school civics teachers) that it did much to end the Great Depression, the New Deal had electrifying effects on the broader relation between the American state and society. With respect to giant corporations in particular, in the eyes of many, it gave excluded constituencies—laborers, small farmers, small shareholders, and many more—a place at the table of the state, a table that previously had been monopolized by the monopolists. In combination with the seeming triumph, after a few years, of Keynesian economics over the vicissitudes of the business cycle (the depression that was predicted to accompany the return of huge numbers of U.S. troops from war in Europe and Asia never having happened), it was a time of great optimism for believers in progress by government planning. In Europe, the horrors of two world wars were, despite the specter of Stalin, about to give way to a brighter future. Having just led his nation through the Blitz and to victory over the Nazis, Winston Churchill found himself cast out even before the war was over for a Labor government that was more suited to building the welfare state and other more genteelly urgent postwar tasks. With respect to the United States, in the eyes of their skeptics on the nonsocialist left (orthodox socialism—state ownership of "the means of production"—never having taken hold among Americans to the extent it did in Europe), corporations were a necessary evil. Their size was essential for achieving economies of scale in production and research, but at the same time it made them a danger to the functioning of democracy. The solution was to place them firmly under the control of the regulatory state that grew from the New Deal embryo.

But given that the regulatory apparatus was by now enough to insure that corporations could be policed with respect to their product safety,[18] their security practices, and their monopolistic excesses, the large corporation in the United States came to be seen in many circles as a national asset, a source of expertise and competence that could be called on by the state when public needs demanded it. Indeed, the postwar period saw the rise of the corporate manager as a species worthy of study in his own right, whose difficult job was to manage corporate affairs once it had outgrown the need for the vision and entrepreneurial drive of its founders—the Fords, the Carnegies, and the like. Corporate managers were now seen as possessing a great deal of socially useful wisdom, authority, and responsibility. The archetypal study of their role and mission was Peter Drucker's *The Concept of the Corporation*, which was nominally a study of GM (General Motors) but came to be regarded as a classic text of modern management and the role of the corporation in society.[19] Drucker, who was perhaps the first "management guru" before the notion existed, thought the corporation not simply a vehicle to maximize profits, and certainly not a bane of society, but rather a means "to enable society to realize its basic promises and beliefs, and [to] enable society to function and to survive."[20] Like earlier authors, to him the corporation was a distinct entity worthy of scientific inquiry, but unlike critics such as Veblen or Ely, he viewed its flaws mainly as problems to be solved within the corporation itself so that it would function better, rather than as concerns for society to correct via the state. His model of the corporate manager not as a social parasite but as a problem-solver in need of guidance was correspondingly different. His book and its view of the corporation would become hugely influential for many years among executives and business-school faculty in the United States.

During this period, it also became widely accepted that the expertise of the managerial ranks could and should be tapped by the government. While in the second half of the nineteenth century even Secretaries of the Treasury often came from the world of politics, in much of the postwar period, people with extensive management experience were picked to run not just Treasury but many other Cabinet departments. (Secretary of Defense Robert McNamara, one of President John F. Kennedy's "Whiz Kids," possessed an MBA from Harvard and was for many years a hands-on manager at Ford, experience that proved inadequate to the task of the Vietnam War.) It is now taken for granted that the high corporate ranks should be drawn on for executive-branch appointments, even in Democratic administrations. Meanwhile, in the world outside Washington, the influence and size of gigantic American corporations seemed to grow relentlessly.

From Harvard to Port Huron

So what was an anti-corporate sort to do? Primarily, take refuge in the world of ideas and wait for the politics to change. Skepticism of unfettered markets, powered by fear of giant corporations and by fresh memories of the Great Depression, was still intact. The social problems generated by monopoly, seen often as an inevitable outcome of economic growth in a market-economy setting, had consumed the economics profession in the 1920s and 1930s, and the postwar literature still revolved around various notions of how a benevolent state could manage market deficiencies in both the macroeconomic—excessively wild business cycles—and the microeconomic—poverty, discrimination, monopoly power—senses. And this was an environment in which the anti-corporate raw materials outlined in the previous section could continue to simmer under the comfortable surface of American society to break out after the Cold War ended.

In the United States, the anti-corporate torch was borne for a time most steadfastly (and wittily) not by conventional academic economists, with their dreary models and impenetrable prose, but by the longtime Harvard economist John Kenneth Galbraith. Galbraith was an extremely gifted polemicist. Despite possessing a PhD in economics from the University of California, he eschewed the tools of his profession. He did not trot out equations hinging on robotically calculating self-interested individuals to prove that the world was one way or another or that an arcane government policy would have this or that particular effect. Nor did he much care for the increasingly complex statistical analysis that came to become the economist's way of testing his theories (although he would cite such work when it supported some point he wished to make). Instead, he used words to paint a straightforward view of the role of large corporations in the world and, in so doing, gave intellectual respectability to much of what would follow in modern anti-corporatism. While his work was plagued by a lamentably patrician dislike of the sorts of choices ordinary Americans made in their lives, his writing—including his skepticism of corporations—reached an audience far larger than any "mainstream" economist could have dared dream of.

While some of his remarks strike the contemporary reader as amiss, they explain much about how he could reach the conclusions he did. In *American Capitalism: The Concept of Countervailing Power,* he asserted that innovation is almost exclusively the result of a marriage between the largest corporations and the government. The government carries out basic research and issues contracts to big companies to have its needs (whether for nuclear power or nuclear weapons) filled. The companies in turn carry out the applied research and produce the ever-more sophisticated goods necessary to provide for the state and keep consumers happy. He called this marriage the technostructure. Conspicuously absent from it was the lone entrepreneur remaking the world, which in Galbraith's view was almost entirely a romantic fiction.[21] There was no role for such a creature in the modern economy, because corporate monopoly had more or less eliminated competition on the basis of price among large firms, news that would shock these firms' managers today. In *The New Industrial State,* he reported upon traveling to the Soviet Union that large Soviet bureaucracies (with the attendant gulags and show trials to prop them up, which went unmentioned in his analysis) and large American corporations were converging to more or less the same structure.[22] And, in a claim soon to be buried by their economic difficulties in the 1990s and the flood of innovation in U.S. high technology in the 1990s still to come, the Japanese and the Germans as of the early 1980s had surpassed the United States in "industrial achievement" owing to lower military budgets. (Interestingly, the effects of globalization per se on the competitive threats the large American firms would face did not interest him much.) Because of all this, Americans would soon accept that the age of national industrial/economic planning was upon us. Since such planning required stable corporations to engage with the state, stability in employment would evermore be a hallmark of corporate managerial life.

While skeptical of many aspects of the dominant corporate giants, Galbraith too was no socialist. He did admittedly place great stock in one idea that meant the technostructure was wasteful—the Veblen idea of large business enterprises manufacturing demand for products through advertising. But his main view was that large companies were unavoidable and the task was to harness their power (and restrain their costly behavior) properly. In both *American Capitalism: The Concept of Countervailing Power* and *The New Industrial State,* Galbraith signed onto and in fact developed in much more sophistication the argument that such firms were an inevitable consequence of modern capitalism.[23] Over time, a new industry would come to be dominated by a small number of corporations. These firms taken as a whole would amass much of society's managerial talent and acquire unique knowledge of cutting-edge technology, which requires massive investment in research infrastructure.[24]

The expense of maintaining and improving the technostructure insulated the ultimate handful of survivors in a manufacturing industry (services, despite their growing importance in the economy even as he was writing, did not enter into the analysis much) from competition from new entrants. But large corporations must make huge investments in research and development and thus need on the one hand to make sure that their products are bought (which prompts advertising to persuade consumers to buy products of dubious social value) and that macroeconomic demand be stabilized so that individual product demand does not fluctuate wildly. The modern knowledge of Keynesian macroeconomic management gave the government the tools to do that, which in turn kept the technostructure going. And so the Galbraith approach is much more sophisticated than one in which corporations simply buy corrupt politicians (although it would be reduced to this in his last years). Large corporations *need* a stable economy, and being as dominant in the economy as they are the government needs to work closely with them. So the model is one of a marriage of necessity and of equals. But the cost of this quasi-insulation of these giant firms (whom competition is powerless to discipline because of their size) is that they potentially obtain monopoly power over consumers and American democracy.

In *American Capitalism,* Galbraith interprets this unfortunate convergence surprisingly optimistically. Americans on their own can form organizations to create what he calls "countervailing power"—labor unions, buyers' organizations, and middleman merchants that can use their own power to negotiate with the manufacturers for lower prices. (Wal-Mart, had it existed on the scale it does now when he wrote, might have been seen by him as an example of this.) It was the job of the state to encourage greater balance between buyers and sellers by using the anti-trust law only on manufacturers and not on retail chains or unions.[25] But by the time of *The New Industrial State,* he had turned pessimistic. Government provision of macroeconomic management and even the promotion of economic growth itself, vocationally oriented education, funding for research that is sometimes basic and sometimes applied, and military spending are all not done for their stated reasons but to serve the needs of the corporate establishment—the "adaptation of public goals to the goals of the technostructure."[26] Large corporations lead, and the government meekly follows. Countervailing power is nowhere to be found. As we saw in Chapter 1, by the time of the Iraq war in 2003, Galbraith's view of corporate power was more sinister still.

Galbraith was the last prominent representative of a genus of econo-mists known as American institutionalists, with Veblen being among the early giants of the subdiscipline. By Veblen's time, standard economics emphasized a universal model of human behavior in which people used such preferences to rationally make their best choices given their resource constraints. Institutionalists inverted that reasoning and thought that historical and social conditions determined the preferences people had. Thus, a Galbraith assertion that large corporations could come to dominate a society, and could manipulate people's purchasing behavior, fit comfortably within that tradition. The field took a substantial blow with the triumph of modern economic modeling, which institutionalists avoided, and ultimately faded away into next to nothing.[27] But his legacy—a rigorous theoretical structure that indicated how corporations could come to be the dominant actors in society—proved ultimately to be unusually important in the development of the modern ACM.

His influence was vividly clear in the 1962 Port Huron Statement, effectively the charter of Students for a Democratic Society and thus the founding document in many ways of the American left in the baby-boom era and beyond. Given the tenor of the times, with corporate executives seen as sources of expertise in government and corporations as such still not dominant in the thinking of the left at the time, it is remarkable how large "corporations," the "corporate economy," "corpo-rate vetoes" over public policy, and the like loomed in the statement. In a document that runs roughly some fifty single-spaced pages, some variant of "corporate" appears twenty-seven times. Among the excerpts:

The economic sphere would have as its basis the principles:

- that work should involve incentives worthier than money or sur-vival. It should be educative, not stultifying; creative, not mechani-cal; self-directed, not manipulated, encouraging independence;

a respect for others, a sense of dignity and a willingness to accept social responsibility, since it is this experience that has crucial influence on habits, perceptions and individual ethics;

- that the economic experience is so personally decisive that the individual must share in its full determination;
- that the economy itself is of such social importance that its major resources and means of production should be open to democratic participation and subject to democratic social regulation.

Many social and physical scientists, neglecting the liberating heritage of higher learning, develop "human relations" or "morale-producing" techniques for the corporate economy, while others exercise their intellectual skills to accelerate the arms race.

. . .

Corporations must be made publicly responsible. It is not possible to believe that true democracy can exist where a minority utterly controls enormous wealth and power. The influence of corporate elites on foreign policy is neither reliable nor democratic; a way must be found to be subordinate private American foreign investment to a democratically-constructed foreign policy. The influence of the same giants on domestic life is intolerable as well; a way must be found to direct our economic resources to genuine human needs, not the private needs of corporations nor the rigged needs of maneuvered citizenry.

. . .

We can no longer rely on competition of the many to insure that business enterprise is responsive to social needs. The many have become the few. Nor can we trust the corporate bureaucracy to be socially responsible or to develop a "corporate conscience" that is democratic. The community of interest of corporations, the anarchic actions of industrial leaders, should become structurally responsible to the people—and truly to the people rather than to an ill-defined and questionable "national interest." Labor and government as presently constituted are not sufficient to "regulate" corporations. A new re-ordering, a new calling of responsibility is necessary: more than changing "work rules" we must consider changes in the rules of society by challenging the unchallenged politics of American corporations. Before the government can really begin to control business in a "public interest," the public must gain more substantial control of government: this demands a movement for political as well as economic realignments. We are aware that simple government "regulation," if achieved, would be inadequate without increased worker participation in management decision-making, strengthened and independent regulatory power, balances of partial and/or complete public ownership, various means of humanizing the conditions and types of work itself, sweeping welfare programs and regional public government authorities. These are examples of measures to re-balance the economy toward public—and individual—control.

If there was a single moment when many of the themes of the modern ACM first cohered, even if (at that time) far from the mainstream of American life, this was it. Many of these themes—the public interest against the corporate, corporate dominance of the government and the corresponding need for "democratic" control, human passivity ("rigged needs"), corporate-imposed changes in the way we live—came together here. Of greatest importance is the frequent use in the statement of "corporate" as opposed to mere "big business" dominance. Finally, lest one be tempted to believe that the scribblings of academics are as a rule of no consequence, note that clearly the SDS had (skeptically) read their Galbraith, with their dismissal at one point in the statement of the potential of "countervailing power." (The document also uses the phrase "affluent society," the title of Galbraith's most famous book.[28]) While other issues—Vietnam, the arms race, Watergate—would dominate the thinking of progressives around the world for several decades, the anti-corporate template was set by Port Huron. From then on, the more the New Left moved into positions of importance in American society, the more important specifically anti-corporate thinking as I am defining it would become.

Also emerging in this era was a man who would become perhaps the most famous anti-corporate warrior of all, Ralph Nader. Often (justifiably) identified as the father of the modern consumer movement, Nader first came to public attention when he investigated the safety of GM cars and published his indictment of the Chevrolet Corvair in particular, *Unsafe at Any Speed*.[29] GM hired then private investigators to seek to discredit him. The president of GM was forced to apologize in testimony before a Senate committee, and a star was born. Nader soon emerged as a hero for a new generation of young people, including a host of lawyers, who sought to have the government aggressively combat corporate malfeasance in the areas of product safety, environmental damage, and fraud. (Even the U.S. Junior Chamber of Commerce saw fit to name him as one of its ten Outstanding Young Men of the Year in 1967). A host of pressure groups (e.g., Public Citizen, the Center for Science in the Public Interest) that viewed corporations as constantly posing a threat to consumers was spawned by his and his followers' activism, as were several government agencies (e.g., the Consumer Product Safety Commission and the National Highway Traffic Safety Administration, both established in the early 1970s). His ability to identify "corporations" specifically as the primary villain in the American political drama and to invoke the word "corporate" as an adjective to be attached to all sorts of nouns where it morally didn't belong (e.g., "corporate power," "corporate government," and "corporate welfare") played a large role in pushing the vision sketched at Port Huron—of corporations as the primary obstacle to achievement of a valid democracy—forward. Ultimately, by the time of his two quixotic presidential runs in 2000 and 2004, he had been at the vanguard of developing the modern anti-corporate foundational belief that corporate power explains everything. It is hard to understate his importance in modern anti-corporate thought.

The Stakeholder View

The 1980s saw the gelling in the United States of the stakeholder view of corporate governance, which holds that corporations should not only serve shareholders or even the vaguely defined broader public interest but also other specific, conflicting interest groups affected by the firm's operation—workers, customers, residents living near factories, etc. The idea is that some form of corporate governance should be found that allows these other groups to contribute to decisions about plant locations and closings, the distribution of firm revenue, etc. In contrast to the Anglo-American world, law and custom in many other countries had for many years organized the country's firms to reconcile the interests of a variety of these groups. Recall that German codetermination, in which employees are guaranteed some (and sometimes as much as half) of the seats on corporate boards of directors and which has roots going back to Bismarck, has been cemented in law for decades.[30] Japan and France too were home to firms chartered to be operated for the benefit of employees and customers simultaneously. A survey of managers in a variety of countries in the 1990s asked whether the firm should serve shareholders or all stakeholders. In Japan, Germany, and France, the percentage answering "all" was 97, 83, and 78 percent, respectively. At the other end, 71 percent of British and 76 percent of U.K. managers answered "shareholders."[31]

Thus, globally speaking, the stakeholder ideal was far from a novelty when it began to obtain a significant foothold in the United States. And the idea had been around in the United States for awhile. One of the earliest rigorous statements of it was half of a 1932 debate in the Harvard Law Journal. While numerous fairly abstruse arguments from economic theory followed on one side or the other, the basics of the modern argument—that corporate operations affect many constituencies, and they should all have a voice in its operations—are more or less unchanged from the one laid out there by E. Merrick Dodd.[32] Soon corporate executives themselves were occasionally speaking in these terms. The chairman of Standard Oil of New Jersey pronounced in 1951 that the task of the firm was to find "an equitable and working balance among the claims of the various directly interested groups...stockholders, employees, customers and the public at large. Business managers are gaining in professional status partly because they see in their work the basic responsibilities [to the public] that other professional men have long recognized in theirs."[33]

The stakeholder idea was a channel through which current anti-corporatism could make its way to the mainstream, in that it emphasized that there were much broader interests beyond those of shareholders. By altering (usually in a gradual, nonradical way) anti-corporate thinking from mere opposition of the corporate interest to those of the broader society to a specific delineation of who (outside of the government) deserved a voice in corporate governance, stakeholder thinking advanced the credibility of more extreme anti-corporate thinking. Unions and neighborhood associations and environmental groups in disputes with particular corporations began to opportunistically refer to themselves as "stakeholders" as they positioned themselves in public opinion. In 1976, Ralph Nader proposed a federal corporate charter to take account of all stakeholders. And the 1980s were when laws adjusting the relation between corporations and various stakeholders began to spread in various states, although not in those where incorporation was most common. Some required that the interests of other stakeholders be considered, and some merely allowed directors to consider stakeholder interests. Altogether, in the Anglo-American world, the stakeholder idea, which had been explicitly present, if not by that name, since at least the 1930s, was by the 1980s finally beginning to assert itself. A crude measure of these effects can be gleaned by counting references to both "stakeholders" and "corporations" in major newspapers listed in Lexis/Nexis.[34] The uses of the term rose from 104 from 1980 to 1989 to 627 from 1990 to 1994 to 2,566 from 1995 to 1999 to 4,640 from 2000 to 2004.

The View from Europe

In Europe meanwhile, the reaction to corporate giants after the end of the war was somewhat different. The ideas that large privately run corporations did not operate in the public interest and that society would be better served with public-interested, democratically accountable public authorities making decisions on what to produce, what to pay workers, etc. were if anything more accepted in the corridors of power in Western Europe than in the United States. And the catastrophic destruction of World War II made Europeans more amenable to the construction of the full welfare state, which was easily expanded to accommodate the nationalization of large private firms. In the United Kingdom, France, West Germany, Austria, and elsewhere, various combinations of electricity production, rail transport, automobile manufacturing, coal mining, steel manufacturing, chemical productions, and other industries were brought under state control. (Sometimes this was done at least nominally on the basis of wartime collaboration with the Nazis, e.g., the nationalization of Renault in France in 1945.) By the mid-1980s, much of this had been undone (although France briefly experimented yet again with nationalization soon after François Mitterand was elected in 1981). The reasons for the reversal were the obvious underperformance, inefficiency, and politicization of enterprise decision-making that followed nationalization. A company chartered for the benefit of shareholders seeks (subject to the constraints of employee shirking) to maximize shareholder value; a company answering to the state must incorporate, through whatever uncertain collective-choice process exists, the conflicting objectives of workers, buyers, ordinary citizens who sympathize with one or the other, and politicians who otherwise benefit from this or that enterprise decision. The catastrophic contradictions inherent in the latter problem were apparent to all by the mid-1980s. It was undoubtedly this failure of state management of large enterprises that would motivate many in the modern ACM to reject any big enterprises, whether public or private.

The View from the Arts

In addition to policy and ideas, anti-corporatism v.2 saw the emergence of much more anti-corporatism in the arts. This took the form of criticism of both the corporation itself as an overpowering, amoral, spirit-crushing institution and the armies of managers who worked for it as either soulless or sinister, or sometimes just plain absurd. In *Catch-22* (1961), Milo Minderbinder is the director of the wartime "syndicate," whose "shareholders" are the other members of the company. He seems to conjure money for himself out of thin air while keeping his shareholders forever waiting for their payoff. In Arthur Miller's 1949 play *Death of a Salesman,* Willy Loman is not explicitly housed in a corporation, but his ultimately catastrophic devotion as a faceless soldier to his employer in the business wars is obvious. Tom Rath, *The Man in the Gray Flannel Suit* (a 1956 film), finds that the money he reaps from joining the United Broadcasting Corporation does not compensate him adequately for the soul he loses. J. Pierpont Finch (whose name of course is meant to recall J. Pierpont Morgan) uses deceit to climb the ladder of the evidently nonmeritocratic World-Wide Wicket Company in the movie *How to Succeed in Business Without Really Trying* (1967). Artists as a whole have long considered social commentary to be at least as important as the pursuit of beauty in their work, and the social commentary regarding the corporation often views it as bumbling and staffed mainly by the duplicitous, greedy, and dishonest. That they are far from efficient producers of goods and services, their nominal goal, of course follows immediately.

ANTI-CORPORATISM V.3: THE MODERN MOVEMENT

Sometimes history seems to turn on the smallest things. On the night of November 9, 1989, the East German Minister of Propaganda, Günter Schabowski, announced that "as far as I know effective immediately, right now" residents of East Berlin could travel to the western side of the city. Schabowski had apparently misinterpreted on live television a note he had received indicating that starting *the next day* East Berliners would be able merely to apply for travel documents to go to West Berlin. But his announcement sent tens of thousands of East Berliners surging to the Wall, and the overwhelmed guards had no choice but to let them through. East Germany and the rest of the Central European Soviet empire were gone within months, and the Soviet Union within two years.

The scene of Berliners pouring through the gates of the Wall was greeted with joy in much of the world and marked a key juncture in the nature and prominence of anti-corporate thinking in the world of ideas and politics. It was a fitting end to a tumultuous decade, beginning with the election of Margaret Thatcher as prime minister of Great Britain. She was brought to power by the Winter of Discontent, the period in 1979 when Britain was brought to its knees by a combination of the macroeconomic dysfunction (particularly high inflation) crippling so much of the industrialized world and the peculiarly British disorder of a society brought to its knees by the (dare we call it monopolistic?) power of its trade unions. Early in her administration, she decided to go beyond what she had previously contemplated and carry out a massive privatization of most of the firms that had been nationalized over the past several decades. In much of the developing world, the 1982 developing-country debt crisis gave birth to what came to be known as the Washington Consensus, the belief that the only way forward for poor countries was to reject state ownership and intervention and vigorously embrace market forces (a task that has since been accomplished with only mixed success).

And so the trend of the times was clear. In 1986, the Socialists were ousted in the French legislature, and the new government more than undid the Mitterand nationalizations. Meanwhile, economic experimentation in Hungary, China, Chile, and elsewhere seemed to demonstrate the falsehood of most of the central propositions then motivating progressive economic thinking: the belief that large organizations inevitably dominated any highly advanced economy and that the public sector had to be intimately involved with managing these organizations. The modern market economy, of which corporations operating relatively freely were a significant part, was embraced around the world.

And yet, paradoxically, it was now that the modern ACM began to truly spread its wings. Its growing number of members received some inadvertent assistance from some members of the management-guru set, who prophesied (far from entirely negatively) the decline of the nation-state in the face of corporations, globalization, or both.[35] This was a prospect that those hostile to business found frightening. At the same time, in various left-wing activist communities, people were exploring what they saw as corporate complicity in environmental damage, factory closing, and other problems. On the policy side, governments negotiated international agreements designed to dramatically increase the free flow of goods and resources around the world—the World Trade Organization, most importantly. That national laws restricting businesses could be and soon were overturned by the unelected adjudication panels of such organizations generated a view that democracy was being eroded in Western countries by corporate power (a topic explored further in Chapter 5), just as it was triumphing in Central Europe.

But if there was a single galvanizing moment for the dispersed, disconnected yearners of the modern, global ACM, a moment at which the disparate strands of anti-corporate thinking and activism in the United States and elsewhere began to evolve into the defining feature of the post–Cold War global left, it was the publication in 1995 of the first edition of a book called David Korten's *When Corporations Rule the World.* Korten's biography is not exactly one of a bomb-throwing radical. He possesses an MBA from Stanford, spent time in the U.S. Air Force and working for the U.S. government's Agency for International Development, and taught at the Harvard Graduate School of Business. This is ordinarily not the stuff of which revolutionary social entrepreneurs are made. But after a number of years working in developing countries, he became convinced that global living conditions were getting worse and that corporations were largely responsible for it. The value of *When Corporations Rule the World* was that at the right moment in history, it knitted together several diverse strands of argument into a single, (all too) simple claim self-evident in the book's title. That it was accessibly written and did not accuse the general public of complicity in corporate rule (which was attributed to subterfuge, corruption, and the machinations of sinister "corporate libertarians" housed in Washington think tanks and funded by corporate money) made it all the more important.

The book is the closest thing to sacred scripture that the movement has. Its achievement was to unite seemingly small and disparate groups who shared repugnance at what the world was becoming but did not know about one another. It fully crystallized the ideas that corporations are driven (by law and the desires of their managers) only to maximize profits; that in doing so they harm the entire species apart from their shareholders, their managers, and the government officials and intellectuals they co-opt; that the tremendous wealth they produce in the course of doing so allows them to buy out governments; that in pursuit of growth, they destroy the environment and impose other "negative externalities" on society; that, pace Marx, they knit the entire human species into a modernist, growth-oriented, standardized model emphasizing personal consumption at the expense of local organization of economic (and indeed all) life; that their success in this task destroys local cultural diversity; and, critically, that they are ultimately the creations of the public, which can revoke their privileges and turn them back toward the public purpose. The book has, according to its author, sold hundreds of thousands of copies and been translated into twelve languages.

Suddenly, without benefit of any book-industry promotion, an entire movement sprouted not just among specialists but the broader public from the seeds that had been planted over decades. All of the previous strands, and more, were tied together into a neat, distilled package. The enemy of the good society was not the rich or militarism or environmental damage. Rather, there was a common cause of all these things—corporations and their incentive structure. In particular, the Korten book and the literature it spawned posited a sort of anti-corporate syllogism (some of whose components must be true if the movement's claims are to hold together but not all of which it may explicitly acknowledge) that goes roughly as follows:

Assumption—inherent corporate nature. The legal requirement that the Anglo-American corporation operate exclusively for shareholders' benefit means that it maximizes profits to the exclusion of all other considerations.

Assumption—life is zero-sum. When the wealth of one participant in the economic system grows, it does so at the expense of others.

Conclusion—corporate growth imperative. By inherent corporate structure, corporations are forced to grow as long as there is room for growth, so as to maximize shareholder returns.

Conclusion—corporations vs. the rest of us. The corporate growth imperative, in conjunction with life being zero-sum, means that when corporations win, we lose—with respect to the environment, wages, and a host of other considerations.

Conclusion—government takeover. By the corporate growth imperative, in combination with corporations vs. the rest of us, the government ultimately comes to be dominated by corporate interests.

In this distressing outcome, the current set of corporate laws cannot be used to overcome these problems. Total social transformation is required. Indeed, the Korten book is notable for spawning a strain of argument, which is popular among anti-corporate thinkers and shapes the dialogue even among many who do not accept its hard-line conclusions, that says that corporate profit-seeking has been fundamental in shaping modern society, which will have to be dramatically remade on moral, environmental, and other grounds. Because of its dire predictions about the likely future under corporate rule, I will call this the apocalyptic school, to be contrasted with the school of thought that argues not against modernity and progress generally but merely that corporations have too much control over society. I will refer to this way of thinking as power-struggle anti-corporatism. In both schools, unlike earlier Marxist and even some socialist beliefs, which essentially argued that the situation was hopeless absent violently revolutionary social change, a cornerstone of the ACM is that locally driven democracy can and will overturn the corporate-driven world. The ACM and its recommendations are fundamentally an act of faith, a belief in the power of the public purpose to ultimately triumph over selfish corporations; unlike the pronouncements of, say, orthodox Marxists, there is no belief that the system is inherently flawed, just its current results. Freed from the corporate stranglehold, human society will naturally return to the local, the diverse, the public-spirited, and the justly governed. The complex corporate, global economy is the way it is not because we want it that way one individual decision at a time but because corporations have maneuvered us into it. The only missing ingredient in curing what ails us is activism. Hence the magic word "democracy"—the ability of the majority to outvote a view that is numerically small but financially large—looms extremely large in the new anti-corporate thinking. The robustness of this syllogism will be tested in subsequent chapters.

Post-Korten, a raft of books was issued that amplified the anti-corporate theme. Given the skepticism that the American Revolutionary generation had of (special-privilege) corporations, some depict the ACM as a gallant effort to take the country (and sometimes the world) back, as rabble-rousing in the best American tradition.[36] Some titles use colorfully angry language depicting corporations and their minions—not just their managers, but those who do their dirty work in the think tanks, academia, and government—as mortal threats to society.[37] While many are published by smaller houses (Berrett-Koehler Press in San Francisco, the publisher of *When Corporations Rule the World*, is especially energetic), at least a few are published by major houses, in apparent ignorance of the irretrievable conflict that the authors posit between the corporate interests of these publishers and the broader public interest.[38] And even those works that are published by smaller firms are widely available on the shelves at the major corporate chain bookstores (in seeming defiance of their private interests), which suggests their continual popularity.

With respect to solutions, the movement proposes revoking all three long-standing legal principles from Chapter 2—the open-access approach to corporate formation, the legal rule granting corporations the right to act as persons not just in contracting but in all other behavior, and the limited liability shareholders have for corporate debts. Corporations, it is argued, have always been creations of the state and therefore serve at the pleasure of the people's representatives. Corporations that behave immorally should have their charters scrutinized by the legislature and, if necessary, revoked. When this happens, all the toxic effects of corporations and their manipulations—the corruption, the annihilation of local life, the environmental damage, the fraud—will all wash away and humanity will return to a more natural state from which it has temporarily been diverted by the corporate interregnum of two centuries or so.

Modern Artistic Anti-Corporatism

The arts too increasingly came to reflect this sinister, all-powerful view of corporations in the last quarter-century. From the art of the 1960s and 1970s that had revolved around individual duplicity, the entire corporate form was now increasingly depicted as a threat to all that was good. In film, some of the work depicts particular corporations as rapacious levelers of small business—e.g., *Wall Street* (1987) and *Other People's Money* (1991). Other work adopts the view of corporations as all-powerful string-pullers, a theme that is particularly popular in science fiction. In the *Alien* movies, the Weyland-Yutani Company is a devious interstellar corporation that engages in illegal colonization and ultimately tries to develop terrifying parasite aliens into weapons. In *The Terminator* series, it is the secrecy of the Cyberdyne Systems Corporation that leads to the creation of a malevolent computer network that threatens to destroy the human species. In literature, the dystopian genre now known as cyberpunk sometimes has large corporations controlling a failed futuristic world. In *Neuromancer* by William Gibson (1984), which served as an inspiration for the very successful series of *Matrix* movies and gave the world the term "cyberspace," it is the Tessier-Ashpool Corporation that rules the world; in the 1982 film *Blade Runner,* the Tyrell Corporation does. Perhaps anticipating these developments, in two of his novels—*V.* (1963) and *The Crying of Lot 49* (1966)—the acclaimed postmodern writer Thomas Pynchon wrote of the strangely conspiratorial Yoyodyne Corporation as a participant, even perhaps the architect, of arcane plots.

Enron and Beyond

The movement certainly knows how to take advantage of an unexpected gift. That gift arrived in October 2001 when the Enron Corporation, depicted for years as a dynamic innovator largely responsible for creating new markets to trade such exotica as electricity futures, announced that it had vastly overstated its earnings. It would soon be forced to declare bankruptcy, and several of its executives would be convicted of white-collar felonies. Along with other cases of overstated earnings and workaday thefts of company funds by managers in companies such as Worldcom and Tyco, the Enron collapse led to an outbreak of coverage contending that corporate America had become rotten to the core during the go-go 1990s. The legislative response, a series of enhanced disclosure requirements known, because of its primary legislative sponsors, as Sarbanes/Oxley, was modest relative to the demands of anti-corporate activists. But the episodes quickly became a cause célèbre for the ACM, which immediately moved to capitalize on them to move for broader anti-corporate measures.[39] Indeed, anti-corporate activists had already during the 1990s learned the value of focusing their attention on particular firms, which they could particularly tar with breathless accounts of various misdeeds. Examples included the Royal Dutch/Shell Oil group, whom activists charged first with culpability in the Nigerian government's execution of the writer and activist Ken Saro-Wiwa and later with environmental devastation; Nike, targeted by college students and labor unions for its allegedly low wages and poor working conditions; and Wal-Mart, whose efforts to open stores in the United States were sometimes frustrated, particularly in big cities, by activists who objected to its wages and benefits and its impact on local retail businesses.

In hindsight, the breathless attention paid to Enron and other corporate-fraud episodes is baffling. For example, the first major announcement of Enron's difficulties—that it would be taking accounting charges in a variety of activities, resulting in a revaluation of assets— appeared in *The New York Times* on October 17, 2001. It was at this point a business story, but after nearly continuous and increasingly breathless coverage, it was by November 10 the lead story on the front page. This was when the country was still reeling after the September 11 attacks, and indeed only 34 days after the beginning of the invasion of Afghanistan, then seen as a highly perilous and uncertain undertaking. And yet coverage of Enron quickly rivaled the Afghanistan campaign for weeks as the most important story in the press. This is understandable as a matter of sensationalistic (profit-maximizing, even) journalism—the brash symbol of the new economy getting its comeuppance. And yet the extent to which its troubles and those of other large corporations with shady accounting were quickly knit into a coherent tale of the entire era was a mistake, given that taken at their worst the abuses involved only a tiny fraction of the thousands of companies trading on the primary U.S. stock exchanges. Even now "Enron" is a term of art for broader corporate skullduggery. The Enron bankruptcy led to unemployment and the destruction of retirement savings for about 4,000 company employees. This was painful (and legally actionable) for these victims but hardly a meaningful description of an entire era. Despite this ultimate unimportance for the broader world, it is almost beyond doubt that these few scattered fiascoes helped set the stage for the prominence of anti-corporate language in the 2004 campaigns, language that is likely to get worse before it gets better.

The Anti-Corporate Moment

While its historical antecedents are now clear, where has this recent coalescence of explicit anti-corporatism come from? Why, in other words, now? Speculation on the evolution of ideas is hazardous, but one possibility suggests itself. The end of the Cold War—whose threats of nuclear war provided a unifying principle for the political left for the entire period from 1945 to 1989—and the increasing desire around the world for more resort to market forces stole from the left its fundamental *raison d'être*. While in foreign policy fears of what they saw as American imperial power unchecked without the Soviet Union quickly gave the global left common ground, the very existence of that power, combined with the pressure on welfare states, on traditional cultural practices, and on state oversight of society, brought about by the rise of global marketization required an explanation. If it is all the doing of all-powerful corporations, suddenly all these things become explicable. In this neatly tied package of an ideology, corporations have an interest in rolling the state back, and the American government and military (along with their government minions elsewhere) are doing corporate bidding. A grand unified theory of war and peace and of economic and social history becomes possible. Such a theory had long ago been offered by Marx and Lenin, but the events of 1989 (combined with the rejection of at least the economic aspects of Marxism by almost every country on the planet) discredited it. The idea of corporate power redeems for the left the possibility of such a comprehensive theory of why the world is the dissatisfying way it is.

Another development also worth noting is the rise of rightist anti-corporatism. In the American context, to be on the right has generally meant to be against regulation of business. Like all conservatives, American conservative wish to conserve that which is (or go back to that which was). But most American conservatives seek to conserve something different from conservatives in other societies, limited government—including limited restrictions on commerce. But commerce is a fundamentally dynamic and indeed disruptive force, and so this type of peculiarly American conservatism lends itself to acceptance of social remaking on economic grounds. But in the United States too, there is now a strain of purely static conservatism. Such conservatism rejects commerce if it upsets traditional mores and institutions. While rarer in the United States, it is more closely related to traditional European conservatism.[40] This conservative anti-corporatism is based on cultural chauvinism (and distaste for commercial activity generally) rather than the class-warfare legacy that motivates the anti-corporatism of the left. This strain of thought is not historically unknown; in 1902, the British writer Frederick A. McKenzie wrote a book attacking American corporations investing in Britain on such nationalist grounds.[41] Very often in this rightist view, modernization itself is something to be suspicious of because of its power in undoing traditional society. And so the nativist right too now has its own anti-corporatism, which partially overlaps with that of the left. This strain of thought objects to corporations as cosmopolitan, disloyal to the nation that spawned them, and destructive of traditional morality. Indeed, what the anti-corporate left calls "local" is often "traditional" to the anti-corporate right.

Still, while it receives aid and comfort from some romantics and traditionalists on the right, modern anti-corporatism is primarily a creature of the left. And the investigation of those claims is the next task, beginning with claims about some of the purely economic aspects of the corporation.

Chapter 4

Corporate Economics

One after another their facilities line the great highway arteries of the American Midwest—not just the corporations familiar to consumers, such as McDonald's, Wal-Mart, and Honda, but others with mysterious names and even more mysterious purposes—MetoKote, MD/MT Picture Displays, Stillwater Technologies, Aida, Grob. Tens of thousands of them trade shares on major and minor stock exchanges around the world, and the opening of such exchanges in emerging economies is often treated as a landmark event. The largest corporations have clearly formed a web that covers the entire globe and draws in most of the world's citizens during many of their daily activities. The economic charges against them make them an increasing target of public skepticism.

The ACM has a love–hate, although mostly hate, relationship with economics. On the one hand, there is a fascination with some of the jargon when it is useful for making the anti-corporate case. And so words such as "externalities" are frequently sprinkled through anti-corporate texts. And yet for the most part, mainstream economic theory is largely ignored in the movement. The Swiss theologian and religious revolutionary John Calvin said that philosophy was "a diabolical science" because it "fixes our contemplations on the works of nature, and turns them away from God." The ACM takes a similar view of much mainstream economic thought, which they dismiss as "corporate libertarianism" when it calls attention to the virtues of competition and free commerce.

As we will see, corporations unquestionably present some intrinsic incentive problems. But as the economics of the corporation is discussed, it is critical to compare the current corporate landscape to the available alternatives and to remember that, fundamentally, corporations are simply a legal structure to motivate people to provide things that other people want, given that those wants conflict with what still other people want. Ultimately, corporations are governed by the same principles as any other form of human organization: their members react to incentives, and among those incentives are those provided by the gains from trade with their customers. If (and this will be an important argument later) corporations are able to provide more of what people want while sacrificing less of what other people want than other forms of social organization, that is a powerful argument in their favor. The first task is to handle the conventional economic criticisms of corporations (which can be drawn from mainstream economic theory) before tallying what economics suggests about their social benefits. Discussion of one purely economic criticism, corporations' alleged economic power, is deferred until the next chapter.

THE TRADE-OFFS OF LIMITED LIABILITY

Limited liability, now the dominant form of liability allocation for joint-stock companies, provides some incentives that are socially useful and some that are socially costly. In this it is like any system of allocation of legal responsibilities. Thus the proper comparison is to the available alternatives. Bear in mind that the term "corporate limited liability" is misleading because, as Frank Easterbrook and Daniel Fischel note, corporations do not possess limited liability. Corporate personhood makes them liable for all debts they incur. It is instead the ability to go after the personal assets of shareholders that is limited.[1]

The primary justification for limited liability is that it encourages risk-taking. Even now business creation is an extremely risky venture. Research by the U.S. Bureau of Labor Statistics indicates that 34 percent of new business ventures fail to survive more than two years and 56 percent fail to survive more than four years.[2] As any small-business owner knows, many mistakes he might make can have catastrophic impacts on his economic experiment. He may underestimate the cost of supplying his product—of acquiring store space or worker time or other needed resources, of learning what consumers really want, or of discovering and mastering the most cost-effective way to bring it to them. He may overestimate how desirable what he plans to sell is to consumers, measured by what they are willing to pay for it. He may fail to anticipate supply disruptions, demographic changes, arbitrary changes in public tastes, or the introduction of alternatives to his product. (He may choose to see this not as a problem of his mistakes, i.e., an inability to correctly forecast the future, but as bad luck or surprises. But economically the effect is the same.)

And the very role of a new business is to gamble that by bidding resources away from some other use to be used for her ends, the owner can generate enough income to more than pay what is needed to procure those resources away from those alternatives. New business ventures are a way of reorganizing society, sometimes in very small ways initially and (if the venture succeeds) to a greater extent later on. The would-be software entrepreneur who persuades a building owner to rent office space to him may bid the space away from an insurance agent; his programmers away from other software firms; his receptionist away from a law office. In doing so, he provides a signal to people that a career in software is slightly more lucrative than before, because of higher demand for the services of people who have the appropriate talents and training. This is how prices coordinate resources use. To found a business is to gamble that currently other businesses have gotten it wrong with these resources, in the sense that there are unexploited opportunities for profit. And the high rate of closure for new businesses suggests that often those beliefs are mistaken, which in turn suggest that competition is vigorous.

But it is the ventures for which these beliefs are correct that generate much human progress. We generally think, not entirely without reason, that much of modern civilization is built on the foundation laid by statesman, scientists, and thinkers. But it is in fact the lowly businessman who often translates these abstractions into tangible things that people may use to improve their control over their own lives. It takes a scientist (e.g., Frederick Banting and colleagues at the University of Toronto) to better understand the natural world (by discovering that injections of insulin can bring diabetes under control). But such discoveries are idle curiosities unless entrepreneurs can solve the equally if not more difficult problems of figuring out such things as how to produce insulin in the most efficient way and how to efficiently distribute it to those diabetics, thus making it available and affordable to the largest possible numbers of them. It takes a large corporation such as Lilly benefiting from economies of scale in marketing and basic research to lower those costs further. And it then takes companies like Genentech to provide the basic technological breakthroughs that allow corporations such as Lilly and Novo Nordisk to improve the product.[3]

And unlimited liability would dramatically increase that risk for business owners, increasing the expected loss of any entrepreneurial venture and thus preventing many such ventures from being launched. Do drug-company executives and workers, possessing less risky alternatives, make the effort to develop a new medicine, knowing their personal assets and even their liberty are at risk if the medicine has unforeseen negative consequences? Surely not, even if the probability of this happening is quite small. This is true even for those entrepreneurs who issue no shares but still wish to incorporate to obtain protection for their personal assets—a medical partnership of a few doctors, say. And so it must be true that the absence of limited liability would have a cost in terms of diminished entrepreneurship. But how big? It is impossible to say for certain, although some scholarship documents the sizable effect of limited liability's introduction on firm survival rates, firm startup rates, firm efficiency, and the rate of creation of organized venture capital in environments as diverse in time and place as family businesses in Scotland over the century ending in 1970, 19th-century England, Ireland, and the United States, and postwar Germany.[4] Given the speed with which other jurisdictions copied limited liability after it was adopted, the enthusiasm with which countries adopt it upon transition to a market economy, the rarity of repeal, and the near-immediate undoing of repeal when it does occasionally happen, there is some reason to think that government officials *fear* substantial political costs if it is not enacted and preserved. Certainly, it is difficult to imagine a speculative venture such as Genentech, launched when "genetic engineering" was still a largely theoretical idea, being able to do what it does if limited liability had not been available.

Of course, lowering shareholder risk is not a free lunch. Risk comes from the inherent fact that there are many possible futures, each contingent on choices made now. That shareholders bear less risk under limited liability than under the alternatives does not change this underlying fact but simply requires that other parties bear more. It is helpful to classify that risk-shifting into two types: risks imposed on others who transact with or within the firm (internal risk-shifting) and risks imposed on those who do not participate in the firm in any way (external risk-shifting).

Limited Liability and Internal Risk-Shifting

The corporation has several constituencies who expect to be rewarded by their participation in it but face risks based on how well it does. In addition to shareholders, others include creditors, employers, and customers. The size of and investment by these constituencies will vary depending on the firm's own prospects and the allocation of liability for corporate debts.[5] If there is unlimited liability, there may be little if any investment in shares, and the owners of the firm may borrow money instead. Creditors will be willing to lend because any debts will be fully secured by collateral, so firm financing will be heavy on debt and light on equity. But borrowing is obviously constrained not to go beyond whatever collateral the firm possesses. If, on the other hand, a corporation selects limited liability, those who lend money to the firm must do so knowing that if the owners of the firm (or the managers they hire) spend money unwisely and the firm ends up in financial difficulty or even bankruptcy, their ability to recover their investments is constrained. Hence, the owners are immunized from some of the costs of their mistakes and will be willing to run the corporation more aggressively. Equity financing will partly squeeze out reluctant creditors relative to what would occur with unlimited liability. This aggressiveness is a double-edged sword, because on the one hand it places other firm constituencies under greater risk of loss, but on the other it enables the financing of some potentially landmark but highly risky ventures that could not occur under unlimited liability.

And so limited liability raises the possibility of excessively aggressive corporate behavior, borne here by other corporate constituencies (creditors who incur a greater risk of default, employees who incur a greater risk of job loss after having made many investments in knowledge and skills that are specific to that business and cannot easily be transferred, customers who run a greater risk of firm nonperformance). And thus legal scholars who argue for a reduction or elimination of limited liability sometimes call for a "piercing of the corporate veil," by which they mean more opening of shareholders to personal liability for firm debts. Of course, a key point in these internal risk-shifting issues is that all participants in the corporation know those risks going in. Everyone who lends money to a corporation, every employee who works for one, every business partner who signs a contract with one knows (or certainly is in a position to easily know) that the corporation's shareholders have limited liability. It is possible to contract around limited liability by demanding that firms soliciting their money adopt unlimited or partially limited liability. The optimal rule with respect to liability is to maximize the number of alternatives available—letting those who wish to incorporate with limited or unlimited liability do so. But of course that is exactly the law now; the only innovations brought by limited liability were to overturn the common-law procedure that treated personal assets as seizable for purposes of settling debts and to make limited liability the rule unless corporations stipulate otherwise.

Limited Liability and External Risk-Shifting

But one type of party does not benefit from prior knowledge of limited liability—the bearer of external risk. The decisions of corporate owners or their agents may impose what economists call external costs or "negative externalities"—in other words, costs on parties who do not participate in the transactions that generate the costs. For example, firm owners secure in their limited liability may choose production methods that produce high risks of calamitous accidents (e.g., oil spills or crashes of trains that release toxic fumes). Nearby residents or other potential victims will be in no position to insure against that risk (except at potentially very great cost, e.g., by moving far away from the facility).

However, in the event of an accident, such victims will have the option of litigation. They may sue the corporation for any damages caused. As long as the damage does not exceed corporate assets (which could be attached in any judgment against the corporation), the corporation and its shareholders will have to fully bear the costs of the imposed externality.[6] And so how frequently corporations are bankrupted by such judgments becomes the key question. (Offset, to those who believe that courts are prone to unjustifiably finding liability or overcompensating plaintiffs in torts involving huge damage claims, by excessive awards to plaintiffs. This is said to occur when juries make liability findings and excessive awards either out of sympathy or out of opportunism—the opportunity to assist deserving plaintiffs at the expense of a deep-pocketed defendant substantially alien to the jurisdiction.[7] This outcome might be plausible at least in the United States, since its litigation system is more sympathetic to plaintiffs than that of other common-law societies because of the easy availability of contingent fees and class-action certification.)

There are no data available on the frequency of bankruptcies from liability findings in particular, although many observers contend they are rare. Famous examples include those resulting from asbestos and breast-implant litigation, although examples of companies being able to pay huge amounts (via settlement before the completion of trial) are also easy to find—Exxon in the Valdez oil spill and the tobacco companies in their gigantic struggle with first the federal and then state governments in the 1990s over damage to smokers' health. That many of the scholarly discussions of bankruptcy and limited liability repeatedly refer to the same small number of examples suggests that the evasion of external costs through bankruptcy is not a significant problem, which in turn suggests that the tort system is adequate for addressing it. To repeat, corporations *are* liable for external claims. The only question is whether bankruptcy allows them to evade these responsibilities. But here the theoretical problem asserted not just by the ACM but many legal scholars must be conceded: there is in limited liability some propensity for taking actions whose costs may fall on outsiders, and it is the function of the tort system to address these externalities. It is certainly a problem in theory, although evidently not a large one in reality. And addressing it by restoring unlimited liability carries dramatic costs of its own, most notably preventing the establishment of highly risky ventures with potentially dramatic payoffs.

There is one final point with respect to shareholder's unlimited liability for external costs. In the law, *all* participants in a corporation enjoy limited liability in a sense. Neither employees' nor creditors' personal assets can be attached. Employees' exposure is thus limited in the event of a liability finding against their employer to lost wages and lost returns on any training and experience they have acquired that is not useful in other employment. A worker may be hurt when his raises are lower due to a large liability award against his employer, but his personal property cannot be seized despite his contribution to the activity generating the award. Creditors' exposure is similarly limited to being unable to fully collect in bankruptcy proceedings the money they lent. These groups are subordinate in firm governance, with shareholders making final decisions, but their consent is nonetheless required to enable the corporation to do whatever wrongdoing it is found liable for. Limited liability simply places shareholders on an equal footing with these other participants.

On Balance

Limited liability has costs, although any liability rule would; the only question is their allocation. The alternatives to it proposed by legal scholars apply equally to internal or external costs. As substitutes, more reasonable critics have offered pro rata unlimited liability (liability for a share of costs proportional to a shareholder's share of ownership), joint and several unlimited liability (every shareholder can be held liable for the entire award), and criminal penalties for corporate managers or shareholders. The question of criminal penalties is most easily dealt with. (In fact, that a corporation can be criminally liable is every bit as much an aspect of corporate personhood as its other rights criticized by the ACM, although the movement never mentions it.) First, note that criminal liability applies only to problems of external cost. Internal costs, like all other disputes over debts, have always been matters for civil law. But the conditions, if any, under which criminal penalties should be imposed for pollution, presiding over accidents that take lives, etc. is an interesting one. Somewhat surprisingly, economic research indicates that when corporate managers commit such criminal violations, they generally do so in their own interests rather than in the interests of shareholders. The interests of corporate managers and shareholders are frequently not aligned, a topic explored further in the next section. And so a manager may fail to adequately monitor the safety of a production process because of the extra work it would impose on him rather than because it is what shareholders want. This sort of shirking is what the evidence shows typically motivates corporate crime.[8] Given that, the preferred approach is to sanction those managers directly. The corporation itself should be sanctioned only if managers cannot be adequately punished given the social cost of the offense and their personal wealth. In cases where the legal regime calls for imprisonment when a private party commits the same act, there is no economic reason not to employ it against any corporate manager.[9] As long as these procedures are followed, there is no obvious economic objection to making managers criminally responsible for offenses of sufficient social cost for which they are directly responsible. But for internal costs any form of unlimited liability poses its own problems, quite possibly fatal ones.

Practicality

If shareholders are to have unlimited liability for internal damage, it will be on a joint-and-several or pro rata basis. Both pose problems. They both require elaborate, presumably expensive record-keeping so that a court can establish who owned which shares when, so that liability may be allocated properly. Widely dispersed ownership and pro rata liability may mean that a huge list of shareholders must be maintained and that many of them must be dunned to pay the judgment, which is impractically costly. With joint and several liability, the largest shareholders will be the first targets of litigation, so that they are deterred from owning shares to begin with (defeating the whole purpose of issuing them in the first place) and shareholders must constantly monitor the behavior of their fellow shareholders with respect to hiding assets and whether their fellow shareholders' wealth grows or shrinks. Such liability regimes seem almost impossible to connect with the world in which we live, of freely tradable shares dispersed throughout the population.

Risk-taking

Presumably, those ventures most crippled by the absence of limited liability would be those seen at the time they seek to float shares as the greatest risks. Sometimes such perceptions are justified, and those are the ventures quickly liquidated by competition. But if the ventures that generate the most social value—say, radically different yet ultimately far more effective medical treatments—are those seen as riskiest beforehand, the social cost of ending limited liability could be profound. For example, corporations were critical in the early development of aviation. In the wake of the successful demonstration of their flying machine in Europe, the Wright Brothers faced huge orders from European and the American governments and incorporated in 1909. And yet the basic product itself was obviously risky, not just in the consumer-safety sense—Lt. Thomas E. Selfridge of the U.S. Army was the first powered-aviation fatality on a flight in which he was only the third aviation *passenger* in history—but in the sense of being so novel and world-changing that it would be difficult to decide whether the breakthrough is even valuable to consumers, and if so in which uses. It seems more than plausible that the inability to incorporate, including the obtaining of limited liability, might have crippled the growth of that industry, of biotechnology, of *any* industry with great risk in its initial phases. If one accepts that the legal system is highly unpredictable, those risks become greater. In envisioning an anti-corporate future, the fruits of the eminently corporate present are invariably taken for granted.

Economies of Scale

One of the most frequently offered original justifications for limited liability was the need for large amounts of capital. Capital can be borrowed too, but for new, highly risky ventures such funding can be harder to get. This is a problem that is most compelling for industries with great investment needs early on. Then, the unwillingness of investors, especially passive ones, to court total financial disaster will be a significant constraint. The Nobel Prize–winning economist John Hicks, in a work that tallied the pluses and minuses of limited liability, argued that "[i]nsofar as one associates economic progress with economies of scale, it must be regarded as a major achievement of limited liability that it has made much of our economic progress possible."[10] If one accepts the contention of, say, John Kenneth Galbraith that economies of scale broadly defined are the key ingredients of the giant corporation and (as every government that has implemented it has believed) that the absence of limited liability makes investors reluctant to fund the achievement of such economies, it follows that the absence of limited liability means the absence of corporate size. To be sure, the ACM is not the least troubled by this argument. Rather, it generally accepts that limited liability is a key ingredient in the size of our larger corporations and criticizes size as a key part of the corporatization of the world they decry.

Unchaining the Small Investor

Much criticism of limited liability assumes that it benefits only the firm issuing the shares, but potential investors as a class actually benefit too. The potential exposure investors face under limited liability unavoidably limits, perhaps sharply, the number of people who are willing to invest in corporate shares. This is because of the risk of what Governor Levi Lincoln of Massachusetts, while campaigning for limited liability in that state, termed "utter ruin" from a corporate default.[11] Under limited liability, there is a vast democratization of investment, as participating in (potential) profit streams from growing corporations becomes affordable to far more people. Estimates of the size of the American shareholding class differ but range from roughly forty to as high, in a 2000 survey by Zogby International, as seventy-eight percent.[12] In modern America, stock ownership and market trends are the stuff of daily conversation for many throughout most of the income distribution. Corporate success is the concern not just of fat cats or mutual-fund directors but of truck drivers, nurses, teachers, and others vested in the stock market either directly or through their retirement plans. While share ownership is not as widespread in other countries, the adoption of full open-access incorporation by France in 1867 also significantly democratized wealth there. While critics of the growing heft of shareholding America cite the risk to which investors are exposed when markets go down, this effect is dominated by their newfound access in the last twenty years to the power of asset-value appreciation and compound interest (through reinvestment of dividends), power previously available only to the wealthy. For investors, unlimited liability is exclusionary, and limited liability, liberating. Through tradable shares of firms incorporated under it, the fruits of the corporation are made available to all.

Adverse Selection

This is a problem that occurs in many contexts where information about a product's quality is uncertain. When buyers are unable to distinguish between high- and low-quality products, it is very possible for the low-quality products to taint the perception of the high-quality ones, so that no buying and selling of high-quality goods occurs. Those who buy a new car and are dissatisfied with it for reasons unrelated to quality find it impossible to sell, because the huge number of low-quality cars offered in such circumstances poisons the market by forcing consumers to assume that any car for sale with only a few thousand miles on it must be low-quality. Health insurers find that if they are required to provide insurance to all comers, they will be flooded by enrollments from those who have just found out they will now be incurring major health expenses (because of diagnosis of cancer or heart disease, say). In this case, the insured is selling his claims risk and the insurer is then the "buyer."

But this problem may also cripple the market for shares if unlimited liability is the presumptive rule. Investors would (rationally) assume that those running a firm that, contrary to the norm, offers a limited-liability contract have negative inside information about its future liabilities and so would spurn it for unlimited-liability firms. At first glance this seems like a nonproblem—shouldn't firms offer whatever terms are necessary to attract shareholders? But the nature of adverse selection is that *no* firms—whether likely to generate large future liabilities or not—would be able to solicit investments on a limited-liability basis. Only those firms capable of soliciting funds with unlimited liability would remain, and the previously mentioned concerns of unlimited liability would then occur. But under the presumption of limited liability, firms still have the option of unlimited liability, and investors would see them as unusually *low-risk.* Such shares have in fact traded from time to time during the open-access era.

Limiting of Competition

Unlimited liability may protect entrants who currently face little competition because of their dominance. Under unlimited liability, it is common for share ownership to be limited to those who have the resources to settle any liability claim. Absent limited liability, shareholders must exert a great deal of costly effort to monitor the performance of the firm's managers (the principal–agent problem, discussed below). Because share ownership under unlimited liability is intrinsically less attractive to potential investors for reasons previously mentioned, the ability of new firms to issue shares in order to challenge existing ones is limited. Such entrenchment of the status quo discourages price competition and stifles innovation from entrants who improve the product or business model of the existing firms or who produce more efficiently. The absence of limited liability thus cements a stable, unimaginative economy.[13]

Overall, the way limited liability has come into such widespread acceptance is instructive. If limited liability causes inefficient risk management, it seems unlikely that either shareholders or creditors would have invested in or lent to firms employing it as aggressively as they have over the years, nor that many jurisdictions would enact and retain it. Unless one supposes that one jurisdiction after another blindly follows the one before it off the cliff into bad law, the resilience of limited liability strongly suggests its social value. Indeed, if one accepts that such landmark achievements as legal protection of collective bargaining and the establishment of the modern regulatory and welfare states are signs of progress in human society, it is difficult to see why the same label should not be extended to limited liability.

THE PRINCIPAL–AGENT PROBLEM

Another problem inherent in corporations of any significant size occurs because those who run the firm are different from those who own it. Shareholders, particularly smaller ones, cannot directly make decisions about how to run the firm because their expertise is limited and their time is costly relative to the size of their investments. And so they hire professional managers to do it for them. The rise of the professional manager, noted in Chapter 2, is the ultimate example of this phenomenon. At some point, a successful firm must hire managers not among its founders to be chief executive officer, chief financial officer, division heads, etc. (Such managers can of course be shareholders themselves.) But these individuals, like all employees, have interests that conflict with pure profit maximization. When the incentives of owners and managers conflict, the managers will tend to take decisions for their own benefit even if it costs shareholders, a problem well-known to Adam Smith.

The end of the stock bubble in 2000 provided several lurid examples of such activity in such firms as Tyco, where L. Dennis Kozlowski, its chief executive officer, was convicted (despite being one of the highest-paid executives in the United States) of misappropriating company funds for such less-than-essential items as a $6,000 shower curtain and a birthday party for his wife in Sardinia.

Problems of owners monitoring managers are particularly acute when ownership is widely dispersed. This is an example of what economists call the principal–agent problem, in which a principal pays an agent to accomplish a task but the agent has an incentive to "shirk" by acting in his own interest but contrary to the principal's. Scholars refer to the corporate principal–agent problem in particular as the separation of ownership and control, and anti-corporate writers mock the idea that shareholders, especially small ones, meaningfully own the company. To be costly to shareholders, agency costs arising from these incentive clashes need not rise to the prosecutable level of those cases brought against the management of Tyco and other firms involved in the corporate scandals of the late 1990s. And fortunately shareholders have a number of weapons at their disposal even when they do not. The most common is the threat managers face from changes in control of the firm in the event of underperformance. While anti-corporate thinkers assume that such discipline is impossible for widely dispersed shareholders, thanks to modern technology, the last twenty years has seen the rise of large shareholders (corporate raiders) who campaign among shareholders, large and small, for changes in management practices or outright takeovers. Because of modern communications technology, it is now as easy to communicate with small shareholders as large, and small shareholders have without question been empowered by the shareholder-activist movement.

Shareholders have other weapons too. If managers have ambitions to work elsewhere, the usual concerns for reputation also serve to discipline them to some extent. And given that agency costs have been well-understood for centuries, compensation schemes have emerged to better motivate managers. Stock options as employee compensation are the most common. While they are not without their own problems (e.g., the temptation they create to overstate earnings), they are part of a large menu of compensation options available to owners. And the stock exchanges where they list shares have a documented historical incentive to police the quality of stocks that list there.[14]

As with limited liability, the discussion here is not meant to dismiss the principal–agent problem as a nonissue. Rather, investors know about the problem and are capable of using their ingenuity to come up with ways to control it effectively, even as they will never be able to completely eliminate it. In no way does its existence cast doubt on the social value of the limited-liability joint stock company. That such tactics cannot completely eliminate the problem (which sometimes extends to criminal fraud or embezzlement) is no more an indictment of the corporate form than are the continued existence of car thefts indictments of laws against car titling. Indeed, sometimes the cure may be worse than the disease. When J.P. Morgan ran his financial empire, he, as was common in those days, placed many trusted confidantes on the boards of directors of companies his firm had a stake in. The presence of these men on these boards forced those companies to become more effective because Morgan's reputation and power insured better performance. But this practice was banned in the anti–big business outburst of the late 1800s as an "interlocking directorate." Many laws aimed at excessive concentration of power (e.g., prohibitions of large shareholders from serving on boards of directors and measures discouraging takeovers) gave managers more power at shareholders' expense.[15] The Sarbanes/Oxley legislation, a response to Enron and other media-friendly corporate disasters, has chased IPOs (initial public offerings) of stock to overseas exchanges as the issuing firms seek lower regulatory-compliance costs, an issue of huge concern to the U.S. financial firms that lose the (often hefty) fees these IPOs would otherwise garner.

And perspective is critical. Most agency problems are not illegal, just inefficient. Corporations and their managers being as entitled to the presumption of innocence as anyone else, some of them accused of felonious shirking have presumably not in fact violated the law, and the ones that have are a tiny portion of the thousands of companies listed on the various global stock exchanges. Lawyers say that hard cases make bad law, and policy made in fevered reaction to scary headlines is generally bad policy. Unreflective media obsession with corporate scandals is unhelpful. The principal–agent problem, like the flaws of limited liability, is real but far from crippling, as firms on their own often come up with ways to control it. Laws up to a point also do so but sometimes cause more (unanticipated) problems than they solve. And so the legal structure of the modern corporation is clearly not without its flaws, provided they are examined in isolation. But this is simply another way of saying that people act opportunistically when given the chance, which is as true in a corporation as in any other organization. While corporate managers may attempt to chisel their clients, so too may the firms that represent plaintiffs in suits against deep-pocketed corporations behave unethically in pursuit of the healthy fees that successful litigation may bring.[16] It requires an almost tragic naïveté to assume that other parties classifying themselves as aggrieved by corporate behavior are not similarly motivated. Reasonable people can disagree about the exact borders of efficient corporate law—whether limited liability should only extend to particular actions, whether stock options are efficient compensation, etc. But the broad contours of such law have played an indispensable role in the creation of the modern world. Indeed, as the most widespread way of organizing businesses of any size, corporations carry very far the benefits of commerce that often go unappreciated.

CORPORATIONS AND HUMAN PROGRESS

One could easily imagine the following scene as a major story on any television news program: a new medicine comes out that promises to significantly treat or even to cure a cruel disease. The tiny pills are extremely expensive because of high development costs (most potential drugs fail at some point in the testing and approval process and never make it to market) and patent protection for the manufacturer, and some in the United States are unable to afford them without cutting back on, say, food or heating their homes in the winter. The reporter finds a patient who, desperate, stretches the medicine out, taking it intermittently or cutting the pills in half. Drug prices, the viewer is told, are considerably cheaper in other countries, particularly those with single-payer health systems. Perhaps the story is leavened with details of how profitable the medicine is for its manufacturer or how profitable the company is overall. The viewer is then quite naturally prompted to wonder, "Why are these prices so high?"

But this is not the proper question to ask. Rather, that question is *"Why is the medicine even there to begin with?"* Bringing all the resources together to manufacture and ship it in the quantities it will be needed to places all over the world is a phenomenally complex task. How does the manufacturer avoid having excess medicines pile up unsold in one part of the country even as it is impossible to find in another? Why, indeed, are medicines to treat cancer, diabetes, artery blockage, or any other disorder produced at all, despite the immense costs these activities occur in resources claimed from other uses and in failed drug-development efforts? The answer is that the price system, or the market economy, or the enforcement of property rights, or whatever one chooses to call it, provides a structure whereby self-interested people can attempt to provide valuable services to others, secure in the knowledge that if their guesses are right, they will keep the rewards. This is how markets solve problems. They do not hand out ballots, nor do they allow one group or society to prevent or require, under penalty of law, that someone else do something. Those things that are valued by consumers relative to the costs of making them available get made; those that don't, don't. To be sure, sometimes one can raise ethical concerns about the choices that individuals make when they interact in the marketplace—drug companies, to take one example, probably devote more resources developing and promoting medicines for erectile dysfunction than for medicines that treat malaria. But that is a consequence of giving drug companies, like all companies, the freedom to try the market experiments they wish to try in the pursuit of greater profits. The only alternative for politicians is to command that those resources be diverted to other purposes, e.g., by enforcing via the police power an artificial desire shared by a (perhaps very small) number of citizens for a more "local" economy through the implementation of laws against multinational commerce or by enforcing the will of the political majority *du jour* that profits not be above some acceptable level. Unavoidably, this lessens the desire of people to take these risks to begin with.

There is almost a subtle aesthetic quality to the way businesses solve problems. It is part art and part science and is admirable and beautiful in total. That an oil company can achieve the proper allocation of gasoline to every station owner so that every car owner can acquire gas, provided only that he is willing to pay the price the seller asks, is a phenomenal achievement, requiring a delicate ballet of orders given down the business chain, of listening attentively to what station owners are telling it about demand, and of great risks taken at just the right moment. Such modern global commerce is one of the greatest and even in a sense one of the most beautiful human achievements. The corporate form facilitates business, thus also facilitating its ability to solve the problem of the proportions in which people and land and skill and oil and metals and an infinite list of other resources should be used for various competing purposes. These are problems that are solved through the cooperation of the market in ways that no central planner could hope to duplicate. (Imagine, for example, that a bureau of democratic economic planning had to decide how much of which resources should be acquired in which quantities to produce which medicines, and how the resultant production should be distributed around the world, without profit signals to guide it.) And the largest global corporations correspondingly solve the largest global problems—how to learn that the talents of workers in China, France, and Michigan can be stitched together to provide services that people in Brazil, Germany, and California find useful. This is not a trivial task. The history of trying to solve such problems with "non-market" means does not inspire confidence. The political directing of resource use has historically led to planned economies with fields full of rotting produce just a few miles from stores with no food on the shelves, goods whose money prices are cheap but whose time prices involve months or years of waiting, and all manner of other problems created or left unsolved. This, ultimately, is what a "post-corporate" world or "corporate democracy," a world where corporations must be operated in whatever enough politicians assert is the "public interest," comes to.

What are the fruits of this world that corporations have helped create? Globe-spanning commercial networks and the erosion of local self-sufficiency (whose effects are discussed in Chapter 6) to be sure, but also an astonishing improvement in human possibilities and sense of self-ownership. Material conditions have improved dramatically during the corporate era; there was a reason that in the seventeenth century, Thomas Hobbes could describe life as "nasty, brutish and short." Per capita income in the United States (in 1990 dollars) grew by a factor of 225 percent from 1820 to 1900, after having grown by 139 percent during the 120 years prior to that. For the United Kingdom, the analogous figures were 163 versus 42 percent; for France, 153 versus 78 percent; and for Germany, 177 versus 18 percent.[17] The launching of the era of the open-access corporation was not the only change occurring during this period, but no one contends that it was not a key part of this story. By promoting higher standards of living, the corporation has been a major force in improving our lives.

But is per capita GDP a good measure of the way we live? Many in the ACM argue not, asserting that it can only approximately measure material things and not other aspects of life that are more meaningful. But of course one of the advantages of greater income is that it can buy the other things—leisure, environmental protection, etc.—whose omission from its calculation is so often criticized. Rich countries have much cleaner environments, safer buildings and workplaces, etc. because they can afford more of these things.[18] And in fact if anything per capita income growth *understates* how much life improved during this period. Nobel Prize–winning economist Robert W. Fogel contends that

> [M]ost of these great advances in health care and education are overlooked in accounts of gross domestic product (GDP), because the values of these sectors are measured by inputs instead of by output. An hour of a doctor's time is considered no more effective today than an hour of a doctor's time was half a century ago, before the age of antibiotics and modern surgery. It has recently been estimated that improvements in health care, if properly measured, are at least twice the cost of health care, but such calculations have not yet made their way into the GDP accounts. In the case of the United States, my own rough estimates indicate that allowance for such factors as the increase in leisure time, the improvements in the quality of health care, and the improvements in the quality of education would come close to doubling the U.S. annual growth rate of per capita income over the past century (from 2.0 to 3.6 percent per annum).[19]

Elsewhere, Fogel notes some of the particulars of this revolution in the way we live:

- In 1850, the average Englishman took in as many calories as the average modern Indian.

- In the 1700s, the average Frenchman had a fifth of the calories available for work as the average modern American.

- The height of the average British male increased by over four inches between the mid-1800s and the mid-1900s.

- Contrary to theories based on the damage to health from widespread pollution and stress, Americans suffered far more from chronic degenerative disease and birth defects in the mid-1800s than now. And if chronic disease arrives, it arrives later. For those born in 1840, the average age for onset of such afflictions as type II diabetes or heart disease was fifty-one. Now it is more than ten years beyond that.

- The gap in life expectancy between the rich and the poor in the United Kingdom between those born in 1875 and those who are adults now fell from seventeen to about four years.

- Homelessness in the United States has *fallen* since 1850 (when it was mostly caused by chronic malnutrition, which made people unable to work) from between 10 and 20 percent to 0.4 percent of the population.

- The average American has 1,400 more hours of leisure time now than in the nineteenth century. While the entry of many wives into the workforce means that husbands and wives combined work more hours than thirty years ago, they retire much earlier—previous generations worked almost until the day they died. In essence, much of what the average wife in a two-earner family is buying with her extra work during prime working years is complete freedom in later years.

- Other than churchgoing, self-actualization activities—travel, enjoyment of the arts, exercise, family time—hardly existed in 1880, when wage earners spent almost six entire days working to put food on the table.[20]

Not all these effects are directly attributable to higher income enabling individuals to purchase better health care, although that is part of the story. The increased production of doctors, modern water and milk purification systems, sewage control, the rise in knowledge about infectious disease, the construction of modern hospitals on the basis of that knowledge, and the cleaning up of urban slums were other prominent factors. But economic growth during the nineteenth century made such technological and scientific progress possible; there would be no modernity without it. To the extent that corporations enabled this growth, they have helped completely remake the way we live.

More concretely, prior to 1900 disastrous plagues were common in all societies. In 1850, life expectancy in Western Europe and the United States was roughly forty-one years. As late as 1865 to 1868, Finland suffered a famine in which 100,000 (out of an initial population of 1,800,000) perished. And modern economic growth, significantly fueled by corporations, was what delivered a portion of humanity from all this and delivers ever more as time goes on. The list of candidate contributors that pushed the West past the rest in the great transformation of human quality of life starting in about 1750 is a very long one. It includes intellectual-property law, a general protection of property rights, acceptance of scientific rationalism, and a host of other factors. But the enabling of risk-taking and economies of scale via modern corporate law is surely a critical part of the story; it is hard to imagine modernity without it.

And so too with control over one's life. Throughout most of human history, most of humanity was utterly subordinate to a centralized, often extremely militarized, state that controlled the finest details of human activity. European serfdom is perhaps the most famous example, but during much of the premodern era, various forms of state slavery were the norm. The Chinese emperor T'ai Wu (who ruled from AD 424 to 452) would have officials in every village meticulously document the agricultural effort put forth by all residents, this being perfectly proper because their lives belonged to him.[21] The English common law famously treated wives as more or less property extensions of their husbands until they were given independent property rights in the nineteenth century. In fact, the history of such legal reforms is suggestively similar to those for open-access incorporation; Connecticut passed the first such law in the United States in 1809, followed gradually by other states in competitive evolution. The introduction of open-access incorporation contributed to the ability of women in England in the second half of the nineteenth century to accumulate wealth, with companies often issuing special classes of shares to circumvent the reluctance of banks to permit women to hold stocks (or most forms of wealth).[22]

It is possible that these laws were all part of a general burst of human progress, but it is far more likely that economic growth forced such legislative changes, because the social cost of continuing to restrict property rights—whether as women's ability to own land or as an entrepreneur's ability to incorporate—became much higher when the potential wealth forgone grew with the available technology. Even the intrinsic dignity that comes from entrepreneurship has recently been demonstrated by a program to acquaint convicted prisoners with the fundamentals of running their own legal business. The Prisoner Entrepreneurship Program has a far lower recidivism rate and greater success in integrating released prisoners toward the mainstream of society than programs based on other methods.[23] This is one of many examples of ways in which free commerce puts people in charge of their own lives, something far more important than the material gains of the corporate era, which are themselves substantial.

Even the accidental and incidental benefits of large corporations, the happy side effects given to the rest of us in the course of their operation, can end up benefiting people in unexpected ways. An increasing body of research shows that the need to solicit multinationals forces nations to improve their governance, liberating not just corporations but their own people too from the grabbing hand of corrupt officials.[24] Venice was always the best-governed of the medieval Italian city-states and also the most commercial; surely this was no coincidence. The U.S. drive against the spoils system, Tammany Hall, etc. and a similar drive in the United Kingdom coincided exactly with the age of corporate expansion in the second half of the seventeenth century.[25] And beyond corruption control, there are many other free social benefits, large and small, that flow naturally from the power of corporations to create wealth. The Billiton Mining Corporation, with large production facilities in Mozambique, found that malaria was exacting such a toll on its productivity that it was best for it to work to simply wipe it out in the entire region, an effort that has been largely successful.[26] Early British industrialists constructed new towns with large parks and gardens for each worker's residence.[27] Large corporations did and do provide critical support to the arts, hospitals, and other causes. (Whether they do it for profitable public relations or because of the public spiritedness of their decision-makers is immaterial to the argument.) Corporate headquarters often provide the most daring and interesting architecture. The ordinary functioning of mass commerce, in short, provides all manner of free benefits—not negative but *positive* externalities—for the surrounding society.

The establishment of the limited-liability, open-access corporation was a big part of the story that so revolutionized the way we live—the release of humanity from the squalor and tenuousness of life that was its lot for most of its history, and its replacement with societies where people are empowered to make their own way in the world rather than be in thrall to those who for no reason other than history are their social betters. Since ideas are perhaps the only boundless resource, the formation of new corporations and competition among existing ones will only further extend human possibility. And perhaps one of the least appreciated virtues of a world driven by commerce, and of global corporations in particular, is the push it gives people who are trying to make something of their life an incentive to do so across racial, religious, and gender lines.

CORPORATIONS AND GETTING ALONG

Loud arguments over diversity and multiculturalism—the former a simple numerical statement of the distribution of the population among various tribal groups, the latter an attempt to acknowledge and subsidize their continued difference—are the bane of our age. But international migration from impoverished and outright failed states to the prosperous, well-governed societies of the West has unavoidably thrust such issues front and center in those societies, and both Western and non-Western societies grapple with how to accommodate the sometimes incompatible claims of their various tribal groups to such government-mediated income streams as affirmative action.[28] Unfortunately, the channeling of such differences into politics is costly, because zero-sum politics is so costly to begin with, the more so when the basis for organizing the struggle over political spoils is tribe. More public jobs or university admissions reserved for some groups mean fewer available for others; government favors for an industry dominated by a particular tribal group take opportunities away from others.[29] Government officials can succeed by redistributing wealth from others to their supporters or by persuading their supporters that they are threatened by real or imaginary forces in society, which all too often are asserted to lurk sinisterly in other tribal groups. And so politics is an environment that unavoidably lends itself to ethnic, religious, and sex-based conflict.

But commerce is different—unlike politics, it has an overall common purpose, making money. (The ACM is the first to point out—before criticizing—this facet of commercial life.) Unquestionably, people participating in it may have their own motives—working at a more leisurely pace, stealing office supplies, failing to report labor-law violations to the government—that conflict with the overall goal of profit maximization. But the existence of the goal allows the owners of a firm, including the shareholders of a corporation, to have a united purpose. There is then a clear incentive to try to limit activities that damage the pursuit of profit. One of the most important ways that commerce contributes to the greater good (beyond its most elemental function of using scarce resources in ways that people value the highest) is in its encouragement of intertribal cooperation for bottom-line purposes.

On August 14, 2006, the PepsiCo corporation announced that it was promoting Indra K. Nooyi to chief executive officer. Ms. Nooyi is an American citizen who immigrated from India after years of working in the offices of various multinational corporations there. The press release announcing her appointment made no mention of her ethnicity or sex, relegating that to a biographical paragraph and stressing instead her impressive achievements with the firm. Ms. Nooyi is at the cutting edge of what will soon be a tidal wave of multitribal management of multinational firms. Another example is Carlos Ghosn, of Brazilian birth and French nationality and employed by the French firm Renault, who become a folk hero in Japan by turning around the Nissan automaker there after Renault purchased it. His foreignness allowed him to take steps that would have been culturally difficult for a Japanese executive.

More concretely, Table 4.1 shows the percentage of female managers in a variety of industrial democracies in the private sector in 2000, along with the percentages of female legislators. There are three things to note. First, there is no overall relation between the percentage of female parliamentarians (which might measure either the extent of government efforts to achieve equality of the sexes or the willingness of the population to vote for female candidates) and the percentage of female managers. Second, the percentage of managers tends to be higher than the percentage of parliamentarians. People, in other words, are more willing to overlook sex when they are chasing money than when they are selecting politicians.[30] Third, while the United States is commonly criticized for having a low level of political representation for women, it has the highest percentage of female managers among all countries in the world for which data are available; not far, in fact, from fifty percent. This is so even though the United States has fewer laws to promote greater female representation in business than many European societies do. (Norway, e.g., now requires that corporate boards of directors have at least forty

Table 4.1 **Women in commerce, women in politics.**

Country	Percent Female Among Managers	Percent Female in Legislature*
1. United States	45.3	13.8
2. Austria	38.3	25.1
3. Belgium	38.3	24.9
4. France	35.0	10.9
5. Ireland	33.7	13.7
6. Spain	31.5	26.6
7. Canada	31.5	23.6
8. Netherlands	30.5	32.9
9. Iceland	28.7	34.9
10. Luxemburg	27.1	16.7
11. Germany	27.1	31.0
12. Finland	25.9	36.5
13. Denmark	25.0	38.0
14. Norway	21.2	36.4
15. Italy	17.3	9.1

*For bicameral legislatures, figures are for lower house.

Sources: International Labor Organization (managers); Parline database via nation master.com for March, 2002 (legislators).

percent female membership.) What it does have is greater business flexibility. As many commentators have noted, one of the greatest economic difficulties some Western European nations face is the combined crippling effect of labor-market rigidities, high taxation, and high unemployment benefits on business formation and job creation. Such measures freeze the male-dominated status quo in place and make it difficult for competition to overcome whatever discriminatory tendencies exist.[31]

So too with ethnic tensions. Figure 4.1 depicts the relation between restrictions on commercial activity and interethnic conflict. On the horizontal axis is a World Bank measure of the total number of legal procedures needed to register a property title, register a contract, or start a business. More procedures mean more government interference with entrepreneurial activity and more opportunities for the government officials who hand out the licenses and permissions to demand bribes.[32] On the vertical axis are the mean responses by country to a question from the World Values Survey, an ongoing research project which periodically asks residents of over a hundred countries a series of questions about their beliefs. This particular question asks the extent to which the respondent is averse to having neighbors of a different ethnicity. (The symbols are standard World Bank country codes.) The results are striking in that more procedures are clearly correlated with more hostility to or fear of other groups.[33]

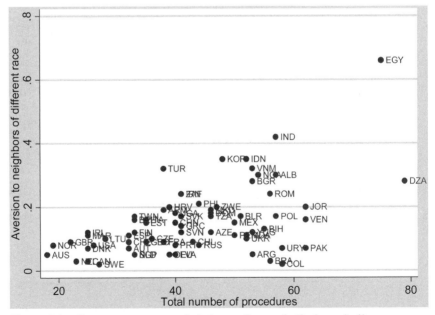

Figure 4.1   Government economic intervention and ethnic prejudice.

Restrictions on commerce prevent people from engaging in mutually beneficial commercial activity across tribal lines and may then force them into the political marketplace, where conflict rather than cooperation is often rewarded. The California constitution of 1879, for example, formed under the influence of whites-only labor groups (whose primary purpose was to restrict competition, by whatever means necessary, in the market in which they sold their services), prohibited the state government or private corporations from hiring Chinese workers. Other states had broader bans at that time against the employment of immigrants on public projects.[34] U.S. labor unions throughout much of the last 120 years used intimidation and the special privileges they gained under law to keep black workers out of unions and hence ineligible for work in closed shops, doing substantial damage to black economic prospects. They could and did do this not because laborers were more prejudiced than business-men but because discrimination cuts against the interests of businessmen in competitive markets while advancing the interests of unions seeking to restrict the supply of labor.[35] In present-day India, in contrast, modern commercial activity brought about through that country's embrace of economic liberalization and globalization since 1991 has promoted oppor-tunity and liberation for members of historically disadvantaged castes and tribes.[36] While many of the residents of rural villages there may still on balance desire (or may be forced by the dead hand of custom) to maintain the traditional links between ancestry and occupation (i.e., the traditional role of caste in much of that society), a technology company that wishes to be competitive cannot afford such indulgences. For the profit-maximizing businessman, discrimination is costly in a way it is for no other group in society.

And the global multinational corporation, with its need for intertribal cooperation not just among buyers and sellers but within the same firm, is the ultimate arena for posttribal cooperation. Firms need managers who know the local terrain, they need people who can speak a variety of languages, and most importantly, they need to maximize shareholder value and therefore promote the best candidate regardless of tribal iden-tity. Along with military platoons and sports teams, modern multinational corporations obliterate tribal barriers more effectively than anyplace on earth, because they must. If it is familiarity with the other that breaks down hostility to and suspicion about them, then the spread of global commerce is perhaps the greatest force in the world today for promoting intertribal cooperation, for dampening the forces that might otherwise tear us apart. Like the other ways in which it creates social progress, promotion of the ability to get along is an inadvertent benefit of the corpo-ration, particularly the global one.

Chapter 5

Corporate Power

What people who fear and despise corporations fear and despise most is "corporate power." Hundreds of books have been published on this theme, most of them since 1990. Broadly defined, there are three accusations—corporate political power, i.e., corporate control of government; corporate economic power, the ability of large corporations to destroy all economic competitive threats and, bolstered by political power, to redistribute wealth in their direction; and corporate social power to influence consumer behavior and the basic organization of society itself.

POLITICAL POWER

Despite the casual way in which the term is used by the ACM, political power is an elusive concept. Failure to think systematically about what power is is a major deficiency of all too many discussions about politics and about corporate power in particular. Typically, the idea of corporate political power is used to mean complete dominance of the political process, even and perhaps especially in nominally democratic societies, by a unitary corporate interest. David Korten sums up the problem as well as anyone in the movement:

> The larger the economic unit, the larger its dominant players, and the more political power becomes concentrated in the largest corporations. The greater the political power of corporations and those aligned with them, the less the political power of the people, and the less meaningful democracy becomes. There is an alternative: to localize economies, disperse economic power, and bring democracy closer to the people.[1]

And democracy, in turn, is a thing to strive for because of the equalizing effect it has on power, as the Harvard economist Elaine Bernard makes clear:

> At least in a democracy each person is formally equal. The humblest citizen, the most prestigious citizen still has only one vote. But when we move that power over to the marketplace, the humblest and the wealthiest are totally asymmetrical. And one has such power that they can literally crush the other completely and utterly and fully. So that's one of the reasons historically we've always felt the need to regulate markets.[2]

Power and Where It Lies

This is strong language—of crushing, utter dominance. The quasi-sacred nature of democracy, and its elbowing aside by corporate power, dominates anti-corporate thought. What makes corporate power so sinister is its toxic effects on the ability of the majority, through its representatives elected through a one-person, one-vote scheme, to implement the public will. But the assertion that power belongs either to the people or to "the marketplace" raises more questions than it answers. In particular, the word "power" cries out for elaboration; it is common for distinguished thinkers to discuss its implications without defining it, and sociologists have struggled for years to come up with an acceptable definition. To Bertrand Russell, power is "the production of intended effects." For Robert Dahl, "A has power over B to the extent that he can get B to do something that B would not otherwise do." But surely these cannot be helpful definitions of "power" in the corporate context. If I buy baseball season tickets only because the owner has signed a star player, neither that player through the exertion of his talents nor the team officials can be said to have "power" over me in any meaningful sense. All they have done is made me an offer which I have accepted.

But not all offers are equal, of course; some are those that can't be refused. Robert Bierstedt thus does a little better by defining power as "the ability to use force."[3] But "force" too is somewhat vague; the threat to imprison someone who doesn't pay taxes is surely an exercise in power, but what about the threat to fire someone for refusing to work overtime? In both cases, people are given choices but unpleasant ones—comply or go to jail in the first case and comply or lose one's job in the second. Where does "force" stop and "choice" begin? And the notion that a vote constitutes meaningful power is especially troubling. A person's vote is one among millions (the power of an individual in a democracy is far less than the power of many shareholders in a corporation, as constricted as the latter admittedly often is), and very often government, elected or not,

is used to get B to do something that he would not do were he not threatened with a fine or jail time for noncompliance. With one vote, I *as an individual* surely have no power over government decisions. I may be an
infinitesimal part of a larger group that can influence government policy,
but my ability on my own to exercise "power" over the government is
essentially zero.

Following the economist Paul Heyne, I will take power to mean
the ability to get another to work for your ends by limiting his options,
as opposed to persuasion, the eliciting of cooperation by expanding
someone's options.[4] Governments and individuals both have power in
this sense, but power so defined is an intrinsic part of government. Whatever power corporations have, they cannot (in the modern era anyway)
put people in prison or invoke the power of taxation, which are ways to
emphatically limit options. The Russian oil company Yukos was depicted
as immensely powerful, and deeply influential in the operation of the
Russian government, particularly under President Boris Yeltsin. But
it took his successor, Vladimir Putin, just a few months to engineer its
takeover and the jailing of its CEO via the interpretation of ambiguous
laws that the government itself had enacted—a tool not available to
nongovernmental actors. Government has intrinsic power that a private
actor, including a huge corporation, may only have by manipulating the
levers of that original power.

Thus government is always about power (sometimes used for good
reason and sometimes not), something that cannot necessarily be said of
business or any other social group or institution. While a monopoly could
exercise significant power as defined here (by continually strangling
or deterring competition), the importance of such monopolies will be
subjected to scrutiny below.[5] Since such political power as corporations
possess runs through the government, it is essential to begin by thinking
about the best principles to shape the use of that power. One useful rule
of thumb is to make, in the words of Hayek, "rules which make it possible
to foresee with fair certainty how the authority will use its coercive powers
in given circumstances and to plan one's individual affairs on the basis of
this knowledge."[6] Government laws and policies should be consistent—
they should obey what Hayek calls the "rule of law" and what I will call
equality before the law. In this conception, crafting laws in ways to expand
rather than constrict the options of individuals requires treating everyone
in analogous circumstances analogously. This concept is observed substantially if not primarily in the breach in the operations of most modern
governments, and so one measure of corporate power is their ability to
obtain special treatment at the expense of other special-interest groups.
A corporation's ability to gain special tax privileges or subsidies decreases
the options of others by increasing the corporation's competitive advantage and increasing the tax burdens of other citizens. Framing power this

way allows us first to focus on whether a particular power in the hands of the government is legitimate to begin with, and only then whether a corporation (or any other pressure group) has gained control of that power. By not thinking carefully about what power is, the ACM ignores the possibility that if its recommendations are taken to heart, its own ability to use the state power to decrease the options of other people will increase in ways explored below.

If corporations earn "corporate welfare," that is because government first has the power to arbitrarily redirect wealth from some individuals to others via its taxation and regulatory powers. Whatever power corporations achieve, in other words, results from their successful use of the original power of the state to limit the options of—to exert power over—others, particularly by handing out special privileges and punishments to particular classes of citizens based on irrelevant considerations. A government that did not possess such power could not hand out corporate welfare or any other kind of special treatment. We do not live in such a society if we ever did, and so the question is how much power corporations possess to influence the government, the ultimate repository of most power, relative to other groups and given the (sometimes essential!) ability of the government to exercise power over individuals to begin with.

The Elusive "Public Interest"

As we saw in Chapter 1, one of the most common themes of the ACM is the contrasting of the public to the corporate interest, the former sometimes phrased as the will of "the people." But appealing to the public interest is a vague and even dangerous thing, all too often used in lieu of an honest confession of the speaker's own private interests. Almost everybody trying to influence government policy in furtherance of his private interest asserts, sometimes even to the point of believing it himself, that he is acting in the public interest even as he is unable to discern or unwilling to confess the hidden hand of his own private interest. The small businessmen may really believe that the public interest is served by giving him government loans at preferential terms, and the hard-line conservationist may really believe that the public interest in fact requires tying up public or private land for generations so that it may be used in the way he wishes it to be used (i.e., preserved as it is) rather than in the irreconcilable ways that some others wish it to be used, e.g., for timber harvests.[7] But these questions can more productively be phrased as the clash of one special interest versus another. Indeed the entire reason for politics is that our conceptions of "the public interest" differ. Almost all interests are private or special interests, in that achieving these interests requires damaging the interests of others. This is as true for environmentalists and patients as for oil and drug companies.

How "Power" Is Manufactured

For these reasons, the "public interest" is often an empty term, mistaken for the evanescent sentiments of whatever majority of special interests happens to prevail today. Both individual corporations and the people seeking to limit their activities are by any reasonable definition special-interest groups. Together they employ the resources at their disposal to exert political pressure, and the government, based on those resources poured into it, makes a decision. The question then becomes one of the political strengths of *all* contending factions. The notion that struggle among factions is an inevitable part of governance played a key role in the construction of the U.S. constitution and the debate over its ratification.[8] But it is unknown to or ignored by the ACM, which sees governance as a potential torrent of public-spirited legislation held back only by the desperately corrupt blocking measures of only one special interest—the corporate one.

Obviously, corporate power as the ACM defines it depends in part on corporations' economic might. The bigger they are, the more resources they can spend on political pressure, by any reasonable conception of how governments make decisions. Are corporations large? Certainly some of them are. But this is easy to exaggerate. The revenues of Fortune 500 companies are often said to be larger than the GDP (gross domestic product) of many countries, but that is apples and oranges. GDP is a measure of net value added, but corporate revenues are a gross measure of sales before deducting costs. And if such gross figures are to be the measure of power, many government agencies would qualify as equally powerful. The annual budget of the BBC is bigger than the GDP of roughly forty percent of the world's countries and would put it roughly in the middle of the Fortune 500. The annual expenditures of Harvard University would put it comfortably in the fourth quintile of the Fortune 500, while the University of California system would not quite crack the top 100 and the National Institutes of Health just would. Whereas once people could assert that the "Seven Sisters" private oil companies dominated world oil production, now they are insignificant next to (and routinely dominated by) the state-owned oil companies in countries like Saudi Arabia, Venezuela, and Malaysia.[9] It would take a special sort of naïveté to believe that corporations try to influence politics while public broadcasters, unions, local governments, students, professors and scientists, ad infinitum do not. And so appeal to gross size is not very informative. We should instead examine all inputs to and outputs of the political process—the extent to which corporations dominate the application of political pressure, and the extent to which the political output serves their interests rather than those of other groups.

Political Outputs

To be sure anecdotes about corporations exercising political power to obtain special privileges are not difficult to find. In 1998, Congress and President Bill Clinton extended the period of federal copyright protection to fifty years after the death of the author for individual creations and seventy-five years after creation for corporate copyrights. This action was taken after pressure by, among others, the Walt Disney Company. Contemporary press reports asserted that it took an outsized interest in the legislation because it wished to prevent Mickey Mouse from falling into the public domain. (Mickey Mouse is actually protected by trademark, which can last until the end of the universe as long as Disney defends it, but many of his early movies are protected only by copyright.) Copyright protection was in fact extended numerous times in the twentieth century despite the fact that all of the intellectual-property owners lobbying for more protection by definition already had adequate incentives to create the existing stock of artistic innovations that they were seeking to further protect. Pharmaceutical companies have had some short-term success in limiting the ability of consumers to import lower-cost prescription drugs from Canada. But, recall, the government's power to limit imports in this way derives from its preexisting immense ability to control the pharmaceutical trade to begin with—to restrict the ability of Americans to buy any medicines that sellers are willing to provide—and from that starting point to hand out special privileges to special pleaders, whether patients seeking cheaper medicines or drug corporations seeking higher profits.

But there are just as many examples of corporations being frustrated by other special interests who block them from pursuing profitable trading opportunities. A very small group, anti-Castro Cuban-Americans and their sympathizers, has been able to maintain an embargo on the movement of goods and people between Cuba and the United States for almost half a century despite the immense opportunities a repeal would generate for some U.S. corporations. Corporate conspiracies in restraint of trade have been illegal since the Sherman Antitrust Act, but labor unions have been explicitly and asymmetrically exempted from antitrust law (violating equality before the law) since 1914.[10] Rather than becoming more subservient to corporate interests, the regulatory state has increased the scope of its authority over commerce during the postwar period. In 1970, the number of federal employees employed by regulatory agencies was about 20,000, and this number had somewhat astonishingly grown to almost 120,000 by 2002. The number of new pages in the Federal Register each year, which is a commonly used measure of the amount of new regulation governing businesses, grew over the same period from roughly 20,000 to roughly 80,000.[11]

The taxation of corporate income is another example of corporations waging political factional warfare less productively than other special interests opposed to them. As many other commentators have noted since the corporate income tax's inception, it represents a form of double taxation, in that what is left over after present costs have been paid is taxed both before it goes to shareholders in the form of direct levies on corporate income and after it goes to shareholders in the form of individual taxation of their dividends. Such double taxation is no more efficient or just than taxing the corporation's wage payments at the corporate level before it is distributed to workers, only then to tax employees' wage income. This burden not borne by any of the corporation's other contracting parties is now accepted as normal. The corporate income tax is taken for granted despite substantial costs when entrepreneurs choose business forms other than incorporation to avoid it.[12] Thus the ultimate question that corporate taxation provokes is not whether the rate at which it is currently assessed is too high or the revenue it currently brings is too low, but *why it exists at all*. Its very existence is in fact a sign of corporate weakness relative to other special-interest groups.

A vivid example of a sustained decline over time in the corporate position relative to the law is the evolution of U.S. product liability law. Such law—which governs the liability manufacturers face when the use of their products causes injury or death—has consistently become less favorable to manufacturers (most of which are corporations, many of them very large) since the mid-1800s. When mass manufacturing first arose in the early stages of the Industrial Revolution, it was governed by contract law. The manufacturer or the seller of his product was only liable for risks explicitly accepted in the contract of sale. The separation between manufacturer and seller (who was usually a retailer who purchased the product from the manufacturer or an intermediate distributor) made it essentially impossible for a consumer injured while using a product to sue the former. In the first two decades of the twentieth century, courts began to hold that the manufacturer could be directly liable if it was negligent (i.e., had failed to uphold some duty expected of it during the design or manufacturing process). But by approximately 1970, the prevailing law had switched to a standard of strict liability, in which the manufacturer was held liable regardless of any negligence in design or manufacturing as long as the product was used normally. In subsequent years, some courts began to extend the definition of "normal" so that even consumer misuse of the product could sometimes result in a liability finding. Economists who study such law disagree over whether this legal revolution is efficient or not. But that the law has changed dramatically in favor of consumers against manufacturers, most of which are corporations, is beyond dispute.[13]

Political Inputs

If "corporations" can be taken as a single pressure group, it is clear that sometimes they do well at the government trough and sometimes they do not. Why are these results so mixed? The first reason is that while corporations give a great deal of money, many special interests do. Table 5.1 shows campaign-finance data from the Center for Responsive Politics for the 2003–2004 election cycle for all donations to all federal candidates both via traditional methods (political action committees, individuals, and "soft money" to candidates and parties) and so-called 527 committees, which were a new development in campaign finance during that election cycle. The bold entries are those from business interests. Undoubtedly, some of this money is from business interests in opposition to large corporations, so these figures overstate, perhaps substantially, the pursuit of some purely mega-"corporate" interest. While business interests dominate conventional political donations, they are a minority of 527 donations, and all kinds of Americans give money for all kinds of reasons. (Given that business dominates "soft money" donations, and that those donations have recently been outlawed, business interests might find the field tilted somewhat more against them in coming years. Then again, political entrepreneurs may find, as they always seem to,

Table 5.1   2003–2004 political donations.

	Standard Donations	527 Committees
Agribusiness	**$52,927,826**	**0**
Comm./Electronics	**101,724,013**	**88,865**
Construction	**71,669,012**	**220,604**
Defense	**16,341,812**	**0**
Energy/Natural Resources	**52,699,546**	**88,000**
Finance/Ins./Real Estate	**334,786,787**	**3,775,263**
Health Businesses	**49,755,029**	**109,943**
Health Professionals	73,984,331	869,804
Lawyers and Lobbyists	**210,187,147**	**29,173**
Transportation	**51,338,278**	**0**
Miscellaneous Business	**207,655,249**	**145,117**
Labor	61,484,080	78,806,694
Ideology/Single Issue	180,705,120	426,136,558
Total Business: $1,153,541,664		
Total Non-Business: $821,986,587		

Source: Center for Responsive Politics Industry Profiles, http://opensecrets.org/industries/index.asp. The CRP defines "Ideology/Single Issue" as Abortion, Candidate Committees, Democratic/Liberal, Foreign and Defense Policy, Guns, Human Rights (gay/lesbian and ethnic groups), Leadership PACs, Pro-Israel, Republican/Conservative, Women's Issues. The CRP lists $1,154,093 in 527 money as "Unknown."

new ways for all special interests to curry favor with politicians for mutual benefit.)

And even these data overstate corporate influence. "Corporations" do not have a single, unified interest. Retailing corporations are often in favor of lower trade barriers, while domestic manufacturers are often in favor of higher ones. Thus some fraction of corporate political pressure simply cancels out other corporate political pressure. In addition, it is taken for granted (not just by the ACM, but by most critics of spending on political campaigns and lobbying) that money is the only meaningful input to political success. This is false. Campaign donations contribute to the achievement of political objectives, but so does the mobilization of the time of political activists. Political parties and candidates devote extensive energies to mobilizing their "ground game" in the run-up to Election Day in the belief that hours of work by mobilized partisans can generate more votes. Activists presumably coordinate phone-calling and letter-writing campaigns because their representatives respond to such pressure. Sometimes massive street demonstrations or other forms of public protest are used to acquire the privileges sought. Unless the groups arranging and participating in such activities are all in the grips of a mass delusion, time spent in political agitation must surely be an input at least as important in the generation of political success as money. Corporate constituents are likely to be relatively disadvantaged in the time inputs to political pressure. Whether time is more or less important than money presumably varies from issue to issue, but the history presented above suggests that while corporations and their shareholders are hardly a victimized class in contemporary society, they are hardly the government's puppetmaster either. Like every other pressure group in society, corporations in general, corporations in a particular industry, and individual corporations win some and lose some. Corporations acquire many special government privileges relative to equality before the law; but then again, so do all pressure groups, sometimes at corporations' expense.

CORPORATE ECONOMIC POWER

Do corporations, especially large ones, dominate the economy? The anti-corporate literature leaves no room for doubt. Through their leveraging of the market power given to them by economies of scale and by their control of the political process, they control the economy of every society in which they operate and indeed the larger global economy. This power is used to cement the economic power of today's corporations over any existing or hypothetical competitors. Evidence on the revenue of the largest corporations as a percentage of the economy is often marshaled (inaccurately, as noted above) to support this hypothesis.

But corporate profits have not, contrary to what anti-corporate theory might predict, risen over time. Figure 5.1 shows corporate profits before and after taxes as a percentage of national income since 1929. After-tax profits are much closer to pretax profits now than they were fifty years ago, but that is not because after-tax profits are rising but because pretax profits have, subject to larger swings, declined. Pretax profits reached their peak in the late 1960s and have broadly declined since, while after-tax profits have more or less revolved around the same mean since the end of the Great Depression. While the corporate tax burden is clearly lower since the early 1980s (in that the gap between pre- and after-tax corporate profits has declined), after-tax profits were not noticeably higher in recent years than in the past. It is difficult to interpret this pattern in a way consistent with a hypothesis of increasing corporate dominance over the economy.

The story of large corporations more and more dominating the economy also fails to account for competition, for the idea that individual corporations do not even posses enough power to prevent their profits being competed away and even their being driven out of business by other firms, let alone to control the government. Of the companies on the *Fortune* 500 in 1970, sixty percent no longer existed by the middle of this decade.[14] Big corporations come and big corporations go. The average life expectancy of a *Fortune* 500 firm (in the United States or in other

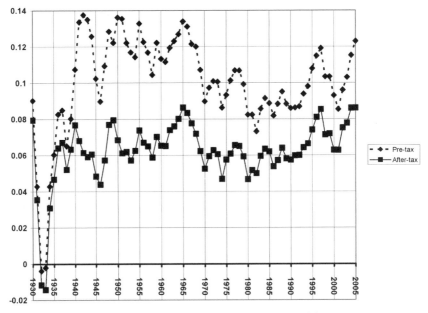

Figure 5.1   Corporate profits as a proportion of national income, 1903–2005.

countries) is forty to fifty years, and 12½ years for all companies large and small.[15] (These estimates include mergers and bankruptcies leading to purchase by other firms, the latter often an example as much of corporate failure as corporate power.) Corporate life expectancy has been shown to have declined in several European countries studied in recent decades.[16] The individual corporation is so weak, so constrained by competition, that it is very possible that half a century from now, Microsoft, Toyota, and General Electric will not exist. And much of this is due to new firms bearing revolutionary concepts displacing now-obsolete ones; companies such as Apple Computer or Wal-Mart are radically different from the sorts of firms that dominated the roll of America's biggest firms in decades past. While John Kenneth Galbraith might assert that huge, immortal corporations are required to do most of the innovating, that holds only if "innovating" is constrained to mean tinkering with the existing products rather than substantially remaking the way we live and do business.

The alleged economic "dominance" of large corporations is easily testable by using another data series. The percentage of all employees who are employed by firms with at least a thousand workers has been approximately constant for years. According to the Statistical Abstract of the United States, such firms employed only 13.34 percent of all working for for-profit firms and not self-employed in 2003, a percentage actually slightly smaller than in 1980. It is true that the share of output produced by the largest firms is much higher than it used to be in the early postwar years, but we would expect that in a world with economies of scale. The interesting question is whether or not this size frustrates competition from smaller, newer firms. Economies of scale, after all, only provide competitive advantage in the absence of dramatic new ideas that make the original corporation's economies irrelevant. These ideas can often be produced at astonishingly low cost.

Figure 5.2 shows the index of net business formation for the entire lifetime of that series, published by the Bureau of Economic Analysis from 1956 to 1994. The rate is adjusted so that the value for 1967 is 100 and is designed to allow comparison from one year to the next. The trend is generally rising over time, although there is considerable variation from one year to the next. Similarly with gross business startups, new business formations per 1,000 population, indexed on the right side of the chart and tracked by the government until 1997, have generally risen throughout the postwar period. Modestly rising rates of startups strongly suggest an economy that remakes itself at an ever-faster rate rather than one increasingly under the thumb of its largest businesses. Indeed, recent research suggests that the rate at which businesses are driven out has nothing to do with any increasing monopolistic domination and very little to do even with the overall ups and downs of the economy. Some new thinking on business success and failure is increasingly seen as very

Figure 5.2   U.S. Business formation, 1955–1997.

similar to models of species survival from biology, where firms fail at a relatively consistent rate at various points in their life span.[17] While anti-corporate activists often invoke the stepchild science of ecology to depict all corporations as a single, overwhelming, invasive species destroying the rest of the global ecological and cultural system,[18] a more productive scientific approach would be to use the parent science, evolutionary biology, and view individual corporations as competing species coming into existence, growing, and dying with a predictable regularity.

The dispersion of ownership of large corporations is also not accounted for; if they are large, but ownership is spread out among many people, any "power" is presumably diluted. In 1962, the Port Huron statement bemoaned the fact that "the modern concentration of wealth is fantastic," because one percent of Americans owned eighty percent of all stock shares. By 2001, according to one analysis, the percentage of wealth in stocks and mutual funds (which is not quite the same thing as the number of shares but a useful approximation) owned by the wealthiest one percent of Americans was down to 44.1%.[19] And this trend toward greater dispersion of ownership will continue. It is generally acknowledged that the rise of the shareholder society in the 1980s and the 1990s through such vehicles as mutual funds and 401(k)s radically democratized the ability of the nonwealthy to tap the wealth-generation capacities of the corporate form, consistent with the analysis in Chapter 4. While the percentage of Americans who owned any stock at all was roughly stable at about one-eighth from the late 1930s through the early 1970s, that percentage has soared since then to, by some estimates, more than half. This expansion of access to present and future wealth has given average Americans more control over their own financial destiny and made them less dependent on government promises to fund their retirements on nothing more substantial than a promise to impose taxes on future taxpayers (the essence of public pension schemes such as Social Security). Recall also the role of shareholding in promoting the economic independence of women in nineteenth-century England. The rise of the modern corporation has changed economic power alright—by decentralizing it to the broad population and away from historically privileged groups.

SOCIAL POWER

Perhaps the ultimate accusation of untrammeled corporate power is that the same corporations that are said to dominate government and the economy increasingly rearrange entire societies to suit their purposes. The argument can differ in the particulars but typically boils down to something along the lines of the following: corporations are statutorily driven to maximize profits at the expense of all other considerations, hence are compelled to grow without relent or remorse, and thus must and do systematically reorganize the world around them, including the goals and desires of the world's people, to obtain this objective. They do this in part by taking control of government, but they also manipulate the way people wish to live, converting them into material slaves whose artificial desires to consume more and more will then drive corporate growth. They convert rural societies into urban ones, healthy, traditional societies into consumerist ones, etc. By controlling all of their vital communication and political nodes (the press, Internet content, etc.), they subordinate societies to their narrow goals. As extreme as this fear sounds, it is widely believed. Consider the remarks of the anti-globalization campaigner Jerry Mander, who likens corporations to a sinister science-fiction villain:

> By its ability to implant identical images into the minds of millions of people, TV can homogenize perspectives, knowledge, tastes, and desires, to make them resemble the tastes and interests of the people who transmit the imagery. In our world, the transmitters of the images are corporations, whose ideal of life is technologically oriented, commodity oriented, materialistic, and hostile to nature. And satellite communication is the mechanism by which television is delivered into parts of the planet that have, until recently, been spared this assault.[20]

Similarly, the eminent sociologist Richard Sennett has criticized what he calls the modern "self-consuming passion." He notes (and seemingly bemoans) that a middle-class home in prerevolutionary France might have only two or three sets of clothes per adult, with all the daily items in the house—clothing, shoes, kitchenware—made by hand and built to last a lifetime. People in the twentieth century in contrast did not, as one might suppose, gladly take advantage of the opportunity but rather had to be trained to periodically replace all the things they used and purchased. This was done through the manufacture of products designed to be obsolete and through manipulative advertising.[21] So too many criticize the way corporations entangle the entire planet into a web of dependence that the corporations themselves have spun. People are deceived into relying less on their neighbors for sustenance and more on people on the opposite side of the planet, through the advertising and price temptations of global corporations. This destroys the local sense of community, which is the natural way that people ought to live. In one of the more colorful manifestations of this worldview, an anti-corporate campaigner even argues that national currencies are made artificially scarce by central banks in part to increase people's competitive drives and thus to channel wealth to "giant corporate conglomerates."[22]

There is nothing new here. Sennett, like many other critics of the modernism of which corporations are an essential but far from the only part, does not devote much thought to what life would be like in the absence of firms rising to service these allegedly manufactured passions. A churl might note, for example, that life expectancy has increased by several decades in much of the world since the dawn of the corporate era. Contempt for mass tastes—the desires of the sorts of people who enjoy the occasional Big Mac, mass-market movies, and brand-name athletic shoes—is also something we have seen before. Consider the words of the nineteenth-century German poet Heinrich Heine[23]:

> Sometimes it comes to my mind
> To sail to America
> To that pig-pen of Freedom
> Inhabited by boors living in equality

So too the German philosopher Martin Heidegger in the 1930s wrote that "Russia [meaning the U.S.S.R.] and America are the same, with the same dreary technological frenzy and the same unrestricted organization of the average man." Note the wording: if "the average man" is organized "unrestrictedly," the solution to this problem is to have him organized *by* someone (by Heidegger, for example). The idea that individuals might choose their own ways of living, rather than be organized or deceived into them, was completely foreign to him. In *Introduction to Metaphysics*, Heidegger asserted:

> In America and in Russia this development grew into a bound-less etcetera of indifference and always-the-sameness, so much so that the quantity took on a quality of its own. Since then the domination in these countries of a cross section of the indifferent mass has become something more than a dreary accident. It has become an active onslaught that destroys all rank and every world-creating impulse of the spirit, and calls it a lie. This is the onslaught of what we call the demonic (in the sense of destructive evil).[24]

Similar sentiments can be found in the works of Nietzsche, for whom the American tendency to work hard was "the true vice of the new world," spreading the country's "mindlessness" into the heart of the Old Continent so that one "thinks with a watch in hand, as one eats lunch with an eye on the financial pages."[25] Engels was repulsed by the democratic tendencies of industrializing London, with its "hundreds of thousands of all classes and ranks crowding past each other."[26] It is striking how much the modern anti-corporate contempt for global consumption shares with older strains of anti-modernist thought, much of which came from the right. In the minds of many such thinkers, it simply cannot be that ordinary people would voluntarily choose to purchase two cars, sometimes large ones, that many of them would have similar tastes in musicians or literature (and that profit-maximizing media businesses might learn these tastes through research), that some would gladly shop at Wal-Mart while perhaps aspiring eventually to move up to something more selective or would, given the opportunity because of greater wealth to replace older devices, do so. Sennett aims his ire at one point at the Apple iPod. This seemingly harmless device has a capacity to store thousands of songs, which is in his estimation far more than anyone could ever listen to and therefore enjoy and which is thus a useless excess. And yet iPod users may among other things have the machine choose songs randomly. A larger database of songs means a greater possibility for surprise and hence greater enjoyment. This failure of Sennett and others to see beyond their own beliefs about how life should be lived, and the corresponding belief that people do not know what they are doing in their consumption decisions and are therefore in need of an expert's guidance (encoded into the law if necessary), is a hallmark of modern anti-corporatism, as it has been in many ideologies before it.

Advertising

Another belief of the ACM is that advertising systematically takes advantage of consumers' weaknesses and cognitive frailties to maneuver consumers into buying things that they wouldn't otherwise buy. Among the most common charges is that consumers are persuaded to want ever more material goods, whether to keep up with the Joneses or for self-validation. Get rid of advertising, the theory goes, and everyone returns to a much simpler, happier life.[27]

Undoubtedly, advertising is an activity prone, like many, to excess. One would have to be unusually stubborn to deny that advertising is sometimes of dubious social value and that it sometimes preys on our weaknesses. The famous behavioral scientist Amos Tversky was quoted as saying that whatever he learned about the way human choices sometimes depart from rational behavior had always been known to "advertisers and used car salesman."[28] Whatever tactics might be used by a used-car salesman to persuade a hapless car buyer sitting fretfully in the sales office to spend even more money on the unneeded warranty or undercoating can presumably also sometimes be used by advertisers to persuade consumers to make purchases that upon reflection they may decide they didn't really need. And some such advertising will surely have little social value at best. Advertising targeted at children, particularly for products of dubious health value, is unethical by almost any code of moral reasoning. (Although it is not clear that it is more unethical than the conscription of children into political battles over public education, illegal immigration, and other public issues, which is increasingly common in the United States, such conscription being a hallmark of totalitarian ideology.)

But much, maybe most advertising is in fact *very* useful. Information—e.g., about which products are available with which features at which prices—is costly, and sellers may be willing to pay to make that information available to consumers. (Sometimes consumers themselves pay to acquire information, as when they join Consumers Union or read *The New York Review of Books.*) Advertising often serves to make consumers aware of information they didn't have before. An obvious example is advertising in the Yellow Pages, which often includes names, locations, hours of service, and contact information for various competing sellers. Even advertisements that make debatable claims about product features provide the raw material for verification by outside testers and are typically read or viewed by consumers not passively and mindlessly (as the anti-corporate assumption of human passivity requires) but as part of a much larger variety of competing claims by other advertisers. Such competing advertisements are thus analogous to competing promises by politicians, competing wooing by romantic suitors, and other solicitations for attention that we take for granted. Advertising can even open consumers to new possibilities that didn't exist before. Thomas Sowell notes that the pioneering camera entrepreneur George Eastman used advertising to persuade Americans to engage in photography for pleasure, a cultural innovation that has changed the way we remember our past and created a whole new form of art.[29]

And many tastes are in fact "manufactured" in the same sense that the ACM accuses advertisers of manufacturing tastes for products—such tastes as political causes and fine literature and classical music are "sold" by novelists, professors, and other traffickers in ideas. Two economists have even provocatively suggested that advertising serves to make the consumption of the product itself more enjoyable. In the jargon of economics, advertising and the products advertised are complements— goods whose joint consumption is far more valuable or useful than consumption of either of them in isolation.[30] Tennis balls and tennis rackets or left shoes and right shoes are literally textbook examples of complements, and advertisements and the advertised product may be similarly paired.

This last argument undoubtedly grates on the garden-variety anti-corporate activist, for whom no useful purpose is served by Nike advertisements and Nike shoes working together to make the purchase of the latter more valuable. But the difference between the hypothesis that advertising has pragmatic uses of one sort or another and the presumption that it is manipulation is the difference between those who default to individual freedom and those who presume that centralized control of how other people live is preferable until shown otherwise. It is more productive and more consistent with freedom to talk of persuasion rather than manipulation, but voluntary persuasion is a term that anti-corporate campaigners typically reject. Fundamental to the anti-corporate worldview, not just with respect to advertising but to the entire criticism about corporate social power, is the belief that individuals are not fit to be in charge of their own lives. Their choices and desires are hopelessly manipulated; it falls to those on a higher plane, namely the anti-corporate activists who see through the manipulative corporate fog, to restore society to the more meaningful life that the movement's members assume we all *must* want. This sort of paternalistically aggressive, coercive undoing of the results of billions of decisions taken over many decades is flatly inconsistent with a free society. Ultimately, this sort of criticism of advertising is unimaginative and supposes, like so much anti-corporate thought, that most of us are sheep being led to the corporate slaughter, in desperate need of being saved by the wisdom of anti-corporate, anti-consumer, anti-modernist thought. There is nothing particularly new or anti-corporate about such criticisms of advertising. (The humorist Stephen Leacock once characterized advertising as "the science of arresting human intelligence long enough to get money from it."[31]) But what is novel is the incorporation by the ACM of such views into a broader theory of corporate manipulation of society for its own selfish purposes.

Perhaps no other type of advertising has drawn more scorn in recent years than that for pharmaceutical products. Many physicians, consumer advocates, and anti-corporate activists argue that such advertising targeted directly at consumers encourages patients to beseech their doctors for medicines that are not in their best interest. In this view, such pharmaceutical advertising as exists should confine itself to a scientific listing of indications, contraindications, known risks, and so on.[32] But the informational function of advertising is much richer than that. It informs potential consumers not just how the drug may help them in a medical sense but about things as fundamental as whether to pursue treatment for certain conditions at all or even the possibility that the consumer may have the condition to begin with. A middle-aged, somewhat overweight man without much experience of doctors or knowledge of medicine may see an advertisement for a new anti-cholesterol drug and decide that the possible symptoms of heart disease about which he is so concerned need not deter him from seeing a doctor, because that doctor may simply prescribe medicine instead of scheduling something as frightening as open-heart surgery. Other advertising may alert a patient to a condition that was unknown to him (e.g., depression), leading him to take the decision to consult a physician.

Advertising, including pharmaceutical advertising, is knowledge; sometimes it takes work to separate more from less useful knowledge, but to censor the knowledge is no answer. If one wants to assess the value of a society that largely permits pharmaceutical advertising, one need only note that such advertising has been criticized for a long time; the Port Huron statement also called attention to the outrageous sums that what it caustically called "the ethical drug industry" spent on advertising. A simple comparison of the total worth to society of pharmaceuticals in 1962 and now suggests that any critics of such advertising have a heavy burden: not simply criticism of individual ads or advertising practices, which is easy, but a suggestion for some other system that would have produced more progress during that time.

Logos

The ACM also views corporate branding and logos with scorn and suspicion. Naomi Klein's anti-corporate classic *No Logo* is built entirely on the premise that corporations in recent years have managed to manipulate the law to enable them to turn brand names into their primary asset, while outsourcing the dreary and unprofitable task of actual manufacturing to low-wage Third World sweatshops.[33] The Nike Corporation, which relies on contractors to do most of its manufacturing while doing little in its headquarters in Oregon other than product design and marketing, is the consummate example. Consumers are mesmerized by the marriage of devious advertising to prominently displayed logos into obediently pledging allegiance to a particular brand, and the corporations that create the brands use the wealth they generate from the resulting high prices they can charge to increase their economic dominance. Bolstered by trademark and copyright protection and the immense profits available from the combination of avid consumers and a cheap, compliant manufacturing workforce, a brand's primary function is as leverage to total market dominance obtained from the conquest of small local businesses and of the minds of consumers. In her telling (which Korten borrows in *When Corporations Rule the World*), there are heroic resisters to Brand World in the form of artists who engage in "culture jamming," the use of brand logos in satire to diminish the brands' value, which is depicted as a bravely subversive act. That corporations can plaster their logos all over the airwaves, the Internet, and the streets, while anti-corporate activists cannot use them satirically in their own information warfare, is seen as both obviously unfair and the result of corporate influence peddling in the legal system.

There is a standard economic theory of brands and what function they perform, and it is nowhere to be found in this story. The over-the-road traveler who stops for the night at a typical exit on the U.S. freeway system is often confronted with a host of chain restaurants and hotels, with a few local establishments scattered among them. Which ones should he choose? The brand names will provide him with things of known if perhaps middling quality (unless he is an aficionado of the particular chains, in which case he views the quality as high). The purely local establishments will provide him with something new but of unknown quality. Absent a taste for diversity for its own sake (which many people undoubtedly have), he may find that the brand establishments are better bets. This is what brand names do—they provide reliable information on product features and quality. A Big Mac is the same in Dallas, London, and Shanghai. To the anti-corporate true believer, this is the sign of a corporate-dominated world of dreary sameness. But in fact the presence of McDonald's and Ramada Inn and all other consumer-product brands provides assurances in a world in which the cost of acquiring information about product quality and features can be high. (Whether cultural and product diversity is in fact decreasing is a topic explored further in Chapters 6 and 7. It is generally true that any American municipality big enough to have more than one or two McDonald's outlets also has many more nonfranchise, purely local dining options.) Brands are essential to help consumers navigate a sophisticated, information-laden world.

In various works, Klein has also developed her concept of "public space," which in her view has been systematically invaded by branded corporations in recent years. The presence of brands in malls is one thing; their presence in the universities (e.g., as operators of the bookstores or sponsors of chaired professorships), in hospitals, and on giant billboards on the streets that everyone uses is another. In *No Logo*, where precisely "private space" stops and "public space" begins is not rigorously developed, but elsewhere Klein has written of the latter all too expansively:

> As our communal spaces—town squares, streets, schools, farms, plants—are displaced by the ballooning marketplace, a spirit of resistance is taking hold around the world. People are reclaiming bits of nature and of culture, and saying "this is going to be public space." American students are kicking ads out of the classrooms. European environmentalists and ravers are throwing parties at busy intersections. Landless Thai peasants are planting organic vegetables on over-irrigated golf courses. Bolivian workers are reversing the privatization of their water supply. Outfits like Napster have been creating a kind of commons on the internet where kids can swap music with each other, rather than buying it from multinational record companies. Billboards have been liberated and independent media networks set up. Protests are multiplying. In Porto Alegre, during the World Social Forum, José Bové, often caricatured as only a hammer of McDonald's, traveled with local activists from the Movimento Sem Terra to a nearby Monsanto test site, where they destroyed three hectares of genetically modified soya beans. But the protest did not stop there. The MST has occupied the land and members are now planting their own organic crops on it, vowing to turn the farm into a model of sustainable agriculture. In short, activists aren't waiting for the revolution, they are acting right now, where they live, where they study, where they work, where they farm. [34]

Leave aside the obvious fact that corporations are bringing something to the table with their activities or sponsorship—the corporation that sponsors a university classroom, e.g., is providing money that can be used for laboratory equipment, student financial aid, and so on. Read straightforwardly, the paragraph is unalloyed praise of vandalism and theft and rejection of the notion of intellectual property, usually because of nothing more profound than an idiosyncratic distaste for corporate brands, a distaste not shared by most of the population. There is a long-standing and unfortunate tendency in some Western thought, and particularly in twentieth-century American jurisprudence, to treat property rights as a conditional grant rather than a "right" as that term is ordinarily understood. (Property rights, in fact, used to be a core element of the

liberty to which citizens are entitled, on a par with free speech and freedom of worship, a development that largely persisted in the United States
until the late 1930s.[35]) And the ACM has sunk its teeth into this tendency
with a vengeance.

But property rights are actually an essential foundation if markets are
to make decisions. It is the ability to buy and sell property, whether as
land, one's time and knowledge, or the creative works derived from the
application of one's own genius in the presence of intellectual property
rights, that allows lesser horizons to be turned into greater ones. The right
to control property, to paraphrase Margaret Thatcher, is valuable not
simply because it enables greater wealth creation (which it certainly
does), but because it gives one control over one's own life. It is fundamental to reconciling people's conflicting goals and desires through consent
and trade rather than conflict. When that which you own—including
intellectual property—is clearly demarcated from that which I own, you
and I spend most of our time in trade for mutual benefit rather than in
political conflict over who needs whose permission to use what.

But a property right is meaningless once it becomes contingent, once it
becomes an abstraction applauded when in the hands of a noble figure
like an artist or a campesino, but revocable when possessed by such
unsavory types as the shareholders of a corporation. Unavoidably, such
attempts to discriminate among different sorts of property holders must
result, if successful, in property rights that are more expansive for some
kinds of people and narrower for others—to inequality before the law, in
other words. Klein acknowledges that intellectual-property protection
has its purposes, which she identifies as securing the income of content
producers (Klein, for example) from their creations. But the use of such
protection to earn income for a corporation is in her estimation a different
matter. The justification for such restrictions on intellectual-property
rights is not always explicitly offered, but excessive corporate power is
generally seen as a sufficient justification in and of itself for fairly radical
changes to legal traditions that sometimes date back centuries. Sometimes,
as in Klein's work, it is corporate trademarks and copyrights that are
the primary offenders. (Despite her reputation as an anti-corporate campaigner, Klein seems unaware that many corporations do not sell branded
products to consumers but perform many other vital social-coordination
functions instead, by managing logistics or serving as distributors,
for example.) And sometimes it is *any* corporation's use of the power routinely granted to other human organizations that function as collective
persons—the right to persuade in the public arena, to contract freely,
etc.—that anti-corporate campaigners object to. (These rights belong
logically in any event not to corporations but to the individuals who comprise them. These individuals do not lose these rights simply because the
corporation is the form of association through which they have chosen to

make the statement in question.) In other words, lesser rights for corporate constituents, greater rights for those who criticize corporations. This is exactly the sort of disparity—unequal treatment for individuals depending on how the state classifies the merit of what they do—that has proven so destructive in the past, and which is a clear violation of the principle of equality before the law as defined above—any invitation to exercise the state's power differently over citizens based on the different choices they make, for fundamentally irrelevant reasons.

WHAT IS THE ALTERNATIVE?

Property rights are of course not sacred to the ACM, and so their destruction is no tragedy. So what does the movement value instead? Democracy. Corporations should be governed "democratically" by some collective mechanism incorporating the voices of all of their constituencies—not just shareholders, but workers and others.[36] For the ACM, democracy is the cure for the disease of corporate rule.

Trimming Corporate Wings

Recall that for anti-corporate thinkers of the old-fashioned power-struggle wing, the existing democratic institutions, while they may need substantial reform via, for example, substantial restrictions on the political-participation rights of Americans who work for or own shares in corporations compared to those who participate through some other form of association (i.e., through anti-corporate "campaign-finance reform"), are more or less adequate to the task. For many anti-corporate activists who agitate for more authentic democracy, legitimate political activity largely begins and ends with voting—everyone gets one vote, the majority rules, and no one can spend money in the public square to try to change the votes of others. It certainly does not include the expenditure of money to achieve political objectives, especially if corporate-connected individuals are spending it. (It is also taken for granted that *time* spent on political activism by anti-corporate campaigners should not be restricted in any way.) For the apocalyptic wing, society must be fundamentally restructured. Most dramatically, global commerce must be substantially replaced with largely self-sufficient local commercial activity, and large production organizations, to the extent that they remain, must be managed democratically, in the "public interest" or for the benefit of stakeholders. In some anti-corporate work, most trade in the postcorporate world is envisioned as occurring with people in your immediate global neighborhood. When, lamentably, you must transact with someone far away (not because you want to but because, in society's judgment, you unavoidably *have* to), you will do it on terms dictated by the rest of society.

The primary problem with such an approach is the uncritical assumption that the "public interest" will be the outcome of public processes limiting commercial rights. At this point in our history, the corporation is a well-entrenched feature of many societies. Huge numbers of people all over the planet make use of the commercial networks of which global corporations are a critical part to navigate their way through life—to eat, to learn, to achieve, to be entertained, to see new places and have new experiences. All of that could not help but be substantially and perhaps fatally disrupted by radical reorientation of corporations away from serving their shareholders. Global commercial networks of all sorts would have to be dramatically altered. The consequences of this are impossible to predict, but there is no reason to think that they would be good. The ACM, particularly its apocalyptic wing, takes it for granted that we would all be happier, more introspective, and more fulfilled in a world deprived of such corporate networks. But it is global corporate networks that enable global contact of all sorts—not just the raw technology that enables flying across great distances and exposure to cultural activities of peoples all over the world, but the widespread wealth that enables ordinary people to take advantage of these opportunities in the first place. It is those who run the airlines, publish the books, distribute the music, and seek out the exotic foodstuffs to sell around the world who make global connection possible. There is no possibility of benefiting from the oft-lauded cultural diversity that we now take for granted without its immense corporate underpinnings. That the ACM is comfortable having the state oversee such a sweeping reorganization of society—by replacing the known shareholder-owned corporation with something as unpredictable as "corporate democracy"—is perhaps its most chilling trait.

A world in which excessively "powerful" corporations are brought under "public" control or eliminated outright is not one of happy self-sufficiency. It is instead a world of parochialism owing to isolation and ignorance of other cultures, of resentment over lost opportunities to pursue one's dreams, of foregone technological progress, of artists and scientists who toil in increasing unawareness of what their colleagues in other parts of the world are doing. It is a world, in other words, of substantially diminished possibilities. Given that people, when aware of a better future denied, will tend to bitterly resist it and lapse into zero-sum political warfare, it is also a world of greater social conflict. It is almost tragic that so many of the bright minds of the ACM have been led down this path and have offered in contrast only vague, pallid paeans to the localized, self-sufficient, and especially the democratic paradise that awaits. Upon a moment's reflection, it seems astonishing that any significant portion of humanity would sign on to an agenda that would limit the ability of humans to use the corporate structure to pursue their own grand ambitions and would prevent the most successful of those dreams from elevating human possibility all over the world. Perhaps the best evidence that anti-corporate thinking is atavistic madness is the way so many people all over the world reject the anti-corporate alternative when given a choice. It is thus not surprising that the ACM falls back on the story of psychological manipulation to explain "pro-corporate" beliefs and choices (the buying of corporate products, the purchase of corporate shares, the selling of skills and labor to corporate managers, the enthusiastic desire in emerging markets for the corporate law we in the West take for granted), which appear to be almost universally held, especially among those in poor countries who can't (yet) make these choices.

Even if it were possible, the notion of the "public-interest corporation" would founder on the rocks of reality. Government is, in its proper sphere, an essential component of any modern and well-functioning society. The private sector certainly cannot be expected to adequately police market failures such as the negative externality, i.e., the social costs imposed by profit-maximizing businesses on others that those businesses ignore unless they are forced by legal sanction to take them into account (e.g., the pollutants that the factory owner dumps into the river). Nor can it be relied on to adequately produce what economists call public goods, goods that are under-provided by the private sector because people can receive benefits whether they pay for those services or not, or common-access goods—goods that are depleted or damaged because none can be excluded from using them. (National defense is the classic public good; clean air and water and the ocean's fish stocks are examples of common-access goods.)

But using the state to substantially constrain how privately owned resources can be combined to produce various combinations of goods and services has a grim track record. The catastrophic state of life in communist societies is well-documented; most of those societies have by now largely abandoned outright public ownership and management of most productive facilities. In developed and developing countries alike, there has been a substantial movement in recent years to transfer many activities from the public sector to voluntary negotiations and transactions among individuals interacting peacefully on the basis of property rights. And it will not do to say that this time wholesale public supervision of commerce will be different. There is no reason to expect that in most activities, such close supervision of private activity by public officials would work any better in an "anti-corporate" context than in the older explicitly socialist one, whether that context is provided by Ralph Nader–inspired substantial legal restrictions on corporate behavior or David Korten–inspired total remaking of the way we live.

Many anti-corporate activists respond by saying that they recognize the failures of social models descended from Marx and reject public ownership of productive facilities in particular. Many of them genuinely believe in their own narrow vision of small-scale "free markets," which they believe have been disrupted by the rise of giant corporations. Small businesses in their world will be allowed to compete, Adam Smith-style, while large ones will be broken up. But as we have seen, whether "free markets" exist or not has little to do with whether some of the participants in that market are very large, but whether participation in them by competitors, large and small, new and old, is legally protected. Large companies can be driven out of business by technological progress or be forced to adapt to that progress, either result demonstrating their lack, at the individual firm level, of economic power. Corporate size is not corporate power, and treating them as the same thing will thus yield few benefits in terms of equalizing whatever definition of "power" one wishes to use, even as it destroys the gains that can be achieved in the construction of global trading networks—not just economies of scale, but the ability to link people scattered all over the planet for the benefit of all. Limitations on corporate size are, like it or not, unavoidably also limitations on the free market. If large corporations are subject to competitive pressures then the kinds of restrictions contemplated by anti-corporate activists inescapably limit the ability of people to trade as they wish.

The Postcorporate Corporation

If the postcorporate world nonetheless comes to pass, how precisely are these once purely commercial titans to be managed? Much of the most popular literature is heavy on such inspiring imprecisions as "democracy." Marjorie Kelly is laudably succinct in expressing what she envisions will happen:

> Under market principles, wealth does not legitimately belong only to stockholders. Corporate wealth belongs to those who create it, and community wealth belongs to all...The corporation is a human community, and like the larger community of which is a part, is best governed democratically.[37]

But of course, it was recognized centuries ago that there are many spheres of human activity for which governance, democratic or not, ought to be off-limits; indeed, this idea has been a cornerstone of Western political thought for centuries, and the Constitution of the United States devotes its first ten amendments and much of the first three articles (particularly those parts devoted to checks and balances) to it. The notion that commerce and government should intermingle at close quarters primarily through government institutions to promote commerce rather than to restrict it is also woven deeply into our history and culture (although admittedly less so in recent decades). To replace what is now the long-established institution of the corporation as we know it with corporations that are "governed democratically" would be quite a change. So what would it look like? The movement has not thought about this question in any detail, confining itself primarily either to specific legislative steps or to vagaries about fair representation of all stakeholders accountability to the public will and the like. Plans and platitudes are plentiful, precedents are not. And so the question deserves attention.

A critical claim of this book is that in politics, as in much of life, we must take people as we find them and not as we wish they were. This observation is especially important when we think about the possibility of using government power, even and sometimes especially democratic power, to frustrate the actions of citizens freely chosen under the existing rules of the game. Although many people think when they hear the word "democracy" of some combination of majority rule, freedom of thought, and a government whose powers are constitutionally limited, what the term really means in its purest form (and certainly in the anti-corporate literature) is merely some form of majority rule. What the ACM often seems to mean in its advocacy of greater accountability and corporate democracy is that all of the corporation's stakeholders should be represented via some sort of voting mechanism. The belief is that such governance will result in the fruits of the corporation being distributed fairly among the various stakeholders—workers most prominently. (Kelly even vests an abstraction—the environment—with a stakeholder claim.) But political theory suggests, alas, that there is no way to get from democratic governance to any definition of the public interest that "the public" will accept. (This insight belongs originally to the French nobleman Marquis de Condorcet, himself an advocate of democratic governance in the public interest, revealed by reason, who was ultimately killed by Jacobin revolutionaries convinced that their goals were the only "reasonable" ones.)

Consider a democratically governed corporation in which there are three stakeholders: shareholders, workers, and consumers.[38] (Consumers are often not listed by stakeholder-governance activists as one of the stakeholder groups, but of course they should be.) Each constituency has a single vote, and the question before them is how to divide $100 in new profits. Initially, consistent with majority-rule principles, shareholders propose to workers that it be split 50-50 among these two constituencies. But then a problem arises because the preyed-upon constituency, consumers, can propose to shareholders that the revenue be split 60-40 between them, with shareholders getting 60. Shareholders being better off favor such a proposal. But then workers can go to consumers and offer to split the income 50-50 again, this time leaving shareholders on the outside looking in. At which point, shareholders can propose yet another 60-40 split to either group, with that new partner getting 60. This can go on forever; it is a problem known to the field of public choice as cycling.[39] While this is happening, the corporation is avoiding the task of improving its operation and is instead consuming some or all of the hundred dollars in fights over how the spoils are to be distributed.

Many other examples of voting procedures failing to reflect plurality or majority opinion exist as well. The legal scholar Gordon Tullock cites the example of the Liberal Democratic Party in the United Kingdom, which might well be able to defeat either the Labor or the Conservative party in a one-on-one election but never gets the chance owing to British voting rules supported by the latter two parties.[40] Corrupt logrolling, the systematic trading of favors by legislators, would presumably also afflict democratic governance by factions with conflicting interests. Suppliers and workers could vote for higher prices paid to the former and then later for higher wages paid to the latter. All of this would of course come at the expense of consumers and shareholders, ultimately driving the enterprise into bankruptcy. (At this point, the stakeholders might choose to let the government take over the enterprise, at which point the debacle would be completely sloughed off on taxpayers.)

In addition, government regulation of business tends to be hijacked by both government officials and various special interests within society for corrupt purposes. As we saw in Chapter 2, societies with more extensive regulation of business tend to have much higher levels of corruption.[41] That is because bribes are often the easiest way to get around such regulation, and indeed such regulations are often imposed precisely because they give civil servants more opportunities to extract bribes. With respect to corporate monopoly power in particular, imposing more conditions on incorporation has been shown to strengthen the capacity of large existing firms and to protect them from competition from new entrants. This is partly because existing firms capture the regulatory process, using it to thwart competition, and partly because the cost of starting a new firm rises when there are more regulatory hurdles to clear.[42] More general close links between the state and the corporations, a primitive form of the democratic governance of corporations envisioned by the ACM, are associated with both economic stagnation and higher levels of corruption.[43] It is no answer to say that these things will not happen in a world thick with regulatory restraints on corporate governance, because that is the world that *has* actually resulted from "democratic" control of business—a world of corruption, of monopolies, and of political and economic chaos.

While in some circumstances (market failure as defined above) properly restrained democracy is better than the alternatives, decades of history suggest that using democracy to operate a profitable enterprise is not one of them. Democratic governance of corporations will be conducted with about as much relation to the public interest as the U.S. tax system—itself a frightful maze shaped by passionate appeals to the public interest—has. This is literally no way to run a business. Indeed, given the role of competition among corporations in promoting progress, the freedom of consumers to buy or not to buy as they wish, and free commerce's capacity to promote individual achievement as opposed to special-interest empowerment via the state (recall, for example, the evidence on the power of commerce in breaking down tribal barriers from Chapter 4), the best way to expand and preserve one's authority over the direction of one's own life is to make it *easier* to start and operate corporations, not harder.

Centuries of business–government interaction suggest the following principle: *governing corporations in the "public interest" would lead to stasis at best, chaos at worst. The more constituencies with legally guaranteed governance roles, the worse this problem will be.* And "stasis" is not simply the inability to decide how to run the "publicly accountable" corporation but the foregoing of all of the advances made possible by competition among self-governing shareholder corporations. There is absolutely no reason to expect that the endpoint of corporate "democracy" differs in any substantial way from the outright nationalizations of private firms that occurred in other societies in previous decades. Such stakeholder governance will lead to catastrophic conflict over how resources should be used that is acceptable, even essential when confined to clear instances of market failure but becomes a destroyer of opportunity and a very effective incubator of social conflict when applied to positive-sum activities.

Of course, shareholder corporations do govern themselves despite having shareholders with conflicting beliefs. But disputes in shareholder-owned corporations are typically not about ends but means. When management decides to reject a takeover offer or not to sell off a division, shareholders all want to maximize the value of their shares but disagree on whether management has taken the proper decision or not. Such disagreements are much less likely when everyone has the same ultimate goal than when everyone is engaged in a zero-sum struggle over how to distribute the proceeds of a theoretically positive-sum enterprise in which they share governance. Even very small collectively governed positive-sum societies—communes, kibbutzes, worker-owned production organizations—often find it difficult to manage their affairs coherently. The belief that even a profitable medium-sized organization (let alone a large one) could be governed by democratic give-and-take requires heroic assumptions about human nature.

In addition to shareholder-owners having common interests, another reason why shareholder-run corporations can succeed is the possibility of exit for the dissatisfied. In a free society, any constituents of a poorly run firm can leave in pursuit of better offers elsewhere. They can seek employment elsewhere, shop elsewhere, start their own businesses, or do anything else that people in free societies may generally do. In addition, in such a society, activities that are not explicitly prohibited are in fact permitted. A corporation run in the interests of shareholders is thus one in which its agents retain substantial freedom of action—freedom to bargain, to propose, to leave—preserving their capacity for ingenuity and creativity. Whether at the small level—a worker who leaves a company because he thinks his job pays too little or is too unfulfilling—or the large—a takeover artist proposing a significant restructuring—a shareholder corporation has an accountable authority to whom proposals can be made. Anyone who doesn't like the status quo makes an offer and if it is accepted is better off and if it is rejected leaves. But a stakeholder corporation, mandated to reconcile several often conflicting interests, has a much tougher problem because it must appeal to corporate opinion across constituencies, a considerably more complex problem. In a zero-sum environment, exit is generally less attractive than struggling harder for a bigger slice of a smaller pie.

Giving people freedom to take it or leave it (or make a counteroffer) within a specifically tailored, easily interpreted, and nonarbitrary set of rules prescribing a narrow set of things they may not do, the outcome most consistent with a free and happy society, is not a likely outcome of "corporate democracy," especially given that alternatives will be few because of the difficulty of forming new corporations. Telling them ever more elaborately and imprecisely what they *must do*, limiting their creativity and flexibility, is far more probable. Simple prohibitions become evermore complex bureaucratic nightmares, ultimately making decision-makers helpless to avoid breaking the rules. This phenomenon is driven equally by the desires of the rule makers to profit from the rules they make, by the inability to predict how distinct individuals with unpredictable goals will react to changed incentives, and by the refusal to believe that people make choices for a reason and that laws that go against their interests had better be simple and vigorously enforced or they will be ignored.[44]

A world of open-access corporations is far more consistent than one dominated by democratically controlled corporations with freedom, *properly defined,* from the arbitrary rule of others—freedom, in other words, to take a particular action or not, to pursue one's interest and reconcile it with the sometimes conflicting and sometimes complementary interests of others, facilitated by the ability to own and trade property. With open-access incorporation, a person may choose to incorporate (for profit or for any other legal reason), to join someone else's corporation, to exit the corporate sector entirely, or to create some other alternative business structure unknown before he thought of it. Open-access incorporation is the ideal legal rule for a free and dynamic society. Subordinating corporations to politics would pave the road to a future full of artificial obstacles to humanity's desire to innovate, to create, to enhance our possibilities as a species. All of that would be submerged in endless squabbling over the distribution of ever-diminishing spoils. The anti-corporate vision of society is fundamentally one that sees our most important problem as seizing the power to command the way others live from those who are seen, erroneously, as currently possessing it. Despite its rhetoric about a brighter democratic future, the ACM operates from a fundamentally dismal view of humanity and our possibilities. The present moment in world history is not in their view the culmination of centuries of creativity and progress but the end stage of a dystopian process that occurs because some people can make money advancing the interests of other people.

In fact, open-access corporations are an engine of freedom, where anyone who thinks he has a clever idea to make money or serve society in any way that appeals to him may pursue that vision freed from personal liability. This competitive, experimental society is consistent in a way that stakeholder governance or political micromanagement is not with the only power that matters—the power of the individual to be in charge of his own life. This is especially true given that limited liability, one of the key features of the modern corporation, does not apply only to for-profit corporations but to corporations established for any purpose. People may establish corporations not just to make as much money as possible but to do charitable work, engage in political activism, or even engage in anti-corporate activity. While democratic corporate governance amounts to people voting on how best to limit someone else's possibilities, under free incorporation all may choose among all the options that currently exist and some that they create themselves.

Corporations, even defined most expansively (and unrealistically) as a single homogenous pressure group, are merely one such group among many. Like members of every other group formed from the right of free association, constituencies of various corporations routinely exercise their right to petition the government for a redress of their grievances. They attempt to shape the laws governing corporate behavior—laws deriving from centuries of evolutionary legal experimentation—to advance their own interests, whether those interests are profits for shareholders, compensation for workers, or better products at lower prices for consumers. Rather than a collective, monotone instrument for domination of the rest of us, corporations are individual entities, each one a device through which the conflicting interests of different members of society can peacefully and cooperatively interact. The society created in the corporate world and, as we will see in Chapter 7, its politics and culture are intrinsically more interesting and vibrant than one in which corporations are subordinated to politics and its discontents.

Chapter 6

Corporate Globalization

In the last quarter century, the notion of "globalization" has seized the imagination of intellectuals, activists, and the public at large as few others have during this time. The *idea* of globalization has if anything risen to dominance in its realm even more than the phenomenon itself, rapidly ensconcing itself in university syllabi, the schedules of the more earnest talk shows, United Nations reports, and pressure-group agendas. And so too it has recently become a key theme of the anti-corporatist movement, which views "corporate globalization" as one of the corporate oligarchy's most grievous sins. Indeed, so closely linked now are the anti-globalization and anti-corporate literature and movements that in many respects they are the same. To be anti-globalization is increasingly to be anti-corporate, and vice versa.

IDENTIFYING THE PHENOMENON

The term globalization is remarkably elastic, carrying different meanings for its friends and foes. This is undoubtedly due in part to its novelty. While the earliest citation for the term in *The Oxford English Dictionary* is in 1962, it is found in only one article in *The New York Times* prior to 1980, in fifteen from 1980 to 1989, 1,038 from 1990 to 1999, and 1,125 between 2000 and 2004. The rapid growth in the use of the term in recent years has spurred a race by supporters and opponents to capture the dictionary space allotted to it, so as to seize the chance to define it in the public mind. What the sociologist Carlos Santos calls "hegemonic globalization" is an annihilating force that "cannibalizes differences instead of facilitating the dialogue among them." For Jassim Asfour, General Secretary of the

Cultural Council of Egypt, it is "an imminent danger that is endangering our [Arab] political, social, cultural and economical stability." Jeremy Seabrook is a British journalist who does not note the irony as he is able to write in his native tongue in the *Korea Herald*, an English-language paper published in a land on the opposite side of the world from his own, that globalization is a "declaration of war upon all other cultures." And so on.[1]

But to its proponents globalization is a force for liberation, an opportunity for people to gain from the new opportunities to trade products, culture, and ideas across national borders that are ever more permeable. For the noted economist Jagdish Bhagwati globalization is the key to prosperity, which is in turn the key to overcoming so many of the world's ills— child labor, slavery, "sweatshops," etc.—so often mistakenly *attributed* to globalization. For the newspaper columnist and best-selling author Thomas Friedman it is unavoidable, full of complications and difficulties, but in the end of potentially tremendous benefit for all the world's people. For the novelist Salman Rushdie, who has more reason than most to know about the dark side of a globalized world, globalization (or at least the spread of some aspects of Western culture) is indispensable in the fight against "tyranny, bigotry, intolerance, fanaticism."[2]

It hardly seems possible that these disparate descriptions can actually be of the same phenomenon. But there are clear empirical patterns that have emerged over the last several decades that show globalization as it has unfolded. Table 6.1 shows the growth in world trade (exports and imports) as a percentage of total global output, foreign direct investment as a percentage of gross global output and gross capital formation, migration to the United States, and the number of regional trading agreements in force over the last fifty years. The trends toward greater interconnection across greater distances are obvious. They are also widespread across a variety of measures, suggestive of a broad remaking of human society. But the issue of interest here is how to interpret them: a spontaneous evolution from below or a corporate plot imposed from above?

GLOBALIZATION IN THE ANTI-CORPORATE MIND

To properly understand how corporations fit into globalization in the mental model of the ACM, it is important to understand how they see globalization overall. And there is no understanding where the movement is without an understanding of how it got there. Most of the anti-corporate view of globalization is a variant of the earlier determinist and especially Marxist conception of the world and the corporate place within it discussed in Chapter 3. It also relies on a description of the global system as a whole rather than giving much thought to the individuals who comprise it. What is known by many scholarly critics of globalization as

Table 6.1   Globalization by the numbers.

World Trade/GDP		
1970	28%	
1980	39%	
1990	38%	
2000	49%	
Number of migrants worldwide (percentage of global population in parentheses)		
1960	75,000,000	(2.5)
1970	92,000,000	
1980	102,000,000	
1990	153,000,000	
2000	176,000,000	(2.9)
Migration to the United States		
Fiscal year 1970	373,326	
Fiscal year 1988	643,025	
Fiscal year 2002	1,063,732	
Regional Trade Agreements		
1970	6	
1990	25	
2006	191	

Sources: World Trade/GDP—World Bank, World Development Indicators; Migration world-wide—United Nations, Department of Economic and Social Affairs, World Economic And Social Survey 2004 Part II: International Migration (New York: UN, 2004); U.S. Immigration —U.S. Department of Homeland Security, Office of Immigration Statistics, 2005 Yearbook of Immigration Statistics (Washington: Office of Immigration Statistics, 2006); RTAs—World Trade Organization, "Regional Trade Agreements: Facts and Figures," http://www.wto.org/english/tratop_e/region_e/regfac_e.htm.

world-systems theory, which powers much of the more abstract criticism of globalization, is descended from the dependency or core–periphery theory of the Argentine economist Raúl Prebisch, which he created to slay over a century of economic consensus about international economics. This conventional wisdom up to the 1930s was inherited from the great classical economists Adam Smith and David Ricardo, who argued that nations should trade freely, the theory (still almost universally accepted in large part today among economists) known as comparative advantage. This argument holds that nations differ, and the members of a nation can benefit by specializing in what they can do relatively well and trading for what they do relatively poorly. This is an uncontroversial insight at the individual level. Left to their own devices, few individuals see self-sufficiency in medical care (treating your own broken leg), the manu-facture of items used in daily life (making your own bicycle), or in most of the wide array of consumption possibilities as desirable. Rather, they engage in a highly specialized activity—they run businesses making locks and keys, they are administrative assistants specializing in insurance billing for physicians who themselves specialize in treatment of highly specific disorders such as gastrointestinal problems, and so on. They exchange the income earned from these jobs for the equally highly specialized production of their fellow citizens. This growing specialization is a hallmark of any growing economy, and has been known to be a key feature of progress for centuries.[3]

The groups of individuals known as businesses also do not try to be all things to all people. They produce a handful of items, pay their shareholders, suppliers, and employees with the resulting proceeds, and rely heavily in their production on the highly specialized output of other firms. Note that even a large conglomerate producing a seemingly wide variety of goods, a form of business organization that is periodically the rage on Wall Street (and can still be found in countries like South Korea today), is not in any meaningful sense highly specialized, in that it produces only a tiny fraction of the millions of goods available in any modern economy. Standard international trade theory is simply the transfer of this theory of specialization and its gains to the groups of individuals known as the nation-state.

Prebisch saw the world differently. In his thinking, what we now call the global economy was the result of conscious organization from on high, and the unit of organization was not class, as in older Marxist theory, but the nation-state. There were two groups of nations in the world, the core and the periphery. The core—the colonial powers of Europe and North America—had through colonialism imposed on the periphery—their colonies and other never-colonized but weak nations such as Thailand—unbalanced economies excessively oriented toward exporting commodities to the core in exchange for high value-added manufactured goods. This exchange was unequal, in that it prevented colonies or newly independent former colonies from developing the manufacturing sector seen as the key to prosperity. One has some sympathy with such a position in light of what was known then, and in light of a cursory reading from history and the contemporary state of the world. Despite preaching the virtues of free trade, for example, the British government practiced the sort of neo-mercantilism that would be familiar to any official in a contemporary trade ministry in France or Japan, enacting protectionist measures to shelter the home country from competition from India's budding textile industry. Upon independence, dependency theorists believed, the periphery only furthered its dependency by participating in international trade. This dependency was fostered by the primary institutions of the postwar global economy—the World Bank, the International Monetary Fund, and the General Agreement on Tariffs and Trade. These entities were seen as the strong-arm enforcement agents of open trading and free markets rather than venues for development assistance and international consensus. Not just in spite but because of the inherently unequal exchange at the heart of the global trading system, all of these organizations, working on behalf of the core, favored the old-fashioned free-trade consensus, and the more they were listened to by poor countries the worse off those countries would be.

Thus, withdrawal from most international trade with the core, at least under the existing terms, was called for. In his defense, Prebisch was in no sense a defender of the crazy quilt of arbitrarily high and nonuniform tariffs common in Latin America during his time. Rather, he believed that industrialization was essential but could be best accommodated through building domestic industry behind protectionist walls, then creating regional blocs of developing countries that could develop and distribute industries among them, and only then trading with the core on an equal basis. This posture is ironically similar to the (misplaced) current enthusiasm for regional economic integration as preparation for full globalization.[4]

Dependency theory lost favor among economists after the debt crisis of the early 1980s and the opening of the Berlin Wall, and of course should have—not just because of the catastrophic failure of so many closed economies to build prosperity but because an implied prediction of the model had failed to hold. Presumably, if the core countries are managing the global economy to divide up a particular amount of wealth extracted from the dependent periphery, simple arithmetic suggests that the core should be as small and the periphery as large as possible. And yet even as Prebisch was writing his most influential work in the 1950s and 1960s, nations in East Asia were knocking loudly on the door of the core by dint of their industriousness and sound economic policy. Several nations such as Australia, New Zealand, and Canada were also able to build prosperity despite significant commodity orientation in their trade patterns.

Noteworthy is that in dependency thinking the nation is still the unit of analysis. It is nations, not classes or regions, that are either in the core or periphery, and it is nations that have to reform their policies so as to extract themselves from an exploitative system. But some of the remaining Marxist intellectuals sought to revamp dependency theory while continuing to use the core–periphery language. One of their intellectual if not empirically accurate achievements was to reintegrate more traditional Marxism, with classes as the unit of analysis, with the Prebisch framework. Such an adjustment was needed because the old Leninist extension of Marxism, which argued that capitalism bred imperialism, which bred the end of the division of the market, which bred revolution, proved inaccurate with the dismantling of at least the external trappings of most of the European empires after World War II. One of the giants in this movement was the sociologist Immanuel Wallerstein, who in a variety of works tried to cram the square peg of the facts of capitalist development into the round hole of Marxist theory.[5]

One of Wallerstein's signal achievements in that work and in a lifetime of Marxist scholarship was to reconcile the old-time Marxist gospel, with its emphasis on historical inevitability, economic determinism, and class warfare, with the dichotomy between core and periphery pioneered by Prebisch. In the conception of Wallerstein and his acolytes, decolonization had occurred because the ruling classes in the core (themselves creations of the global capitalist economic system, whose needs determined how they ruled) simply decided that tacit empire was more efficient than explicit colonization. The essence of the global economy is not a division among countries in which the strong nations dominate the weak, but once again an organization that benefits ruling capitalists. Globalization—the penetration of modern industrial production and exchange mediated via market prices—is thus a creation of these capitalists, and an unstable one at that. According to world-systems theory, Lenin was right to claim that the capitalist stage of history ultimately exhausts itself by pushing workers and the possibilities of productivity enhancement to the breaking point, but it will occur only after the capitalist classes have finished converting all of humanity to the market, at which point, presumably, revolution takes place. In 1995 the sociologist Linda Sklair spoke in terms of a "transnational capitalist class," and multinational corporations as a vehicle "to harness the transnational capitalist classes to solidify the hegemonic control of consumerist culture and ideology" in "the many struggles for the resources of the global system."[6] We are thus back to where we started, with the creaky Marxist model updated to accommodate all the events that didn't seem to play out as Marx and his followers had predicted.

And yet we are not quite there yet, because the corporation hardly appears in the Wallerstein system. A corporation is primarily a passive instrument through which the ruling capitalists obtain the necessary legal privileges that enable them to increase production, capitalize on economies of scale and continue to create and absorb the Marxist notion of labor surplus. It is a vehicle through which capitalism coped with the "capitalist crises of the 1970s and after (oil price shocks, rising unemployment, and increasing insecurity as the rich countries experience problems in paying for their welfare states)."[7] The corporation is merely a symptom and not the disease.

It is only in recent years that the corporation as a peculiar entity has come to dominate the discussion of the global system and how it came about. There is no definitive starting point, but several milestones are clear on the road by which globalization became *corporate* globalization.

The campaigns against economic-reform plans imposed on developing countries in financial crisis by the International Monetary Fund (known as structural adjustment, and imposed, it should be noted, only after countries requested them because of severe economic difficulties) took hold in the late 1980s, although the concern was mostly with destruction of the social safety net and local sovereignty rather than corporate domination.

In the runup to the approval of the North American Free Trade Agreement in 1993 anti-corporate attitudes took a back seat to more traditional concerns about "fair trade," as well as the potential for the handover of U.S. sovereignty to unelected NAFTA adjudication panels. Much of the opposition to NAFTA was scattered around political groups with no other obvious points of contact—protectionists concerned about low wages and regulatory protection (including politically ambitious people such as H. Ross Perot and Pat Buchanan), environmentalists worried about subversion of U.S. environmental protection, and old-line leftists concerned about the penetration of modern "capitalism" post-1989 into regions of the world that until then had kept it at bay.

It was approximately at this time that the theme of corporate globalization began to cohere. By 1996 two articles featured on the cover of the storied progressive magazine *The Nation* depicted globalization as mostly a corporate phenomenon. One was authored by a former advertising executive named Jerry Mander, whose grim views on the dominant corporate culture were discussed in Chapter 5. He had earlier authored a book on the perils of excessive use of technology, particularly communications technology, which he believed served to enhance corporate control over society. Now he argued that globalization itself was a no-win game (corporate elites aside) constructed by corporations for their benefit and at everyone else's cost. The article cleverly tied together such seemingly unrelated strands as the imposition of structural adjustment, the putative growing strains on the global environment from the spread of modernity, and allegedly growing numbers of the poor in both developed and developing countries, and tied them all together into an all-too-neat package: corporations promoted globalization to enhance their profits, despite these catastrophic negative effects.

In a companion article Helena Norberg-Hodge, an anti-corporate activist and cofounder of the International Forum on Globalization (IFG), who is best known for her efforts to "protect" aboriginal peoples from cultural despoiling by the modern world, argued that globalization was the result of a corporate effort to promote a biological and cultural uniformity, which she termed, borrowing from biology, a "monoculture." These arguments are sufficiently important and widely believed that they are investigated in detail below. For now it suffices to note that the mainstream birthing of the idea of globalization as a force imposed from on high by

powerful multinationals took place at roughly this time. The existing bed-
rock of anti-corporate thought combined with the huge amount of press
attention paid to globalization by this time allowed the ACM to easily
absorb anti-globalization sentiment, and to reinterpret it as corporate bul-
lying.

Elsewhere during the 1990s the anti-corporate interpretation of globalization took flight, as more and more global events began to be seen by the
movement, and sometimes the larger media, through this prism. In 1990,
the McDonald's corporation had served writs of libel on five campaigners
of the London Greenpeace group (a group unaffiliated with the better-
known Greenpeace International) who had for some time been handing
out leaflets making assorted unsavory charges against the firm. Two of
the defendants contested the charges. Their defense campaign—an attack
on McDonald's, fast food and corporate agriculture—proved very popular with the world media, and after the longest trial of any sort in the history of British jurisprudence, a judge partly vindicated the defendants. By
this time the trial, the publicity efforts surrounding it and the finding that
the defendants had proven some of their assertions made the case and its
underlying theme—of Ronald McDonald as the head of a gang of corporate exploiters insistent on squelching free speech and selling poison
worldwide—a cause célèbre. The notion of a large, impersonal corporate
Goliath being slain by ordinary citizens was a key aspect of how the story
was interpreted in the press and in the growing anti-globalization movement.

In 1995 the IFG, which would go on to become a clearinghouse for literature promoting the anti-corporatist view of globalization, held its first
conference at Columbia University. In August, 1999, an unknown farmer
named José Bové led a group of protesters to dismantle a McDonald's
under construction in Millau, France and dump the rubble in front of city
hall. His theme was that the global power of the fast-food chains ultimately destroyed local culinary distinctions and good eating generally.
In 2001, anti-globalization activists organized the first World Social
Forum in Brazil as a counterpart to the better-known World Economic
Forum, the annual conclave in Davos, Switzerland that draws leading
activists, corporate officials, and political figures to discuss global economic and political change.

This period also saw the publication of several acclaimed books which
laid out the basic indictment. While Korten's *When Corporations Rule the
World* does not (particularly in its first edition) devote an inordinate
amount of time to globalization as such (although the World Trade
Organization and other multilateral economic institutions are painted as
corporate playthings), William Greider devoted an entire book to globalization and where it came from, with an extensive emphasis on corporate
intent, in *One World Ready or Not: The Manic Logic of Global Capitalism.* In

2000, Michael Hardt and Antonio Negri could make the contention in their surprise best-seller *Empire* that corporations were a part of an American imperial plan. In their conception transnational corporations did indeed control the global flows of goods and the resources needed to make them, but as subsidiary components in the larger U.S.- (rather than capitalist-) dominated organization of all human society. In 2001, Naomi Klein's *No Logo* assayed the march of Nike, Starbucks, and other multinational brand names across a world largely helpless to resist. By 2003 the affable television personality (and longtime employee of a global corporate media giant) Lou Dobbs could pen *Exporting America: Why Corporate Greed Is Shipping American Jobs Overseas,* whose first sentence is a warning that "[t]he power of big business over our national life has never been greater."[8] An idea's time had come.

That idea, simply stated, is that globalization is merely another manifestation of corporate control, rather than a phenomenon that has been constructed over decades, one buyer and one seller at a time. It is noteworthy that the primary villain in the anti-corporate assessment of globalization is termed the "transnational corporation." In business-school textbooks and ordinary journalistic accounts in the United States, the anodyne term "multinational corporation" is used to describe the businesses that produce in and are owned by residents of multiple countries. It is purely descriptive rather than bearing any moral freight. But the prefix "trans" means "over" or "through," and so a "transnational corporation" is a much darker entity—a corporation capable of running over or through the nation-state, the crime being all the greater if the nation would otherwise implement some Rousseauvian popular will. And so the corporation emerges finally not as a passive receptacle into which the ruling classes pour their efforts, but as the central controlling entity in the global economy, the erector of globalization and its sole beneficiary. In this view it is the function of responsible citizens to take their world back by undoing what the multinationals have done. The indictment has several particulars, but all of them derive from a specific view of why globalization is happening, which is related to the larger anti-corporate view of what corporations are and why they exist.

WHY IS GLOBALIZATION HAPPENING?

There are two dominant theories in popular commentary and in much scholarship about the source of globalization. The anti-corporate view contends that globalization is a creation of corporate will. All of the major trade-opening treaties such as NAFTA and the WTO exist simply because corporations have used their influence over (or purchased outright) nominally democratic governments. Much is made, for example, of the dominant role corporate lobbyists allegedly played in the talks to create both NAFTA and the WTO.[9] Absent these formal legal enabling mechanisms, there would presumably be much less global trade and investment. Nations would be largely self-sufficient and have more diverse economies. What we observe is simply the inevitable result of releasing the lock on the caged corporate tiger. Fairly representative is the following claim by the Canadian journalist Linda McQuaig:

> The growing power of corporations and diminishing power of governments these days is usually attributed to mysterious forces operating out there in the global economy, well beyond our control. Here's another possibility: governments are less powerful than they used to be simply because they keep signing trade deals that reduce their power and enhance the power of corporations. It's likely no more mysterious than that.[10]

But is it in fact more mysterious than that? There is another commonly held view that suggests that globalization is not imposed from the top down but proceeds in an evolutionary way from the bottom up. In this view globalization is primarily a function of fundamental technological changes. Throughout most of human history, the vast majority of humanity lived their entire lives within a distance of just a few miles of where they were born, and their sustenance was almost all locally produced. The reason, according to the evolutionary view, is that transportation costs were too high to make long-distance commerce profitable. There was, to be sure, some trade in the preindustrial and precolonial world— the Silk Road most famously. But most of the basic consumption of life —food, clothing, etc.—was produced within a very small radius of where one was born, lived and died.

The increased dispersion of production across great distances, which accelerated tremendously beginning in about 1870, is a simple response to the fact that transportation costs became a much less important component of total production cost for more and more products. Distance is in some sense a production input like labor or machinery, and the cheaper distance is the more it is employed by producers. The rise of modern shipping, rail networks, and air travel make distance less relevant for production. Even something as mundane as the standard shipping crate, which allows the suddenly eponymous container ship to be loaded mechanically by crane rather than by hand, was an immense contribution to lower transport costs.[11] Perhaps even more important, the declining cost of information has made the purchase of that critical commodity much cheaper. A transatlantic phone call that cost over one hundred dollars in 1940 can now be made for less than one. A laptop computer costs several hundred dollars while a boxy mainframe might well have cost several million in 1960, and the former gives the user information-acquisition capabilities that were unimaginable in the mainframe era to boot. In the evolutionary model globalization is built one transaction at a time, as traders—producers, consumers, and investors—realize that these declining costs provide them with options they didn't have before. Production is globalized, investment is globalized, science and knowledge are globalized, and consumption is globalized simply because people can do all these things when they could not previously.

Which view is more nearly correct? The thought experiment to conduct is to ask what the global dispersion of commerce, information, etc., would look like if it were in fact planned by large corporations. We would presumably expect that these large corporations would benefit from globalization. One way that corporations in the anti-corporate mindset become dominant and benefit at everyone else's expense is through monopoly power. And monopoly profits must be successfully defended against new entrants. A world organized for the benefit of a certain set of corporations must surely seek to keep new entrants from siphoning off profits.

An empirical implication of the corporate-design hypothesis is that the set of existing corporate beneficiaries remains stable. If globalization is engineered by a corporate elite we would expect that those elite would design it so as to preserve and expand their gains. One way to erode those gains is for those firms to face growing competition, especially from other nations. Why would the existing set of corporate recipients of the inordinate wealth transfers described in the anti-corporatist literature—these corporations, remember, are powerful enough to run roughshod over all other social institutions in creating globalization in the first place—stand idly by while other entrants begin to take advantage of the same globalization features? The puzzle deepens if many new entrants are in the very countries whose poverty several years prior was what drew the corporate masters there in the first place. And yet that is exactly what has happened. The 2006 *Forbes* 2000 list of the world's largest companies is, to use a word that ordinarily brings approval nowadays, remarkably diverse. While the U.S. contingent is the largest, at 693 firms (a number gradually shrinking), there are over 300 from countries that either now qualify or twenty years ago would have qualified as still industrializing, including fifty from South Korea, forty-one from Taiwan, thirty-three from India, twenty-eight from China, seventeen from Mexico, and fourteen from Malaysia. The most straightforward interpretation of this spread of the large corporate form is that the efficient body described in Chapter 4 has spread to more and more of the world as more and more of the world has arrived at a position to take advantage of it.

To claim that technology is the primary driving factor is not to ignore the immediate importance of political events. Undoubtedly, the establishment of such institutions as the European Union and world-trade law accelerated globalization. However, governmental decisions do not come out of nowhere. The trauma of the protectionist outburst of the 1930s, when world trade plummeted after the imposition of the Smoot–Hawley tariff in the United States and retaliatory tariffs elsewhere, is really another way of describing the benefits globalization was already bringing at that point in history. The salience of the 1930s experience and the need after 1945 to quickly stitch together a prosperous alliance of Western democracies, including West Germany, in light of the incipient Cold War is testimony to the extent to which contemporary decision-makers *believed* that freer trade promoted prosperity. There is little reason to suppose that the recent expansion of the global free-trade architecture was any different. No one can seriously contend, for example, that the opening of China to the outside world beginning in the late 1970s was corporate driven, even though that decision was one of the most important in the current globalization era. India's reforms and especially its economic opening, more tentative than China's as this is being written but potentially as important, are similarly hard to think of in any terms other than the need to improve the functioning of the Indian economy and hence (substantially) improve the lives of Indians.

Others argue that the opening to market forces and global commerce is due to the triumph of pro-market ideology. But this does not really get us very far. To credit "ideology" begs the question of how the ideology comes to be so widely accepted in the first place. Corporate control—relentless propaganda, lobbying, etc.—is one possible explanation, but the empirical track record of the ideology—in this instance, the link between implementing the ideology of openness to global commerce and rapidly expanding prosperity—is another. There is a compelling reason that openness to globalization, corporate or otherwise, is on the rise—it is indispensable to lifting hundreds of millions of people out of the most desperate poverty, as shown below.

RACE TO THE BOTTOM 1: GLOBALIZATION, ECONOMIC GROWTH AND INCOME INEQUALITY

The ACM makes several criticisms about the effects of globalization, in addition to asserting that corporate muscle brought it about. A key claim is that globalization fattens corporate profits while harming living standards worldwide. The most frequently proffered mechanism is the "race to the bottom." In this view, multinational corporations have been liberated by a series of agreements to free trade and investment flows, particularly since the early 1990s. There are two reasons why this opportunity presents itself. First, the North American Free Trade Agreement, the agreements establishing the WTO and similar sets of internationally negotiated rules sometimes prohibit nations from closing off their economies to penetration by transnationals. Second, governments (presumably at the behest of corporations) can under these agreements challenge regulations enacted in other countries that are not directly based on trade, and the adjudication panels established by these agreements take only trade effects into account. The only question considered, in other words, is whether the trade effects violate international trade rules, rather than whether the restriction is justified for some other reason.

The injustice is exacerbated because other groups, i.e., anti-corporate and other pressure groups, are not given a voice in decision-making. Instead, an unelected body of accountants, lawyers, and economists evaluates only the question of whether national policies violate international trade rules, without considering whether the rules are democratically legitimate to begin with.[12] The resulting ability to import goods without barriers imposed by national governments in their assertion of what the public interest is allows corporations to play one country off against another. If the U.S. government decides to increase worker collective-bargaining protections, American corporations can simply threaten to move their operations to the low-regulation haven of Mexico, secure in the knowledge that international-trade agreements enshrine their ability to export from there to U.S. consumers at will. If Mexico in turn reacts to the environmental damage and poor working conditions that corporations bring by proposing to upgrade its own regulations, corporations simply move again to, say, Vietnam. The regulatory power of the nation-state is eliminated by the ability of corporations to threaten to move. The result is that regulation and wages drift down to the lowest common denominator, with a concomitant collapse in the standard of living and the quality of life worldwide. The only people who benefit are a small circle of corporate shareholders, corporate managers, and corrupt politicians and civil servants in developing countries who are able to extract bribes from these corporations as a condition for allowing them to locate in their countries. Many of the most serious claims of a race to the bottom involve the ability of corporations to promote a globalization that results not just in lower wages but child labor, environmental devastation, and other horrors because of the inability of national governments to protect against these abuses.[13]

The race-to-the-bottom argument is striking in that it claims not only that globalization is zero-sum, but *negative-sum*. Corporate mobility creates immense losses for most citizens of countries rich and poor as wages, working conditions, and the environment collapse. One might suppose that at least this would be offset by lower prices for consumer goods, but the monopoly power of large corporations is said to prevent even this benefit from being passed on. But the virtue of staking out such a dramatic claim—that corporations have built the globalization monster for their benefit at the expense of the rest of us—is that it makes empirical assessment easier. It will be useful to first investigate the overall relation between globalization and global income, and then that between corporations in particular and living standards broadly defined.

The overall research findings on the effects of particular types of economic engagement with the rest of the world—open trade, openness to foreign investment and portfolio capital, migration polices, etc.—are largely positive. But there are exceptions. Eminent economists well within the mainstream of the profession can be found who argue that openness to trade as a promoter of prosperity is exaggerated, and that openness to capital flows is in fact destabilizing and destructive.[14] But there is a striking series of basic indicators, collected in a study by David Dollar and Art Kraay of the World Bank, which strongly suggests that globalization promotes higher standards of living across the board. They divided developing countries into two groups. The first has since 1980 enacted policies that promote growth and foreign investment as well as property rights and corruption control, while the other actually trades significantly less than in the 1970s. Note that because China and India are both in the first group the number of people in it, roughly three billion, is significantly larger than the number in the second group, even though the number of countries in the second group is actually much larger. In fact, one of the criticisms Dollar and Kraay make of much analysis which purports to show that globalization has harmed standards of living is that it compares only country averages, without taking account of the fact that beneficial change in a large country has much bigger effects than negative change in a small one.[15]

The most basic indicator of changing material prosperity is growth in real per capita GDP. The globalizing group in the Dollar/Kraay analysis saw average annual growth in real per capita GDP rise throughout the study period, from 1.4 percent in the 1960s to 2.9 percent in the 1970s to 3.5 percent in the 1980s to 5.0 percent in the 1990s. Note that because of compound interest the latter figure, if sustained, is enough to double the average standard of living in fewer than fifteen years. This is thus potentially a remarkable human achievement. The nonglobalizers, in contrast, saw average annual growth rise from 2.4 percent in the 1960s to 3.3 percent in the 1970s (a period of large increases in commodity prices) before collapsing to 0.8 percent in the 1980s and 1.4 percent in the 1990s. At that latter rate it takes nearly fifty years for the average standard of living to double. So this is already a substantial difference.

Critics of globalization counter that economic growth is not a particularly good measure of the quality of life. The most commonly offered concrete reason (the less concrete ones are explored below) is that growth has been accompanied by increasing inequality. And so it is not hard to find statements such as those linking globalization to "increasing poverty, inequality, and environmental degradation virtually everywhere," or that globalization is the single most powerful reason for rising worldwide income inequality.[16]

But two pieces of evidence suggest that inequality too is declining among globalizers. First, the faster economic growth is, the faster the incomes of the poorest twenty percent of the population grow across a large sample of countries, with the two varying at almost the same rate. Growth, in other words, is good for the poor. Second, overall global inequality has declined since 1975. Using data from numerous sources, Dollar and Kraay note first that inequality increased relentlessly from the beginning of available data in 1820. This is not surprising, as industrialization began in a specific area—Britain—and only gradually spread out across the globe. Industrialization increases inequality at first for the same reason that at the start of a charity walkathon distance inequality increases before eventually decreasing—some walkers are faster than others, but most eventually arrive at the end. In the Dollar/Kraay data inequality ceases to deteriorate roughly between 1970 and 1980 and then begins to improve. Discussing the question in these terms raises the further question of whether equality is a moral goal per se, but even if it is the globalization era is very probably the first in human history with rising average income *and* substantial lessening of inequality.

But the improvement is merely in per capita GDP, and in many outposts of anti-corporate thought this is no improvement at all. A central tenet of much of the movement is that per capita GDP is in fact not only a poor approximation of the quality of life, it is actually a negative correlate. Among the putatively obviously costly consequences of high material standards of living are, according to David Korten, reductions in "the normal human contacts and interactions that used to be a regular part of village and urban life."[17] In developing countries, emphasis on economic growth is asserted to disrupt traditional society and to replace a preindustrial idyll with a sort of soulless rat race that destroys all that is valuable in life.

Is GDP associated with a higher quality of life? There are two approaches that would answer this question. The first is simply to ask people how well off they are, and to test whether being richer is associated with more happiness. Numerous studies matching survey answers on life satisfaction with characteristics of countries or individuals have been conducted. Two noteworthy earlier economic studies failed to show such a link after measuring changes in happiness in particular societies over time during a period of rising incomes, a result which threatened to cut the heart out of elementary microeconomic theory. The economists James Dusenberry and Richard Easterlin separately argued that one's income relative to that of one's peers was the most important determinant of happiness, with Easterlin also finding that reported happiness in the United States did not appear to increase over several largely prosperous decades.[18] However, more recent literature has contradicted this finding. Work by David G. Blanchflower and Andrew J. Oswald finds that in fact greater monetary wealth is strongly although not exclusively associated with more happiness. (Among other effects are unemployment, never marrying, and being divorced.) They confirm one finding of the earlier literature, that the income one earns relative to others is also important, but that the absolute level of income is a substantial contributor to happiness.[19] (Whether the former result is a documentation of envy as an important motivator of emotional well-being or a taste for what the eager redistributionist might refer to as "economic justice" is left for the reader to speculate on.) Additionally, people in wealthier nations tend to be happier than those in poorer ones, although there are diminishing returns to increasing wealth, so that the extra happiness when per capita income increases from $1,000 to $6,000 is significantly greater than when it increases from $30,000 to $35,000. Still, if the issue in question is whether modernization of poor economies—which raises income dramatically in percentage terms—increases self-assessed well-being, the available research very strongly suggests that it does.[20]

But survey results, with all their vagaries, are not necessary to persuade a reasonable reader that income is a strong predictor of satisfaction, at least globally if not necessarily within the narrower range of income distribution in a particular country. An alternative to measuring what people say is measuring what they do. If people migrate, for example, from poor countries to rich ones despite immense differences of language and culture, there is a strong inference that higher income promotes a better quality of life. A casual glance at the newspapers suffices to establish that there is overwhelming migration from poor countries to the wealthiest parts of the world, the United States, Canada, the European Union, and Japan. Even in South America, the relatively prosperous country of Chile draws migrants from the collapsed economies of neighboring countries. Fortunately, economic research largely confirms this obvious intuition, in that migration among countries depends on income differences even after accounting for political oppression, distance, and other factors that might plausibly explain it.[21] Indeed, a benefit of using migration as a proxy for quality of life is that it puts a tacit assumption of anti-growth ideology—that people do not want more material goods if it means sacrificing the things the ACM believes are more important—into sharp relief. As long as one supposes that people are sufficiently capable of being trusted with major choices such as whether to migrate, global migration patterns provide strong evidence that the basic economic insight—more income means more choices, which means, on average, more satisfaction in life—is correct.

If per capita GDP differences are at least a first approximation to differences in the quality of life, particularly in the amounts by which income in the richest countries exceeds that in the poorest, growth is itself a fundamental way to advance the human condition. (Recall the amazing transformation in the quality of life brought about by industrialization in the West described in Chapter 4.) In poor countries growth then becomes a moral imperative. The corporate role in globalization is then important not because globalization is a phenomenon to be feared, but rather to be applauded.

RACE TO THE BOTTOM 2: CORPORATIONS AND GLOBAL LIVING CONDITIONS

To argue that globalization rises up evolutionarily from below is not to argue that corporations have an important role in it, nor that any corporate role that exists is healthy. But there are a number of empirical tendencies with respect to multinational investment flows that indicate that beyond the general benefits to globalization outlined above, inflows of corporate foreign direct investment in particular are a harbinger of liberation rather than an agent of oppression. Several of the most common charges against multinationals by the ACM vanish and indeed are turned upside down upon brief inspection. These tendencies do not involve per capita income, but do involve claims of a race to the bottom.

Multinational Corporations and Wages

Do multinationals cause wages to decline because of race-to-the-bottom pressure? The evidence to the contrary is now broadly accepted in studies of multinationals and wages in the countries in which they invest. Given the quarrelsome nature of economics this is an extraordinary result. Examples of foreign direct investment promoting higher standards of living are legion. Specific studies indicate that multinationals raise wage levels in Thailand, Indonesia, the United Kingdom, Ireland, Africa, and Poland.[22] Most important, comprehensive surveys of this literature indicate that the initial entry of such firms raises wages.[23]

There are two reasons that the literature has discovered. The first is that, even in the most advanced economies, multinationals tend to adopt production methods that rely heavily on resources that add to a worker's productivity—computers, highly automated factory lines, worker training, etc. A worker using state-of-the-art machinery will produce more output than one who must produce without such assistance. Multinationals bring with them investments that increase worker productivity. Many of these investments (e.g., many kinds of worker training) stay with the worker even when she subsequently leaves the multinational to work elsewhere. Second, multinationals often pay higher wages even for equal levels of productivity. Elementary labor economics makes this result almost unavoidable. Multinationals, upon entering a market, enhance the demand for labor and must therefore bring about an increase in wages.

Not only does the presence of large corporations enhance the standard of living as measured by wages and per capita income, it also accelerates the conquest of specific abhorrent features of global poverty. Not only is the race to the bottom argument—that corporate mobility promotes more abuses of labor and the environment—not true, it is actually backwards. Corporate invasions, by promoting more rapid modernization, provide people with an opportunity to buy their way out of constraints that result, in the absence of modern economic growth, in so much of the misery for which corporations are erroneously and even disgracefully blamed.

Child Labor

Consider child labor. Globalization has been said to have promoted a dramatic rise in this phenomenon. Appalling stories of children trapped in debt bondage, forbidden to leave what are in effect slave factories or plantations, are not difficult to find.[24] The standard indictment attributes it to globalization. Of greatest interest here is the claim, as with wages, that corporations constantly chase lower costs by playing one country off against another, with child labor accompanying low wages, the decimation of labor standards and union-busting as the "bottom line of the global economy."[25] UNICEF has also endorsed this view of race to the bottom as one of several causes of an increase in child labor.[26] The most oft-proposed remedy is twofold: sustained public campaigns against the practice generally and particular corporate malefactors in particular, and greater efforts to use laws to combat the practice.

But ultimately prosperity will be a far more effective remedy. Given that parents in India, Pakistan, Haiti, and other places where child labor flourishes must generally be assumed to love their children as much as any campaigner against child labor loves his, the latter must first consider why the former would ever agree to place their children in such circumstances. The answer to that question is strongly suggestive of the best way to combat child labor, and indeed all of the seemingly dark sides of globalization. The answer, surely, is that *the alternatives are worse*. The worse the child's lot seems to the Western observer, the more limited and brutal the parents' alternatives must be. Parents whose children have better opportunities to contribute to their family's collective welfare and to live a dignified, rewarding life will be less likely to place them in the labor market. There are numerous ways to do this—raising the attractiveness of education through lower fees and higher quality, improving the education of women (and indeed men) to improve their labor-market opportunities and thus lessen the need for the child's income, and other steps that strike directly at the point of the parent's child education/child labor decision.

But another broader and perhaps critical factor is to simply make the country richer. Richer parents have more room to avoid painful options. Child labor is something bad that is borne as a cost of something good —more family income. To decrease it requires enabling parents to buy whatever it is they must provide for their families with less sacrifice—in short, to make them wealthier. Child labor was commonplace in the early industrial histories of the United States, the United Kingdom, Japan, and elsewhere before largely vanishing over time.[27] The most important factor in reducing it was not laws but higher standards of living. Laws against child labor are commonplace in developing countries, as is a broad unwillingness by governments where child labor is common to make the sacrifices (and, more to the point, to force parents to make the sacrifices) necessary to make the laws meaningful. And yet child labor persists, primarily in the world's poorest countries. Writing laws is easy; achieving their objectives is harder. As an empirical matter, there is ample reason to believe that the promotion of prosperity is much to be preferred to more lawgiving as a way to combat child labor. Again, the research tells the story. Recent work (which is, owing to the novelty of data on child labor, all the work available) suggests both that economic openness to trade promotes less child labor by raising incomes and that foreign direct investment by multinationals in particular promotes lower levels of child labor.[28] These effects work both directly, because multinational corporations do not wish to engage in such practices, and indirectly because they raise local standards of living.

The Environment

The charge of environmental abuse by corporations falls similarly flat. Again, there is a *prima facie* argument to be made on behalf of globalization in general and corporations in particular promoting lower environmental standards and therefore greater environmental damage. Environmental protection is costly and unlike, say, hiring higher-quality workers (which is also costly), the costs incurred provide no direct benefit to the polluting firm. Firms will avoid those costs to the extent that they can, mindful of the fact that doing so may in turn incur other costs, from consumer pressure, the imposition of more stringent government regulation, etc. At the same time, controlling pollution is also costly, in that production declines, and so the country imposing the regulation sacrifices other things. In developing countries such sacrifices are often no trivial matter. To have more environmental cleanliness may mean to have less food for a population already suffering substantial malnutrition, to have lesser ability to travel (which is not valuable just for its own sake but because it allows people to connect with more extensive trading networks), to have fewer resources available for elementary medical care, and fewer of all sorts of other opportunities whose production and consumption generate environmental damage. There is no obviously right amount of pollution for any country, but whatever the right amount is, it is certainly not zero. Nor are environmental cleanliness and more income likely to trade off at the same rate in the preferences of people who live in rich and poor countries, because the needs of ordinary people in poor countries are more pressing than the needs of those in rich countries.

Particularly in the apocalyptic wing, the ACM sometimes fetishizes a sort of idealized premodern world where, because there are no factories and no motor vehicles, there is also little pollution. A cornerstone of this Edenic world is self-sufficiency. To David Korten, the "healthy society" seeks "local self-reliance while freely sharing information and technology, avoiding both external dependence and local isolation." Even households are to be self-sufficient to the extent possible.[29] Perhaps the oddest concept to emerge from this wing of the movement is that of "food miles," the distance the combined ingredients of a meal travel from where they are produced to the diner's plate. Greater food distance is assumed to intrinsically connote greater environmental damage and poorer quality of life, even if environmental practices and regulations in local communities are inferior to those in distant production locations, especially in developed countries; even if technology and environmental laws make long-distance transport environmentally safe; even if global transport enhances food variety; even if globalization promotes the prosperity that is the best remedy for environmental damage; and despite the absence of concern over "medicine miles," "clothing miles," "housing miles," or other computations for the distance traveled by other equally important products. Sometimes quite elaborate attempts are made to calculate food miles, with greater mileage drawing the proper amount of opprobrium.[30] The argument is frequently made that the global food trade is itself inherently inefficient because distance translates into inefficiency. How could it be efficient to transport food from thousands of miles away instead of from local farmers?

Fundamentally, this is a matter of core belief as much as anything. Either one believes that what is created by the ability to trade and to move products over great distances is worthwhile—i.e., one believes in both the value of economic growth and the theory of comparative advantage—or one does not. When global production is dispersed more of everything, including essentials, is available for more people. And the alternative— insistence on local self-sufficiency—is upon a moment's reflection frightening. Modern medical care, for example, is utterly imaginable without a global economy, which enables the sharing of knowledge both old and new and the transport of products critical to physical well-being. Even medical consulting is increasingly conducted across thousands of miles, using high-speed communications technology.

As for the false equating of distance and inefficiency, since transportation costs have been falling for most goods as a percentage of total production costs for over a century, there is little reason to suppose from a purely economic perspective that there is anything inherently inefficient about sending products over great distances. That such costs are so inconsequential is a key part of the reason why dispersion of food production, for example, is not obviously "inefficient." In various outlets Helena Norberg-Hodge has made much of the fact that Mongolia, a country with a long history of dairy production and a large number of cattle, now gets a good portion of its butter (how much is never made clear) from Germany. To the extent that Germany, a highly productive country, can produce butter at a much lower social cost than Mongolia even after taking account of inconsequential transport costs there is no particular reason why Mongolians should not be consuming butter imported from so far away.[31] (The story is different, of course, if the reason for the low German prices is heavy subsidization of German farmers or dairies, which raises the full social cost of producing the butter even as it makes it rational for European governments to market it in Mongolia at below production cost. But that is a problem of inefficient farm subsidies, not inefficiently dispersed food production.) Indeed Africa, where local food diversity and self-sufficiency are the greatest, is not coincidently the continent where malnutrition is also most severe.

Assuming the proposed alternative of highly self-sufficient localities is rejected on moral grounds (and make no mistake about it, in a world racked with desperate poverty lower production costs are a profoundly moral ground), to what extent do multinationals and global commerce exacerbate the very real problem of pollution? Recognizing that preindustrial societies, while having very limited life possibilities by most philosophically tenable criteria, may be largely pollution free (although they may be much more prone to other sorts of even worse environmental problems),[32] it has to be acknowledged that progress comes at an environmental cost. What is the best way to minimize these costs?

In the early 1990s, the economists Gene Grossman and Alan Krueger published a series of papers showing that both air and water pollution tend to rise in the early stages of industrialization before then declining. The reasoning is not hard to understand. Desperate poverty plus the grafting of modern industry onto a preindustrial society lead to environmental deterioration. Eventually income rises enough that people are willing to forego some economic growth to have cleaner air and water.[33] There are many examples of this landmark moment arriving in the moment of crystallization of public thinking; it typically occurs when some best-selling work or badly damaging environmental incident convinces the public that it is time to adjust this balance. The London fog of 1952, the Japanese Minamata mercury disaster of 1962, and the publication of Rachel Carson's landmark environmental polemic *Silent Spring* are good examples of this phenomenon.[34]

Foreign multinationals also often bring with them state-of-the art technology much less environmentally damaging than the productive capacity it replaces.[35] More recent research, with one conspicuous exception, has shown that if anything the relation between prosperity and environmental quality is even more direct, in that newly industrializing economies such as China appear to be making environmental progress much more quickly than European and North American nations before them.[36] Contrary to casual journalistic accounts of Shanghai's dirty air, the ability to, for example, replace charcoal heating inside homes with less damaging central climate control has helped air quality, made affordable only by the fact that Chinese are richer. To be sure, this must be weighed against the increasing number of factories and cars in Chinese cities, but overwhelmingly, the evidence shows that prosperity promotes environmental quality; there is a reason that the environment is so much better in rich countries than in poor ones. Further, the air quality in the capital cities of the three developing countries with the most foreign direct investment—China, Brazil, and Mexico—was significantly cleaner in the late 1990s than in the mid-1980s, after years of substantial inbound foreign direct investment.[37] And particulate pollution in Chinese cities, while worse than in the West, is actually improving rapidly and already significantly better than in South Korea, Japan, and the United States at similar stages in their development.[38] Again, to fight the ills observed to coincide with a rapidly growing world the most effective remedy is to promote prosperity as rapidly as possible.

Perhaps the most provocative research investigates what in essence is a controlled experiment in regulatory competition. Several papers find that the freedom given U.S. states to set their own environmental standards under Reagan-era rules was followed by *improved* environmental quality and that investment was not driven by lower environmental standards.[39] Even "sustainable development," economic growth that does not deplete natural resources, is positively associated with openness to trade and foreign direct investment.[40] Carbon dioxide emissions in particular may be subject to this "race to the top" effect. This is surprising because, taking at face value the claims about their damage to global climate, most of the effects of these emissions are borne by others in two senses—geographically and across time. Pollution is a problem because people operate in ways that minimize their private costs but pass along some of the social costs to others. The person who warms his car up for five minutes on a cold day is avoiding wear and tear on his engine, but only by poisoning his neighbors' air in addition to his own. If political pressure can approximately reflect the public willingness to trade off environmental purity and growth, as long as the pollution stays within the government's jurisdiction and does much of its damage right now there will be political pressure to lessen it if the material costs are not too high. Rich countries have thus all enacted and, more importantly (because they are rich enough to afford to), enforced rules governing emissions into the air and water that damage human health locally or despoil the view.

But carbon dioxide is less subject to this effect. It operates across space —a car in Nebraska generates emissions that may change the climate on the other side of the world. It also operates across time—most of the worst effects would be felt by future generations. And so there is no reason to be optimistic about the prospect of politics effectively addressing this problem as it does pollution that does its damage here and now. Yet even for carbon dioxide the greater desire for environmental protection as income rises seems to be effective in combating it.[41] And with carbon dioxide, as with the empirically empty term "sustainability" generally, it is a mistake to assume that the answer to such challenges should involve wholesale rolling back of the vast material gains that have, as a side effect, generated these problems. Those who reflect seriously on how to deal with such sustainability issues know that it is very often less damaging to global society to accommodate these changes rather than futilely try to undo them. The great masses of the world's desperately poor will not sign on to any "solution" to climate change or any other sustainability problem that requires them to continue to live in poverty. This is all the more true when such changes can be accommodated relatively cheaply—e.g., through improving flood control or ceding some coastal land—rather than imposing immensely costly restraints on human progress (much of which, in the form of technological progress, will lower these problems in any event).[42] Indeed, in countries as far flung as the United States (which is more forested now than in 1900) and the extremely poor West African state of Niger, the extension of property rights to individual citizens over land rather than assertions of ownership by the state often motivates care of trees and other botanical resources, itself a key to many of the asserted sustainability problems brought about by modernization.[43]

It is finally worth noting that the track record in the last several decades of those who predict that economic growth and technological progress will bring about all manner of disasters has been poor. Examples include the fears about global cooling in the 1970s, genetic engineering, and the famine that overpopulation was once known with certainty to be bringing about. The Chernobyl nuclear accident was predicted to ultimately kill tens of thousands of people, a number that looks ludicrous in hindsight. All of these pessimistic predictions understate the capacity of human ingenuity to solve problems, and overstate the capacity of novel technologies to bring about catastrophe. While theoretically tenable, the environmental race to the bottom falls empirically flat. If anything, globalization and corporations empirically promote faster environmental improvement.

Human Rights

Anti-corporate campaigners also claim that corporations actively seek out repressive regimes so as to avoid public pressure from unions and other interested pressure groups that are stronger in freer societies. Friends of the Earth levels that charge specifically against the anti-corporatist villain *par excellence* Halliburton, and Amnesty International can muster several anecdotes of corporate complicity in abuses in particular countries.[44] The rationale is again plausible but not obvious: a tightly controlled society may indeed be one in which the multinational earns higher profits, but only as long as the dictator's brutal enforcement of the corporation's property rights are not turned against the multinational firm itself, say through seizing the factory and turning it over to the dictator's cronies. An example would be the mining firm whose facilities are protected by the regime's armed forces, the same forces who as needed participate in the suppression of the political and economic rights of the country's citizens. As long as the mines are protected, the corporation is at best indifferent to and at worst outright supportive of the dictator's suppression. An oft-cited case is the Augusto Pinochet regime in Chile, one of whose first steps after seizing power was to restore property-rights clauses that had been unceremoniously stripped from the Chilean constitution by the prior government of Salvador Allende. Post-1979 China too is sometimes said to be a symbiotic relationship between the brutal and corrupt Communist government and the multinationals that operate with a free hand (the need for bribery of government officials aside) because of the social order the dictatorial government creates.

But it is not at all clear that dictatorship is attractive to a multinational, even if the dictator promises to defend the multinational's property. The essence of dictatorship is arbitrariness and unpredictability. The more concentrated political power is, the more rapidly and dramatically government policies may change direction. A corporation that believes it is in the good graces of a dictator today may find that tomorrow's dictator (or even today's dictator if he changes his mind tomorrow) believes differently. All the investments made by foreigners who were confident in the stability of the Fulgencio Batista regime looked foolish once Fidel Castro marched into Havana. Even stable dictatorships can be unreliable, as Western corporations find when their contracts are extralegally voided in China. This is fundamentally a question of how vigorously the multinational's property rights will be enforced, with the multinational preferring that all its contracts be honored, that the law be as predictable as possible, etc. That foreign direct investment is attracted by economic freedom—i.e., stable contract, tort and property law, low taxes, little arbitrary interference with commerce, etc.—is both commonsensical and empirically confirmed.[45] The critical question is whether dictatorships or liberal democracies are most likely to protect those rights for the multinational contemplating where to invest.

And this question can easily be tested. The Heritage Foundation compiles annual ratings of what it calls "economic freedom" around the world. The pressure group Freedom House compiles similar ratings on the degree of political rights and civil liberties. The political-rights rating reflects the extent to which "[t]hose who are elected rule, there are competitive parties or other political groupings, and the opposition plays an important role and has actual power." A further criterion is whether "[m]inority groups have reasonable self-government or can participate in the government through informal consensus." The civil liberties rating measures "freedom of expression, assembly, association, education, and religion...[and] an established and generally equitable system of rule of law."[46] The former rating thus measures the competitiveness of elections and the latter measures the extent to which people are free from personal abuse of government power. All of these ratings are widely used in social-science research. The Heritage economic freedom measure is strongly related to the sum of the two Freedom House measures. Figure 6.1 shows the relation between each quintile of the distribution of economic freedom and the average value of political freedom. The latter clearly rises with the former, and the overall correlation is also strong.[47] Even a casual glance around the globe strongly suggests that those countries that rely the most on markets and property rights to guide resource use also tend to be the most democratic and free. More sophisticated academic research, while limited to date, supports the proposition that dictatorships tend to protect property less than liberal democracies, both in theory and in fact.[48] Economic freedom and political freedom go hand in hand.

It is thus not terribly surprising that empirically the charge that multinationals covet dictatorial regimes is a canard. Directly testing the relation between foreign direct investment and political freedom, two earlier studies have shown that indexes of democracy and the aforementioned Freedom House indicators are positive determinants of foreign direct investment in a country, after standardizing for other relevant considerations.[49] Multinationals, in other words, are now drawn to political freedom, not repelled by it. In no case does research using broad samples indicate that repression draws *more* foreign direct investment. Like the charges of child labor and environmental desecration, claims that corporations through their global activities promote government repression

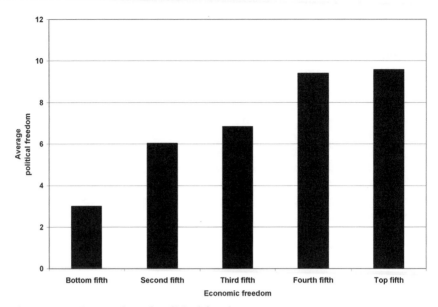

Figure 6.1   Economic and political freedom.

and human-rights abuse do not withstand serious empirical scrutiny. If anything, corporations appear to prefer nations where the rule of law is strong. Government adherence to principles that protect corporate investments also protect human rights broadly defined, regardless of whether corporations explicitly desire it. If corporate investment is desired, human-rights protection in the long run must increase to attract it, other things equal.

THE MONOCULTURE

The final indictment of corporate globalization is its creation of the monoculture. There are two versions of the theory. This section investigates the claim that corporations are eliminating local distinctiveness in diet and instead promoting a global, standard food-production system with harmful ecological consequences. The second, the charge that corporations destroy global cultural diversity, is left to the next chapter. Both monoculture arguments are based on the premise that corporations desire standardization of product lines, because standardization enhances profits. Like anything else, product differentiation pays up to a point—customers prefer more product diversity to less, other things equal—but the profits to differentiation are subject to diminishing returns, and if the costs of differentiation escalate rapidly we might expect the level of differentiation that maximizes profit to be very small. An automobile manufacturer, for example, might choose to manufacture many models on only a few chassis. Manufacturing costs are lowered by maintaining fewer distinct chassis production lines, at the cost of having models sold under different names but which are so similar that they detract from consumer satisfaction.

So too, it is said, with the corporate food culture. Here, the world's food diversity is erased as corporations try to impose a small number of crops grown identically worldwide as humanity's diet, in lieu of much more diverse but less profitable local food webs. For example, corporations benefit when the world eats not just the same industrial-agriculture foods—e.g., bananas, corn, rice—but even a specific variety within those species. Even if a standardized food product is not appropriate to a particular location (say, because the bland bananas perfected on land in the Philippines are not appropriate for Costa Rica), the local ecosystem is bludgeoned into compliance through extensive use of agricultural chemicals. In contrast, in the ideal anti-corporate world people are dependent on local production to satisfy almost all of their food needs. As we have seen, there is said to be almost an intrinsic immorality in importing food over great distances. In the corporate food system native food webs disappear with the introduction of global supermarket chains and transoceanic food shipments, and that is a loss in and of itself. (This intrinsic value of diversity assumes even greater importance in the cultural monoculture argument.)

But most urgently, the lower genetic diversity of the world's food supply makes it more vulnerable to shocks, whether introduced from inside or out. This charge relies on a claim derived from biological theory that more diverse ecosystems are more stable, i.e., less vulnerable to outside disruption, whether from biological invasions or meteorological, geologic, or other environmental changes. Standardization-induced monocropping—raising only one crop on a vast acreage, perhaps even in large plots around the world—raises a nightmare scenario in which an external pest is introduced through the global transport system, and immediately spreads through and devastates, say, the world's corn supply.[50] In locally based food systems both the potential for the pest to migrate and the damage it would do to other genetically distinct varieties of corn in distant places if it did would be substantially lower. But in the global corn monoculture modern transportation networks rapidly spread the infestation all over the world, and the pest is thus uniquely poised to substantially eliminate a crop that much of the world is now unnaturally dependent on.

The borrowing from biology is reasonable up to a point. The belief that ecosystem diversity promotes food-web stability is not universally accepted among biologists. However, a recent survey of the literature in the prestigious science journal *Nature* contends that the evidence on balance favors the hypothesis, although the proposed reasons for the link have changed over time. In particular, it does not appear to be diversity as such that promotes stability, but the presence of critical dampening species (which can presumably be introduced by for-profit entrepreneurs if need be) that serve to deter invaders from crowding out native life. On average more diverse ecosystems are more likely to contain such species, but the relation between diversity and stability is weaker than what is claimed in the anti-corporate literature.[51]

But a weaker argument is still a defensible one, and even if monoculture is not more vulnerable to attack it is still possible that if an attack succeeds the uniformity of a crop worldwide increases the possibility of a global catastrophe. And so it is worth considering the incentives operating on both corporations and other institutions that contribute to the evolution of the global food system. Note first that while a cornerstone of the anti-corporatist worldview is that corporations operate only for profit, and that this profit is what brings about the monoculture in the first place, the notion of how profits are generated is not well thought out. Because corporations are such all-powerful entities, they are believed to maximize profits strictly on the cost side (through the low costs achieved from the monoculture) while *forcing* consumers to buy whatever is produced. But of course profits are revenues less costs, and revenues must be created against the constraints of what consumers are willing to buy. If consumers are nothing more than passive recipients of whatever corporations feed them, than the monoculture danger may follow. But if consumers have any sovereignty at all the food producers will be forced to take account of what they value.

And one source of ultimate value to consumers is biodiversity itself, by the very construction of the argument. The very premise of the monoculture argument is that excessive monoculture, though cheaper, is dangerous. While there is indeed an incentive to drive down costs by standardizing (and even here the argument has limits if standardization is subject to increasing marginal costs), revenues go up by catering to different local conditions. Different varieties of plants are more appropriate for different climates, different surrounding food webs, etc., and indeed this differential fitness is the heart of the monoculture argument. But it thus pays to some extent to maintain genetic diversity within a firm's product line to enable growing in different conditions, especially since storage costs for seed—i.e., genetic—diversity are tiny. In addition, consumers themselves may have a taste for diversity in food consumption, as a brief consultation of the restaurant section of the phone book in any large American city suggests. Genetic diversity pays for a variety of reasons, and providing what pays is what any private firm is about. So the only question is which effect dominates.

Do private firms make any substantial effort to maintain and offer genetic diversity in their seeds because consumers value it (or because it is a form of insurance against ecological surprises), or are their payoffs dominated by the cost benefits of standardization? One study finds a surprising amount of genetic diversity in the product lines of private tea companies, horse breeders, and in particular providers of maize seed. In the latter instance in the entire United States no single variety of maize seed accounts for as much as five percent of U.S. land under maize cultivation, and over 300 varieties are offered.[52] Clearly, on the consumer side, the average American supermarket also has far more food diversity than it did twenty or thirty years ago. Once exotic products such as shiitake mushrooms or prosciutto, previously available only to a fortunate and wealthy few outside their native areas, are now ubiquitous in any decent-sized supermarket in every corner of the United States and, increasingly, the world. Diversity is sufficiently valuable that if anything the pursuit of profit *compels* corporations to enhance it.

Even if the worst predicted outcome occurs, it has a certain 1930s B-movie quality to it, in that the ACM assumes that the consequences are nightmarish (Helena Norberg-Hodge has predicted "starvation on a massive scale")[53] and that passive, static human society is in no position to do anything about it. But of course the world and especially the United States maintain a massive research infrastructure designed in part precisely to combat problems such as these. Numerous universities in agricultural areas of the United States devote sizable resources to agricultural research, and in light of historical experience it seems unusually pessimistic to presume that the sorts of scenarios envisioned by anti-corporate campaigners would simply be allowed to proceed unchecked. The proper question to ask is not just whether there is some scenario so frightening that the global agricultural trade should be largely shut down to avoid the remotest chance that it might happen, but rather what is the best way to accommodate and insure against whatever weaknesses exist in the global food system. To make the worst-case scenario the master of our choices, perhaps forcing a centrally planned remaking of the global food system, is to fall into the trap (common to many pessimistic prognosticators) of ignoring the human capacity for ingenuity in the face of smaller, novel problems that arise in the course of solving bigger, more important ones.

One such gigantic problem is malnutrition, a problem the global food system is increasingly solving. The UN Human Development Report from 2003 notes that between 1990–1992 and 1998–2000 the percentage of the population that is malnourished declined in every region of the developing world save the Arab countries, where Iraq, crippled by war and sanctions, was largely responsible.[54] And local food diversity/independence is a sign of weakness, not strength; sub-Saharan Africa has both the most localized, diverse food systems and the greatest prevalence of malnutrition. The quiet miracle of the progress against the age-old scourge of hunger is a continuation of steady progress made for decades. The corporate food system, in conjunction with the scientific break-throughs on which it relies, makes it possible to imagine a world in the near future where, thanks to technological progress and especially global integration and expanding global division of labor, most humans are for the first time in the history of their societies not at nature's whim with respect to meeting basic food needs. Measured against this, even the worst plausible consequences of the global food system are minuscule, eminently manageable problems. In fact, there is ample reason to suppose that it is the barriers to *more* global food trade, in the form of rich-world farm subsidies and agricultural protectionism, that are extremely damaging to efforts to combat severe poverty in the developing world.[55]

HOW DO PEOPLE LIVING IN A GLOBALIZED WORLD SEE IT?

Ultimately the anti-globalization movement is a small minority world-wide, albeit a loud and (because of its overrepresentation in the opinion-manufacturing industry) influential one. If one wishes to evaluate globalization, one might actually ask people affected by it what they think of it. In 2003 the Pew Center for the People and the Press released a study as part of their ongoing Global Attitudes project that investigated the attitudes of people in forty-four countries toward, among many other things, globalization.[56] The answers by country to several questions are shown in Table 6.2. In the first three columns the public support for "trade and business ties" with (Col. 1) and "different products" (Col. 2) from other countries is overwhelming in almost every case. The third column asks respondents for assessment of "the world becoming more connected through greater economic trade and faster communication," which is a rough measure for views of globalization overall. Here too public approval is astonishingly high by the standards of most opinion polling. Even in Western Europe and the belt of Muslim countries stretching from North Africa to Pakistan, areas often felt to be under siege by globalization's pressures, support for greater integration is remarkable.

An interesting contrast can be made with the responses in Columns 3 and 4, with the latter asking for an assessment of "globalization" by name as opposed to the idea of greater interconnectedness, which is itself the essence of globalization. On the former question support is still quite high (with the exceptions of Jordan, with great opposition, and Argentina, coming out of a major financial crisis in 2001–2002, with a bare majority of those with an opinion finding that its effects are bad), but in most cases less than support for interconnectedness. This suggests that globalization opponents have had some disturbing success in stigmatizing the term

Table 6.2 Attitudes toward a globalizing world (percent saying "some-what" or "mostly favorable"/"somewhat" or "mostly unfavorable").

Commercial Ties	Different Products	Overall	Connectedness	"Globalization"
N. America				
United States	78/18	81/16	88/9	62/23
Canada	86/12	93/6	92/7	69/23
Latin America				
Argentina	50/31	55/38	75/15	35/39
Bolivia	77/19	54/44	79/16	49/31
Brazil	73/18	73/23	79/12	45/18
Guatemala	73/14	90/9	89/8	52/20
Honduras	93/6	95/4	92/4	65/13
Mexico	79/13	76/17	85/7	45/18
Peru	83/13	68/26	88/5	52/20
Venezuela	86/12	92/7	92/6	77/17
W. Europe				
United Kingdom	87/9	94/5	92/6	68/21
France	88/11	91/9	94/5	60/36
Germany	91/8	86/13	82/7	51/30
Italy	79/13	78/19	85/9	67/26
E. Europe				
Bulgaria	89/6	81/14	79/6	33/14
Czech Republic	84/14	88/11	96/3	69/26
Poland	78/15	70/26	79/10	38/30
Russia	88/7	77/19	89/3	31/14
Slovak Republic	86/12	65/34	94/5	65/29
Ukraine	93/6	57/43	87/10	43/22
Africa				
Angola	89/6	71/26	83/12	61/18
Ghana	88/5	92/6	80/2	73/5
Cote D'Ivoire	96/4	93/7	96/4	75/11
Kenya	90/5	83/15	94/4	82/7
Mali	95/3	84/15	88/7	42/11
Nigeria	95/3	94/9	94/3	90/5
Senegal	98/1	81/19	96/4	69/17
South Africa	88/9	83/13	86/9	70/9
Tanzania	92/7	88/7	44/6	47/7
Uganda	95/4	84/5	94/4	73/12
Asia				
Bangladesh	84/9	73/25	83/4	63/8
China	90/3	89/7	90/2	76/5
India	69/7	77/14	79/7	45/6
Indonesia	87/10	88/10	90/8	79/13
Japan	72/22	83/14	91/5	53/5

Table 6.2   Attitudes toward a globalizing world (percent saying "somewhat" or "mostly favorable"/"somewhat" or "mostly unfavorable"). *(continued)*

Commercial Ties	Different Products	Overall	Connectedness	"Globalization"
Philippines	83/13	74/21	84/10	63/17
South Korea	90/7	69/30	92/6	84/12
Vietnam	98/1	94/4	97/0	79/2
Muslim Belt				
Egypt	67/15	60/31	66/17	37/21
Jordan	52/48	60/40	57/42	27/64
Lebanon	83/14	82/18	83/14	44/29
Pakistan	78/2	57/22	62/6	33/9
Turkey	82/12	84/11	80/11	45/23
Uzbekistan	97/3	68/31	93/3	25/4

Source: Pew Research Center for People and the Press, Views of a Changing World, How Global Publics View: War in Iraq, Democracy, Islam and Governance, Globalization.

itself. As for overall views of the phenomenon, the Pew Center itself notes the distinction when it contrasts the disquiet about globalization among policy makers and intellectuals with favorable attitudes of the "global public." The Pew Center's own summary of global opinion is that, opinion-makers apart, "[t]o varying degrees, people almost everywhere like globalization."[57]

Table 6.3 contains assessments of both foreign multinational corporations and the anti-globalization movement. In all but two of the countries (again Argentina and Jordan) more people have a favorable than unfavorable opinion of corporations, and often by overwhelming margins. In twenty-five of forty-three countries (the question was not allowed in China), more people have unfavorable than favorable opinions of anti-globalization protesters. To be fair, the number of people with no opinion is often higher in the latter case. But the ratio of favorable to unfavorable views is higher for corporations than for anti-globalization protesters in every country of the forty-three with responses to both questions except Argentina, Bulgaria, and Turkey. This suggests that there is something seriously deficient with the narrative of multinationals foisting an undesired globalization on a global population that doesn't want it. Perhaps the best hint of a better mental model emerges in the finding that while the global public overall is enthusiastic about globalization and the participation of multinational corporations in their economy, it is people in the most misery-laden areas of the world who appreciate it the most. Comparing the ratio of supporters to opponents of multinationals it is those in Latin America, Asia, and especially Africa who are the most

Table 6.3   Attitudes toward corporations and anti-globalization activists (percent saying "somewhat" or "mostly favorable"/"somewhat" or "mostly unfavorable").

	Large foreign cos.	Anti-globalization protesters
N. America		
United States	50/39	30/49
Canada	39/38	39/50
Latin America		
Argentina	25/60	24/31
Bolivia	61/30	47/32
Brazil	63/26	31/39
Guatemala	68/23	44/38
Honduras	67/20	46/17
Mexico	64/26	37/28
Peru	57/30	28/20
Venezuela	75/22	34/42
W. Europe		
United Kingdom	61/34	49/43
France	5045	44/55
Italy	51/39	27/54
Germany	57/39	34/55
E. Europe		
Bulgaria	55/21	66/15
Czech Republic	60/33	18/72
Poland	44/42	21/34
Russia	42/35	9/24
Slovak Republic	71/25	32/58
Ukraine	55/33	20/23
Africa		
Angola	69/18	27/32
Ghana	85/8	36/18
Cote D'Ivoire	85/14	43/36
Kenya	78/18	21/45
Mali	65/8	20/16
Nigeria	75/21	28/42
Senegal	83/11	22/52
S. Africa	78/16	44/32
Tanzania	53/21	20/17
Uganda	83/8	22/37
Asia		
Bangladesh	48/22	22/21
China	76/9	N/A
India	46/25	24/19
Indonesia	71/23	20/31
Japan	63/26	17/27

Table 6.3   **Attitudes toward corporations and anti-globalization activists (percent saying "somewhat" or "mostly favorable"/"somewhat" or "mostly unfavorable").** *(continued)*

	Large foreign cos.	Anti-globalization protesters
Philippines	74/23	54/32
S. Korea	66/34	21/19
Vietnam	93/3	23/34
Muslim World[1]		
Jordan	42/56	23/57
Lebanon	57/45	24/40
Pakistan	29/18	9/12
Turkey	41/40	29/27
Uzbekistan	76/8	5/19

[1]Surveys for Egypt not available in this sample.
Source: Same as Table 6.2.

enthusiastic. (There is no obvious pattern in geographic variation in sentiment about anti-globalization protesters.) For such populations, globalization is the compelling opportunity they have ever had.

The problem of how best to coordinate the conflicting desires of over six billion people is a phenomenally complex one. The increasing commercial connectedness of the world's people has not occurred because of the decisions of a handful of corporate barons and their government handmaidens. Globalization is the evolutionary response, one person at a time, to technological advances that make distance less relevant, as well as to the declining appeal of government attempts to plan particular economic outcomes. It is humanity's decentralized solution to this very difficult problem, and corporations are a key part of the underlying phenomenon, but not the phenomenon itself.

Instead, it is perhaps better to think of globalization as liberation. Life in much of the developing world is characterized by poverty utterly unfamiliar to most in the West, including, one supposes, to many members of the anti-globalization movement. It is also all too frequently marred by varying degrees of corrupt and brutal governance. People embrace globalization because it is the path to something better than what they have always known. Corporations, while not synonymous with globalization itself, are one of its primary transmission channels. They are the standard-bearers of the transparency, competition, and creativity that openness to new ways of seeing the world brings. It is helpful to those accustomed to hearing talk of corporations and globalization framed around the objectively meaningless term "sweatshop," discussion of races to the bottom and corporate abuses to take precise account of the astonishing transformations that globalization has already brought to hundreds of millions of people. Consider what workers at Nike's factories in Vietnam have told the Swedish writer Johan Norberg:

Today Nike has almost four times more workers in Vietnam than in the United States. I travelled to Ho Chi Minh to examine the effects of multinational corporations on poor countries. Nike being the most notorious multinational villain, and Vietnam being a dictatorship with a documented lack of free speech, the operation is supposed to be a classic of conscience-free capitalist oppression.

In truth the work does look tough, and the conditions grim, if we compare Vietnamese factories with what we have back home. But that's not the comparison these workers make. They compare the work at Nike with the way they lived before, or the way their parents or neighbours still work. And the facts are revealing. The average pay at a Nike factory close to Ho Chi Minh is $54 a month, almost three times the minimum wage for a state-owned enterprise.

Ten years ago, when Nike was established in Vietnam, the workers had to walk to the factories, often for many miles. After three years on Nike wages, they could afford bicycles. Another three years later, they could afford scooters, so they all take the scooters to work (and if you go there, beware; they haven't really decided on which side of the road to drive). Today, the first workers can afford to buy a car.

But when I talk to a young Vietnamese woman, Tsi-Chi, at the factory, it is not the wages she is most happy about. Sure, she makes five times more than she did, she earns more than her husband, and she can now afford to build an extension to her house. But the most important thing, she says, is that she doesn't have to work outdoors on a farm any more. For me, a Swede with only three months of summer, this sounds bizarre. Surely working conditions under the blue sky must be superior to those in a sweatshop? But then I am naively Eurocentric. Farming means 10 to 14 hours a day in the burning sun or the intensive rain, in rice fields with water up to your ankles and insects in your face. Even a Swede would prefer working nine to five in a clean, air-conditioned factory.

Furthermore, the Nike job comes with a regular wage, with free or subsidised meals, free medical services and training and education. The most persistent demand Nike hears from the workers is for an expansion of the factories so that their relatives can be offered a job as well.[58]

Vietnam, remember, is still in the early stages of "corporate globalization." It is roughly where South Korea or Taiwan was thirty-five years ago. Ultimately, globalization is emancipation—from limited choices, from arbitrary, cruel rule, from the inability to pursue one's own dreams because of obstacles generated by others. History will mark the current globalization era as the one in which the prosperity, freedom, and opportunity that Westerners (particularly anti-globalization activists, who are far more common in the West than in the Rest) have long taken for granted began to take flight worldwide. We are not there yet by a long shot, but globalization and the corporations that power it give us a map to getting there.

Chapter 7

Corporate Culture

American society is disproportionately shaped by the outlooks, interest, and aims of the business community—especially that of big business. The sheer power of corporate capital is extraordinary. This power makes it difficult even to imagine what a free and democratic society would look like.[1]

What is the effect of large corporations on the broader human culture? One of the most striking claims of the ACM is that they use their economic power to shape the public culture and conversation in the directions they prefer. Two specific charges—that these firms produce mass culture at the expense of far more interesting and profound culture that does not appeal to leaden mass-market tastes and that the "corporate media" stifle dialogue about unconventional political views more generally and about anti-corporate arguments in particular—loom large in anti-corporate hostility. These subsets of the "social power" argument offered in Chapter 5 are not economically implausible, as we will shortly see. But they are false.

The term "culture" is extraordinarily elastic, and I will investigate several indictments of the alleged corporate culture. I will use the term "cultural products" to refer to books, movies, music, and other forms of human expression. The economics of these products are often similar to the economics of ideas, especially political ones, and the anti-corporate hypotheses about these markets are very similar. And for both products, it will also be helpful to distinguish between static culture on the one hand and dynamic culture on the other. In economic language, a static model tries to explain the state of affairs at a moment in time—e.g., why a country has a particular pattern of imports and exports right now. A dynamic model explains changes and patterns over time—why a country's exports might change as it industrializes. Neither type of model is right nor wrong; each one can be appropriate, depending on the question that is asked. While most of those making the argument do not know it, the framework generally employed when alleging corporate cultural domination is a static model; its ignorance of dynamic culture will be one of its main weaknesses. When discussing dynamic culture, it will be worth distinguishing between cultural products as defined above and what I will call "cultural institutions"—different habits of thought, behavioral choices, and views about the world associated with particular cultures.

CULTURAL PRODUCTS

Static Culture

The movie business had been largely dominated by the major studios in Hollywood; TV, like radio before it, by the triune axis of the networks headquartered in New York; magazines, primarily by Henry Luce (with many independent others on the scene); and music, from the 1960s, mostly by the major record labels. Now all those separate fields are one, the whole terrain divided up among the giants—which, in league with Barnes & Noble, Borders and the big distributors, also control the book business. (Even with its leading houses, book publishing was once a cottage industry at both the editorial and retail levels.) For all the democratic promise of the Internet, moreover, much of cyberspace has now been occupied, its erstwhile wildernesses swiftly paved and lighted over by the same colossi.[2]

Simply stated, the ACM's indictment of corporate culture is that large multimedia corporations are because of their size able to obtain control over the primary producers of all forms of and hence to shape and limit the spectrum of ideas and cultural products. Often this is done when single multimedia corporations dominate many output platforms. For example, Disney makes movies; it also owns several television outlets (the Disney Channel, ABC, and ESPN), subsidiaries to produce and distribute content (e.g., Miramax pictures), and even a news outlet (ABC News). So too with the other giant media corporations—Time/Warner, Rupert Murdoch's The News Corporation, etc. Such power allows these firms to dominate cultural content, because no other producers are capable of achieving enough size to compete with their offerings. This dominance has been entrenched in the last quarter century by a series of mergers of previously distinct media companies across platforms (television, films, publishing) and across functions (creation of cultural products versus their distribution). The emergence of the Internet as a vehicle for cultural products has only furthered this phenomenon, as these same media giants also gobble up the access portals. They control culture by their market dominance and produce work designed to appeal to mass tastes. The result of all this consolidation is that these firms strangle cultural variety, as the cultural theorist Douglas Kellner makes clear:

> Since the forms of media culture are structured by well-defined rules and conventions, the study of the production of culture can help elucidate the codes actually in play and thus illuminate what sorts of texts are produced. Because of the demands of the format of radio or music television, for instance, most popular songs are three to four minutes, fitting into the format of the distribution system. Because of its control by giant corporations oriented primarily toward profit, film production in the U.S. is dominated by specific genres and since the 1970s by the search for blockbuster hits, thus leading to proliferation of the most popular sorts of comedies, action/adventure films, fantasies, and seemingly never ending sequels and cycles of the most popular films. This economic factor explains why Hollywood film is dominated by major genres and subgenres, explains sequelmania in the film industry, crossovers of popular films into television series, and a certain homogeneity in products constituted within systems of production with rigid generic codes, formulaic conventions, and well-defined ideological boundaries.[3]

And the cultural-domination argument asserts not just that the corporate culture is all the same, but that it is bad—ever more uniform, lowbrow, and drearily middle-of-the-road. From *I Love Lucy* to Stephen King to *Survivor*, it is one mindless mass-market opiate after another. This is not simply a criticism by the anti-corporate left; no less a traditionalist American conservative luminary than Russell Kirk, in the course of a speech lamenting neoconservatives, decried their beliefs that capitalism would promote "a world of uniformity and dull standardization, Americanized, industrialized, democratized, logicalized, boring."[4] That globalization promotes the extermination of local cultures through the aggressive offering of lowbrow Western culture is perhaps its most disturbing aspect. Why does a young woman in Cairo or the Bolivian countryside cling to her ancient culture when the temptation-laden culture of the West is hanging on the tree, ready to be picked?

And this uninspiring pap is sinister beyond its mere mediocrity, because its goal in some tellings is actually to bolster cultural domination by propagandizing for a consumption-oriented life and by serving as a distraction from more important social and political concerns.[5] Everyone who watches *American Idol* is encouraged to dream of being a star and is kept from paying attention to the corporate colonization of the society around him. Control production and distribution, and you control the culture. Control the culture, and you control the society. This argument reaches its zenith in passages such as the one below by Thomas Frank, who is more famous for his argument (in his best-selling book *What's the Matter with Kansas*)[6] that the right wing in the United States has craftily deceived working-class Americans, particularly rural ones, into abandoning their economic interests to vote for politicians who promise to address social issues (abortion, gay marriage, etc.) but never deliver on those promises. Frank has elsewhere argued that the entertainment we consume has been manufactured of, by, and for large corporations as part of a larger project to control the way we live:

> The wiring of every individual into the warm embrace of the multinational entertainment oligopoly is a conquest of a different sort, the crowning triumph of the marketplace over humanity's unruly consciousness...Denunciation is becoming impossible. We will be able to achieve no distance from business culture since we no longer have a life, a history, a consciousness apart from it. It is putting itself beyond our power of imagining because it has become our imagination, it has become our power to envision, and describe, and theorize, and resist.[7]

This argument of manufactured mainstream culture as the key to the kingdom of total corporate social control is hardly new. It was a hallmark of the so-called Frankfurt school of cultural criticism in the first half of the twentieth century and refined by such influential intellectuals as the Italian socialist Antonio Gramsci. In this line of thinking, corporations promoted bourgeois attitudes through the popular culture not just for profits per se but to perpetuate a system that would otherwise, for the standard Marxist reasons, eventually collapse. (Gramsci's belief that the left should try to exert its influence through such fortresses of high culture as the universities to counter the corporate influence allegedly so dominant elsewhere is popular even today.) This notion of workers mesmerized by empty material plenty into overlooking their own best interests is clearly present even now in writing such as Frank's. Note again the bias against individual self-determination: the only possible reason that the masses cannot see what is good for them, as the anti-corporate campaigners can, is that they have been first seduced and then sedated by corporate-manufactured distractions.

That the largest corporations would tend to produce culture and advocate political ideas within a narrow spectrum is very possible economically. (Whether the mass-market culture produced is insipid or not is an aesthetic question, not an empirical one.) We can think of the popularity of cultural products—songs, books, etc.—and the political appeal of ideas as being distributed, like so many phenomena in both human society and the natural world, according to a bell curve. The height of the curve represents the popularity of a particular cultural product—a particular book or type of book, CD or genre of music, etc. Even within genres, it is possible to think about a bell curve of tastes. In classical music, many people will purchase recordings of the music of Beethoven and Mozart, while the work of other composers, especially innovative or newer ones, may be relegated to the tails of the distribution.

If there is only one producer of a particular cultural product, and every cultural product costs the same to produce, then that producer should obviously shoot first for the middle portion of the distribution. Products pitched to the middle can sell many copies, products pitched to tastes at one tail or the other will sell few. It is more profitable to promote a book likely to sell one million copies than one with likely sales of only a few hundred. The more cultural goods the producer can afford to offer, the more its production will shift out in each direction from the center, but in no sense is there any gain to producing the idiosyncratic, the radical, the groundbreaking. And dominating the middle of the distribution may give this company market power. A giant like Disney will make so much money catering to the mainstream that it may be in a position to destroy any firm that would try to make money servicing the tails of the distribution by creating television shows that few people watch or producing ideas that, without strong effort by the distributor of the idea, few people will be inclined to listen to. Disney can afford to tie up the cultural producers who make the most popular output, offer more favorable deals to merchants to carry their products instead of those from smaller producers, etc. In this kind of world, we have only a handful of very large companies catering only to the most mainstream tastes. Those tastes farther out from the center of the curve go unserviced.

But it is not obvious that that is the kind of world we live in. Like any producer, our hypothetical Big Media, Inc. firm is at least theoretically subject to competition. Competition need not come from existing firms, but from new entrants as well. And there is substantial reason to think that entry costs in the market for culture and ideas have in fact fallen considerably in recent decades. It is true that the establishment of big cultural conglomerates and television and radio networks has taken decades, and it is probably not reasonable that an ambitious entrepreneur could wake up tomorrow and, in the manner of a romantic high-tech entrepreneur, overthrow the existing media order with an idea he dreamed up in his garage. But it is in no way necessary to duplicate the full spectrum of products that a major media company offers to provide effective competition for it. In the end, one need not be a giant like a Disney to take customers from Disney. It is the breadth of cultural products offered by all firms, not the size of any particular firm, that is the proper measure of how vibrant the culture and politics are.

In his recent book, *The Long Tail: Why the Future of Business Is Selling Less to More,* Chris Anderson, the editor-in-chief of *Wired* magazine, describes how the Internet is revolutionizing the economics of cultural products. [8] For much of the twentieth century such products were relatively expensive to manufacture. They required extensive investments in physical retail stores and networks to produce and ship products which had to move quickly off the shelves or otherwise waste valuable shelf space. This meant that unless the market was big enough, a cultural product was often not profitable. Indeed, part of the reason a handful of stars in entertainment have historically made so much money is that they are the ones with the mass cultural appeal that will move product. Their salaries are thus bid up to incredible heights, even as Los Angeles is full of dreamers seeking these incredible payoffs who never get any closer to a big music or movie contract than the Hollywood restaurant at which they wait tables. Anderson refers to this as the economics of hits, and it has almost completely characterized cultural-product distribution for the past several decades. A creator who wished to write a book or record an album that would only sell a few hundred copies either had to be one of the few accepted by a relatively small number of nonprofit outlets (e.g., university presses in the case of books) or use a very local distribution network such as a record label or press that specialized in works about and from a particular area.

But the digitization of society has meant the digitization of culture too. The book industry is no longer synonymous with bookstores ordering huge numbers of copies of books and sending many of them back, or Hollywood studios gambling on a limited number of movies released on a huge number of screens. Instead, cultural works can be created and stored on computers and reproduced as needed and may be distributed without even relying on traditional bookstores or movie screens. Internet-only movies and the essentially infinite catalog of Amazon.com mean that it is possible for individual companies and therefore the cultural industry as a whole to move farther and farther down the bell curve in both directions, thus vastly *increasing* the diversity of cultural products. Producers can offer a wide range of products, even when almost all of these products sell very few copies, because there are essentially no storage costs for a digital work and the cost of producing copies on demand is also small. This effect is accentuated because digitization makes it easier for consumers to search for particular titles and to learn about new ones they are likely to find appealing via Web software that matches consumers to works they are likely to value based on their past behavior, to the greater ease of discovering people online who share similar interests, and through something as mundane as being able to search for a work when in possession only of its approximate title on Amazon.com or iTunes.

In fact, one of the signature features of the Internet in economic terms is its ability to lower search costs—the ability to find information on alternatives. The very idea of search costs dates to an older, brick-and-mortar era. It was the economist George Stigler who first realized that lower prices or a higher starting salary do not help if the consumer or job-seeker is ignorant about them. The consumer therefore has to solve the problem of how much searching to engage in. The more he searches, the more likely he is to find a better deal, but the more he must spend on searching. The partial replacement of paper catalogs and browsing through physical stocks of books and music with search engines and online music sharing and such networking sites as myspace.com (which make it possible for cultural producers to distribute their wares much more widely than if they have to be discovered by a publishing or music company)[9] has dramatically lowered search costs. This cannot help but increase the leverage of consumers, including consumers of culture and ideas—freeing them from the tyranny of the hit-machine model of cultural production. Adjusted for inflation,*Gone with the Wind*, a movie almost seventy years old, is still the most popular movie of all time, and (as Anderson notes) Michael Jackson's*Thriller*, released in 1983, is still the best-selling album. We will never see the likes of this again; it will more and more be a world of more culture for more people in smaller doses in smaller production runs (even books or song copies "produced" from the digital inventory one at a time as ordered).

Collectively, the items that sell relatively little each add up to a huge amount of total revenue; according to one estimate, while the average Barnes & Noble carries 130,000 titles, over half of the books sold at Amazon come from titles below the 130,000 best-selling. [10] By any reasonable definition of diversity—one involving the number of people who can access a cultural product farther away from the center of the bell curve—lower production and search costs must produce more of it. Critics of the influence of giant media corporations over the popular culture see the tree of John Grisham bestsellers and endless Hollywood sequels directly in front of them, even as they miss the forest of vibrant cultural diversity around them. It is quite possibly true that a giant media producer—a large corporation that produces and distributes cultural works—must shoot for the center of the public distribution of tastes; it is not true that such producers dominate the production of all culture.

Indeed, what is most striking about the current cultural era is that the new technology of culture has undone the previous decades of media consolidation driven by the needs of the older technology. Whereas the old economic imperatives may have motivated consolidation both vertically (the same corporation buying television networks and television production operations) and horizontally (one media conglomerate buying another), we are now seeing a re-fragmentation of culture. It once fell to a traditional music firm housed in a place like the Capitol Records tower to find and sign talent and distribute its work. Now music is often either self-produced or produced in conjunction with the very small music labels that used to have such difficulty distributing their product globally, and their work in turn is scooped up by "music aggregators," who make it available to various firms that then sell it to consumers via online subscription services. The new developments give music seekers access to more variety than any independent disk jockey, once the hero of independent-minded music fans but long since purged by the index card-sized playlists of "corporate radio," could ever have dreamed of.

That "corporate" FM radio may have an ever-more mind-numbingly dull playlist, even if true, is not the issue. The overall availability of musical diversity, and the diminishing importance of such radio as a musical source, is. The traditional media operating by their traditional systems are longer where the cultural action is; it is instead in the far more variegated system of linking those who make music to those who want to listen to it. The number of movie tickets sold is declining; so are terrestrial radio audiences, audiences for broadcast television, the number of CDs sold by members of the Recording Industry Association of America, and the market share of a host of other organizations increasingly referred to scornfully as the "legacy media." But this is emphatically not to say that the consumption of culture itself is declining. People are not listening to music less, watching video less, or reading fewer books. They are simply accessing greater variety through new channels.

This development is the modern corporate world in a nutshell. Driven by ambition, protected by limited liability, and enabled by personhood and the power to issue shares, risk-takers create ventures that enable a whole new approach to culture. And this is simply the acceleration of a process that is as old as culture itself. Once upon a time, culture was a strictly local activity. If you had access to any of humanity's artistic achievements, it was locally created and witnessed in person—via a traveling musician or a church choir, for example. The advent of mass-entertainment technology—radio, television, motion pictures, recorded music—gave us the culture of the mass audience, threatening local variety. But the newest technology keeps to some extent the mass-market hit (although hits will never be what they used to be in terms of audience size or as a common cultural reference), while opening the door to a far broader world, where we have access to types of culture that were once vital to those few who could access it but unknown to most of the world. In culture, as in medicine, food, shelter, and the other most vital aspects of human society, the corporate world and the innovation it fosters have enabled a much broader array of human possibilities.

Static Politics

Although Anderson does not explore it, there is no reason the long-tail effect should not also apply to political and social arguments—turning ideas into ones and zeros should allow people to be exposed to more ideas than ever. When there are few producers of political information and ideas (a handful of newspapers, nightly news on the networks, etc.), then political "hits"—the ideas in the center of the distribution of American political opinion—will dominate the political conversation. If you want an unconventional idea, you have to aggressively go out and look for it. Unusual ideas currently held by relatively few Americans but which they would be willing to consider if exposed to—stories that explicitly or implicitly advocate such end-of-the-tail ideas as banning gun ownership outright, adoption of a Canadian-style health-care system, complete American foreign-policy isolationism—will be unlikely to get much of a hearing in a media geared toward the middle.

Thus, the ACM has contempt for the media sources that in its judgment promote exclusively corporate interests, but which many Americans actually see as *excessively* hostile to commerce—The New York Times, CNN (where the commentator Lou Dobbs makes a handsome living harshly criticizing American corporations for their inadequate sense of citizenship), and so on. The scornful term of art for the dominant overlords of the opinions to which most Americans, and increasingly people around the world, are exposed is the "corporate media." (This term is used even though the BBC, ultimately an arm of the British government no matter what its disclaimers say, is probably the single most important news source in the world.) Because of their need to cultivate and preserve a bland bourgeois stability, and because they are themselves large corporations dependent on the current corporate system to pay the bills, these media firms systematically exclude anti-corporate thinking. Or so it is said.

Ben Bagdikian is a former reporter, newspaper ombudsman, and dean of the Graduate School of Journalism at the University of California. In the 2004 edition of his book *The New Media Monopoly*, he documented that five corporations control approximately ninety percent of America's mass media, which he defines as newspapers, magazines, TV and radio stations, books, records, movies, videos, wire services, and photo agencies. The book begins by ominously announcing that "Clear Channel is the largest radio chain in the United States."[11] Bagdikian proceeds to lay out an accusation that these gigantic corporations, through their control of these opinion outlets, do not simply reflect a narrow spectrum of opinion by selling to the middle of the distribution but actually manufacture the opinions that, through their aggressive efforts, dominate the market. Indeed, the conservative revolution in the United States dating at least to the first half of the Reagan administration is said to be largely a result of this aggressive manufacture. To its enthusiasts, the book is all the more compelling because in its first version in 1984, it took approximately fifty corporations to achieve the same market share of mass media. Accepting these newer calculations as true (which is highly questionable)[12] and that media conglomerates create opinion rather than provide it as demanded, media consolidation may be inevitable absent government restraint of it but is especially insidious because of its toxic effects on democracy—its exclusion from the political conversation of ideas that threaten corporate interests. The censoring of alternative points of view by the corporate media and their replacements with pro-corporate views make for voter alienation, cynicism, and unaccountable government.

But the key question is again not the market share of particular corporations in markets for traditional media. What matters in a free society is the cost of making an opinion available and the cost to others of accessing it. If a few corporations dominate broadcast television, but the number of broadcast television viewers is declining rapidly, that lack of competition in the market for TV-generated opinions is hardly a compelling problem even if large corporations are trying to manufacture them rather than passively giving customers what they want or trying to be objective. (Even that dominance is questionable. As I write this major newspapers are wrestling with long-term circulation declines, and mighty Clear Channel is in serious financial difficulty.) But the same forces that are unleashing artistic creativity will do the same for political ideas.

Perhaps nothing illustrates this better than the fate of the notion of "corporate power" itself. The anti-corporate movement, particularly in its more recent apocalyptic version, is the very example of an idea that began by lobbing rocks from the outside at the citadel of mainstream opinion before storming into that citadel to become more and more a mainstream idea. As we saw in Chapter 3, the ACM percolated among the New Left after Port Huron. It was able to obtain some modest victories at the height of the penetration of New Left ideas into American politics in the late 1960s and early 1970s (e.g., through the establishment of the National Highway and Traffic Safety Administration and the Environmental Protection Agency), but always as an outsider's movement. As American politics began to turn away from the heady big-government optimism of the 1960s to the anti-government Reaganite optimism of the 1980s, the notion of corporations themselves as a major social problem began to recede. The zeitgeist of that later era was of course the standard one found during economic booms, of commerce as a virtuous activity and of corporate titans as not just public figures but out-and-out celebrities. The ACM was left to labor in the obscure vineyards of the alternative print media. But like so many ideas, anti-corporate ideology was unleashed by the great cultural equalizer of digital technology. A Lexis / Nexis search suggests the ability of the ACM over time to penetrate more mainstream media. In major newspapers, the phrase "corporate power" appeared 56 times in 1988, 190 in 1996, and 298 in 2004. (Whether the references were supportive or critical is irrelevant; what matters is whether the idea was discussed or not.) Indeed, numerous media outlets where belief in corporate rule is very well-represented—*The Guardian* and *The Nation* come to mind, along with many strictly anti-corporate outlets such as *Yes!* magazine—have been able to make their ideas far easier to access by placing their archives online for free. If anti-corporate opinion were truly suppressed, there could be no ACM of any size.

How can it be that in a time when the diversity of available opinions is greater than ever, there is an increasing belief that the "corporate media" constrain the permissible range of discussion? The most likely explanation is that ideas that have not yet obtained full political success are mistakenly and impatiently assumed to have been censored. When Cornel West, in the quote at the beginning of this chapter, argues that a "free and democratic society" is nearly unimaginable because of corporate power, he is really unknowingly lamenting the lack of appeal (at least so far) of his vision of America among the American people. But rejection of an idea is of course not the same as never hearing it, and no political idea has ever succeeded in a liberal democracy without years of persuasion by its early advocates. The spread of political ideas is perhaps more easily thought of as epidemiology than as the sort of horror story of repressive censorship that might be told in a university media-studies department. In the digital age, any idea can spread literally at the speed of light, almost in the manner of an infection. If the idea is not an attractive one, it quickly dies out just as a new virus fails to take hold because its infectious powers are not very strong. But if it reaches a widely visited website, it may spread rapidly into the larger population. Perhaps the best example is the ultimately successful work of the International Campaign to Ban Landmines, whose goal was an obscure idea until it began to spread rapidly in an age when the Internet itself was just beginning to take flight. (A treaty enacting such a ban was ultimately negotiated in 1997.) Ideas are easier to distribute than ever, whatever Rupert Murdoch or Disney wants. Whether the ideas take hold or not is another matter—a matter of the ideas' persuasiveness, not of corporate censorship.

In fact such threats to opinion diversity as remain primarily emanate from government rather than from corporations. The repeal of the fairness doctrine, under whose authority the Federal Communications Commission used to insist that all licensed broadcasters examine public issues from all sides, has provided for far more vigorous debate than the anodyne and timid conversations that used to occur on the airwaves when broadcasters were fearful of running afoul of the FCC. Conservative talk radio reflects the large number of people who believe in unrestricted gun ownership or oppose gay marriage, views to which many officially accredited journalists (in the sense of having the proper degrees from proper institutions) are hostile. (Talk radio is of course not strictly a right-wing phenomenon, and what we care about is not that talk radio, a particular market, be diverse, but that political speech taken as a whole be. Talk radio is simply one vendor in the broader political marketplace.) To take another example, the subsidy of public broadcasting is a subsidy of particular points of view, in this case those that happen to be held by these sorts of people who work in public broadcasting. These biases may be ideological on such questions as the Middle East conflict or abortion rights (and it is the existence of the biases rather than their direction that matters from the point of view of encouraging maximum competition of ideas), or they may even involve promoting a philosophy most employees of public broadcasting might be expected to share, that of active government management of society, which is every bit as much in the interest of public broadcasters as "pro-corporate" stories are in the interests of "corporate media."

Admittedly, all of this analysis with respect to opinions and cultural products alike assumes that ideas compete for attention rather than being imposed, like a high-pressure telephone sales pitch, on helpless consumer-citizens. For popular culture, this is not such an important debate; whether a popular singer is popular because her work has features that the public likes or because the public is persuaded to like what she does (in other words, whether public tastes determine singing success or entertainment-firm behavior shapes public tastes) is not really a critical question. But the assumption that citizens are subject to manipulation by special-interest political opinions, especially "pro-corporate" ones, and hence that the marketplace for such opinions needs to be tightly regulated, is an extremely dangerous one. Policing of the opinion market requires policing *by* someone, and that is where the peril lies. Regulation of production of speech through such tactics as the fairness doctrine or public broadcasting *must* generate zero-sum social conflict over who can say what using other people's printing presses, web servers, and microphones. [13]

To say that the airwaves belong to "the public" is an evasion, a way of saying that they belong to no one, that conflict over their use will be relegated to politics rather than to the market. The history of public broadcasting is littered with attempts by particular pressure groups to combat perceived bias or to obtain more coverage of particular points of view. Under such presidents as Johnson, Nixon, Reagan, and George Herbert Walker and George Walker Bush, there have been campaigns by officials for more "objectivity" and less "bias," with those efforts often undone under subsequent administrations. The federal government and religious and anti-religious groups have squabbled over whether or not public broadcasting frequencies (those at the low end of the FM dial) should be available for use by religious groups, or whether such groups should be frozen out. Turning speech into a zero-sum political conflict is a sure recipe for risk-averse opinion producers to draw in their horns rather than cultivate trouble with the government—a recipe, in other words, for less (and less interesting) speech. As with culture, the key task for a vibrant market in ideas is to lower the entry costs of new ideas and to improve the ability of consumers to search for them. And as with culture, the new corporate-driven technology accomplishes that.

There are two further points to make in this account of a future of much more robust and interesting political speech. The first is a cautionary one. There is no reason to expect that more diverse political speech gives us a republic of ideal Jeffersonian deliberation. Some recent evidence suggests that when people have views that are broadly similar, but which differ in degree, group discussion of the issue makes the median view more extreme. A group that is on balance pro-choice (or anti-corporate), for example, becomes noticeably more so after discussion. This means that if people can seek out views online or elsewhere that broadly reinforce their own, there is a tendency toward greater extremism. It is not a sure thing that simply increasing the general number of opinions available for the entire markets makes for better governance; the common ground necessary for self-government may shrink when people primarily cluster together with people who see the world more or less as they do. That is not an argument for going back to the old world of a false middle-of-the-curve consensus made possible only by the technological constraints of the media business, but it does suggest the importance of creating mechanisms in the existing media or in the new ones, and especially in civic structures, whereby citizens are exposed to views quite different from their own.

Second, the arguments to this point in the chapter are entirely technology-driven. It is not corporations or even business as such that diversify the culture and our politics. However, we saw that the corporation is a key social innovation that has helped technology of all kinds to improve and has raised the standard of living to such a degree that people can afford political and cultural indulgences that would be unavailable to them if day-to-day sustenance were their only concern. (It is much easier to afford to spend hours at a City Council meeting, writing a blog, or starting and running a pressure group if you are wealthy enough not to have to spend twelve hours a day on household chores or working the fields, as so many people did prior to modern prosperity.) It is business, powered by the corporate framework, which has made a scientific and academic oddity like the Internet into something so profoundly useful to so many of the world's people, including its political activists. It is corporations large and small that market and distribute the vastly expanded universe of cultural and political offerings, giving cultural and political entrepreneurs new opportunities. The increased efficiency promoted by the corporate form creates a better world in politics and culture as in everything else.

DYNAMIC CULTURE

Perhaps the greatest deficiency of the criticism of the modern, allegedly corporate-driven culture is its ignorance of the idea of cultural dynamism. Culture is not an unchanging set of fixed categories, each of which simply competes with the other. Instead, cultures merge, evolve, and interact with one another in ways that leave them changed. At any moment, there is a bell curve of cultural products, but the culture changes over time. This is mostly a story of "corporate" globalization, which, far from providing a way for Western culture to trample the rest of the globe underfoot, allows the producers of culture to learn about what people in other societies are doing and to use that culture as raw material for their own experimentation.

The Cultural Indictment of Corporate Globalization

Perhaps the most impassioned charge against corporate culture and corporate globalization is their alleged annihilation of the world's cultural differences and their replacement with a mindless diet of Western (mostly American) pop culture. A popular legend in the late 1990s had it that the most popular television show in the world was the empty skin-and-surf frolic *Baywatch*. The Jerry Springer show too has been one of our most visible cultural exports. And television is hardly the end of the problem. Everyone who is consuming these sorts of cultural dregs is neither consuming (nor producing) considerably more vital fare. The conquest of the world's cultural diversity by an allegedly banal popular music, cinema, manner of dress, etc. emanating mostly from the United States but also from elsewhere in the West and even Japan (whose cultural products are bitterly resisted by some in countries like South Korea) is one of the most lamented aspects of corporate globalization. As the argument has it, the world more and more gets its nutrition from McDonald's, its footwear from Nike, its news from CNN, and everything else from Wal-Mart.

The cost of this is that locally distinctive cultural products—native foods, artwork, etc.—are displaced by the corporate junk culture. Every meal bought at a fast-food restaurant in China is one less signal given to growers of culturally specific food ingredients there that what they do is profitable and thus worth continuing. And the triumph of the overall corporate culture of Western-style consumption is the wholesale elimination of distinctive local culture, which is a tremendous and permanent loss to the human storehouse of knowledge. And the habits encouraged by Western pop culture also become ways of looking at the world. Western pop culture erodes traditional family ties, social hierarchies, and promotes an irresponsible individualism. And so anonymous government officials in Paris tell one of their British counterparts that they fear the encroachment of the English language because it has "not only brought Shakespeare but also Milton Friedman and Margaret Thatcher."[14]

While the argument that corporations dominate culture in the global sense is basically the same one presented above—corporate desire for standardization requires appealing to the dreary middle—the argument made by the ACM in a global context is accentuated by resorts to ideas about the spread of capitalism generally attributed to Marx and Lenin. In particular, in addition to having a standardized product, the manufacturers of culture are said to be required to extinguish all local culture that might serve as an alternative. It is not enough for Hollywood just to market its wares in China or Mexico; it must crush any competition from Chinese and Mexican movies as well. The term "cultural imperialism" that is now so much with us is linguistically suggestive of earlier Marxist/Leninist conceptions of imperialism, and the coinage of the term is sometimes credited to the Marxist sociologist and media critic Herbert Schiller.[15] And more recently it is corporations themselves, with their built-in incentives, which promote standardization.

But why people would abandon local culture for such cultural offerings from overseas is a profound question. In many respects, cultural consumption goes to the heart of what it means to be distinct from the rest of humanity. The natural inclination as a Salvadoran, a Basque, a Berber, or a Gujarati is to gravitate toward the books, movies, and beliefs with which one is most comfortable by dint of familiarity. The search costs for culture expressed in a language and with cultural references with which one is familiar should be lower. Why would Western culture, junk or otherwise, prove so popular, particularly when the touchstones within it—cityscapes, parochial references within the work, etc.—are so unfamiliar? In part, the story goes, the depravity of Western corporations' mass-market offerings, their appeal to the lowest common denominator, makes them irresistible to people who should know better. And in part the explanation is the sinister marketing prowess of the multinationals. The political scientist Benjamin Barber has stated the claim about as straightforwardly as it can be stated:

> Because sales depend less on autonomous choices by independent
> buyers than on the manipulated habits and shaped behavior of

media-immersed consumers, those who control markets cannot help but address behavior and attitude. Tea drinkers are improbable prospects for Coca-Cola sales, so when it entered the Asian market, the Coca-Cola company quite literally found it necessary to declare war on Indian tea culture. Long-lunch, eat-at-home traditions obstruct the development of fast food franchises. However, successful fast food franchises have inevitably undermined Mediterranean long-lunch, eat-at-home rituals, inadvertently corrupting "family values" as thoroughly as Hollywood action movies have done. For fast food is about accommodating a culture in which work is central and social relationships are secondary, in which fast trumps slow and simple beats complex. Highly developed public transportation systems attenuate automobile sales and depress steel, cement, rubber, and petroleum profits. Agricultural life styles (rise at daybreak, work all day, go to bed at dusk) may be inhospitable to television watching. People uninterested in spectator sports buy fewer athletic shoes. The moral logic of austerity that might appeal to serious Muslims or Christians or secular ascetics gets in the way of the economic logic of consumption.[16]

Several aspects of this claim, in which corporate marketing is in essence an act of war on local cultures, are striking. First, as usual, human nature is profoundly weak, in that we are not capable of being masters of our own fate. Rather, we are passive drones, making choices not because we evaluate them as being on balance beneficial but because we have been manipulated into doing so by devious global advertising firms. Second, the choices we are seduced into making are poor ones. One cannot in this formulation abandon the agricultural lifestyle in the Indian or Chinese countryside because it is a hard life and the city offers something potentially better. Instead, in the Barber view, it must be because of the Western temptress. Third, we are all converging rather than diversifying: instead of adding new types of shoes or food to what a culture already had, people from all cultures exposed to corporate globalization are increasingly mesmerized into purchasing simply "athletic shoes" at the complete expense of what they were shod in before. Global food culture in all its variety similarly metamorphosizes into only "fast food." Fourth, it is once again the incentives of profit-maximizing corporations that drive this destruction. Making the last argument in his book *Jihad vs. McWorld,* Barber argues that culturally dominant multinational corporations can pursue profit only by "intervening actively in the very social, cultural, and political domains about which they affect agnosticism."[17] The idea of an emerging global culture as uniform, inferior, and imposed from above on people unable to resist is a key part of the story of what corporations are doing to the global culture.

In Defense of Cultural Globalization

[India] is a culture which is very ancient, which has form, which has classical music. At the same time we are living in today's world. So you know, we have influences while we travel to the Western countries. What comes naturally to us is to bring both of these experiences together.[18]

In fact, there is a far superior model of the emerging global culture that can be composed from a number of compelling objections to the corporate-imperialism model that have emerged in recent years. This alternative vision depicts global culture as, like globalization generally, the result of exchange among cultures rather than of domination by an all-powerful Western master. The anti-corporate model is once again zero-sum—a model of conquest rather than adaptation. Western culture simply replaces local culture. People consume Starbucks lattes, wear Manchester United jerseys, and listen to Madonna only because they have been tempted away from their own better and more authentic culture by corporate marketing power. But the economist Tyler Cowen has argued that what is really being created by the increasing distance cultural products can travel is a culture of exchange—literal trade in cultural products that behaves exactly as trade in more conventional goods and services does.[19]

Global culture is not a series of sealed boxes that have historically been isolated from one another and consisting of practices sufficiently fragile that they must be protected in the manner of laboratory bacteria samples from the contamination by other cultures that is allegedly an unprecedented feature of the modern globalized world. Rather, cultures are constantly borrowing from one another to create something novel and better. In describing how culture behaves, Cowen uses the phrase "creative destruction," created by the economist Joseph Schumpeter to describe growth in market economies through replacement of inferior technologies with better ones.[20] Schumpeter argued that the essence of capitalism is change, as firms old and new create new ideas and recombine the existing resources, enabling them to replace the old way of doing things with something better suited to human needs. In fact, such destruction is often gradual rather than dramatic, as much adaptation as destruction. The new generation of, for example, computing technology inescapably builds on what came before rather than emerging from nowhere. There can be no telephone without the telegraph, no digital telephone without the rotary phone before it, no fax machine without digital telephones, and so on. Throughout, the underlying thing of value—the ability to transmit information over great distances and to great numbers—improves in efficiency, complexity, and ease of use, with each "breakthrough" inconceivable without the one before. In culture the process is similar. One culture comes into contact with another—perhaps a primarily isolated one meets influences from the broader world for the first time. Eventually the recipient culture changes as it adopts influences from the global culture. (Some of its culture may feed back to the broader global culture.) The new culture is some new and improved balance between local and global influences, not a wholesale colonization of the local by the global.

And contrary to the claim that isolated cultures may disappear upon contact with the global culture, global communications technology may actually provide the members of that culture with the means to save it. One could think of weavers in the Andes who, faced with relentless financial pressure in the collapsed economies in Peru, Bolivia, and elsewhere or the rural unrest fomented by guerilla groups, may be inclined to abandon their culture as they move to cities in search of work. But if the world becomes aware of their plight, it may be easier to invest in activities to preserve the traditional arts to a much greater extent. Besieged minorities threatened with assimilation may more easily make an appeal to humanity in an interconnected world than in a compartmentalized one. This is both because modern communications technology allows them to transmit information to the rest of humanity about their difficulties and because greater global wealth brings with it a greater desire to consume cultural diversity—wealthier Americans and Japanese, for example, may become interested in the weavers' handiwork and pay them enough to keep them from having to abandon their villages to begin with. The world learns about and from the Andeans, and the Andeans learn about and from the world. The Andeans have a much better chance in the modern world with its two-way consensual cultural flows than they did against Pizarro's armies. They continue to make their products, but use modern technology and business tactics to sell them. The global culture is thus enriched.

And cultures may trade influences and create new cultural life forms. Anecdotal evidence of cultural forms borrowing from one another to produce something novel is everywhere. Tappan Raj, whose quote begins this subsection, is a member of an Indian music group specializing in a form of music known as bhangra, which began in India's Punjab and quickly spread to other parts of the Anglosphere. The group's very name, MIDIval PunditZ, is suggestive of the cultural fusion made possible by modern technology. They take classical Indian music and use electronic techniques made popular in the West to create music that is new and exciting, neither entirely Western nor traditionally Indian. (Their work was even recycled back to the West to create yet more cultural forms when it was used in Nokia advertising and in the American television show *Six Feet Under*.)

As Cowen notes, even reggae music is a powerfully illustrative example of the dynamic corporate/global culture. Jamaica in the cultural imperialism model often represents, via its globally popular yet seemingly purely indigenous music, a shining example of the little country that could. Located in the shadow of the gigantic pop-culture machine of the United States, Jamaica has nonetheless managed to invent and retain a distinctive musical form that has become popular around the world and in a short amount of time has come to serve as the soundtrack both for rebellion against Western dominance and more generally for the emergent global religion of Rastafarianism, itself a Jamaican cultural innovation.

But reggae, it turns out, is neither entirely Jamaican nor invulnerable to outside influences. Cowen notes that Jamaica, a country with no recording studios prior to 1951, was nonetheless heavily influenced, especially via radio catering to Jamaicans who had returned home after working in the U.S. sugar industry, by rhythm and blues and other American musical styles. Calypso from other Caribbean islands was also well-known in Jamaica. Bob Marley himself spent time earning money in an American automobile factory. And the invention of the basic rhythmic element of ska, a forerunner of reggae, is often attributed to the American pianist Roscoe Gordon. Jamaican musical innovators took these influences and ran with them, creating a music form that was in fact a hybrid of what came from the United States and of "indigenous" Jamaican forms, themselves products of African and European influences. Once the United States discovered reggae in the late 1970s, it was adopted and adapted by many American and British musicians even as it was being reexported. All of this led to an ultimately pointless controversy among reggae purists over what was "authentic" reggae. Like other such controversies over various types of music, literature, etc., this one was based on the false premise that if one goes far enough back in time there is a pure uncontaminated cultural form.

But that is never so. The Yale music professor Willie Ruff has unearthed evidence that bluegrass and gospel music, thought of as quintessentially American, were in fact influenced by music brought by immigrants from Scotland and what is now Northern Ireland. What was created in the United States was different from but shares similarities with the so-called Celtic music that continued to evolve separately in Scotland.[21] While his thesis has drawn much criticism from those who believe that it amounts to stripping black Americans of their cultural heritage, that is not a sensible way to think about how culture is created—cultures cannot be "owned." So too with sushi, which was exported to the United States, then stuffed with chilies, cream cheese, avocado, and (to the sushi traditionalist) other cultural atrocities and reexported to Japan as a novelty for younger diners to occasionally indulge in.[22] And having created jazz, Americans may only watch in the manner of proud parents as the music moves out to be reformulated by innovators worldwide.

Free trade in culture thus seldom replaces indigenous forms outright but typically creates new ones as artists in different parts of the planet learn from one another. And it does so not because a corporation has force-fed the hapless locals with it but because individual innovators have created it, one cultural experiment at a time. Most of these experiments in artistic styles are never heard of again, but those that stick enrich the world's cultural heritage. To the extent that corporations are involved, it is as carriers of information rather than as imposers of alien and unwanted cultural forms. Perhaps the best way of thinking about their role in the cultural-exchange model is as broadband data lines, facilitating massive transfers of cultural information that dramatically accelerate the pace of experimentation and innovation.

And culture has *always* been this way, but simply not to this extent until recently. Bach was influenced by composers from Italy and France; a director like Bergman or Fellini influences his colleagues around the world. To imply that we could, or should, adopt a model of autonomous, highly localized cultures, utterly protected against any contact with toxins from other cultures, is to guarantee stagnation and to deprive humanity of a flowering of an infinite number of cultural recombinations. Further, to prevent individual choice from governing the cultural market by definition necessitates government restrictions on cultural exchange. This is a point worth emphasizing, because the culture that gets produced under any set of incentives is that which artists are willing to produce. Artists must eat, and so either private buyers or government incentives will determine the rate of return on various types of artistic investment. There is no way of avoiding this simple truth.

Unfortunately, to insulate cultures from contamination is the path of cultural protectionism, whose effects are analogous to those of protectionism for other goods—lower quality, higher costs, and less variety. Just as surely as when a corporate paymaster writes the checks, governments imposing cultural policy have their own objectives. But unlike free-market culture, government control of culture via the power of the purse is not much subject to competition, and so can be expected to produce worse results. The limit case is outright totalitarian control of culture, the history of artists under which provides some of the most somber cultural moments of the twentieth century.

Consider Yin Cheng-Zong, one of modern China's most gifted pianists. Identified as a prodigy at a young age on his home island of Gulangyu, he trained at the Shanghai and Leningrad conservatories and in 1962 took second place at the Tchaikovsky Piano Competition. The U.S.S.R./China split forced him home only to see one man, Mao Zedong, exercise his totalitarian power to ban Western music as reactionary. At the outset of the Cultural Revolution one of the first targets of the Red Guards was pianos, which were actually smashed into pieces wherever they were found. In desperation, Yin took the extraordinary step of bringing a piano into Tiananmen Square and playing for three days in an attempt to save the instrument in China. He was successful, but then assimilated by the Communist Party, which closely supervised his subsequent work. Under the direction of a Party committee, he composed his most noted work, *The Yellow River Concerto*, but was eventually arrested when his photographs from the Tchaikovsky competition were discovered by Red Guards. He left for exile in 1983 as a stark symbol of how the state can subvert, alter, and destroy culture for its own purposes.[23] The more well-known artistic struggles, humiliations, and compromises of Shostakovich and Prokofiev under Stalin are similar.

These totalitarian cases are of course the most extreme examples of mixing government and culture, but even in modern liberal democracies there is reason to be suspicious of relying on government to manage the production of art. It is certainly true that in centuries past the donations of *individual* government (and church) officials were critical in promoting artistic production, along with those of wealthy private citizens. But the mechanism was substantially different from modern cultural protectionism. In an age of monarchies and nobility individual donors funded individual artists whose work they found valuable, so that the process was more akin to one of continuous competitive experimentation than to the sorts of highly politicized, sausage-and-laws decision-making in modern government agencies. Whereas under the old form of pseudo-state support for culture King Ludwig of Bavaria could provide debt relief and subsequent support to prop up the opulent lifestyle of the composer Richard Wagner without suppressing other nobles who wished to support other composers, in the modern cultural state Canadian broadcasters are flatly prohibited from offering a selection that is not sufficiently "Canadian," no matter how costly this restriction is. Indeed, this policy is vaguely reminiscent of the former East German government, which used to issue pink licenses to its officially licensed popular musicians, with others prohibited from performing. In Canada no band may be expelled from a stage for performing too many American songs, but any group may be scrubbed from the radio and television airwaves if his work is not sufficiently Canadian.

In the modern nation-state, whether a liberal democracy or not, the decision to award government benefits to artists (money, permission to operate on state-owned airwaves, etc.) is taken after some sort of elaborate political decision-making process, in which some spectrum— perhaps wide, perhaps not—of pressure groups is allowed input as to what constitutes good and bad art. In the end, the output of the political process is a choice that reflects both these prejudices and the self-interest of various artistic communities (e.g., Canadian musicians seeking protection from competition). Politicized state restrictions of necessity *limit* cultural experimentation. And government assistance to artists inevitably becomes government restraint on artists.

It would be surprising if the process that resulted from funneling art through the state were much different from those of manufacturing cars or running banks the same way. And in fact many of the characteristics of modern state cultural policy, including centralized decision-making dominated by an artistic elite, tend to produce relatively uniform types of art and to crowd out artistic innovation. The late French philosopher Jean-Francois Revel once noted that in Italy the most compelling films (e.g., work by Fellini and Rossellini) were produced in the years where government subsidy was minimal, while in Spain the rebirth of the industry in the 1980s occurred under similar circumstances.[24] In many of the most vigorous film industries in the world—not just in the United States, but in places like India's Bollywood and Hong Kong—filmmakers do not have to answer to a ministry of culture.

A number of economists have provided substantial empirical support for the harm done by entanglement with the modern state to innovation and quality in the related field of religion, something noted over two centuries ago by Adam Smith in *The Wealth of Nations*.[25] Official state sponsorship of churches tends to be associated with lower levels of religious participation, particularly in the state churches. Religious creativity, in contrast, is fostered by a state that does not play favorites. The oft-cited example is the United States, whose constitutional separation between church and state coincides with over 1,500 religions competing for adherents, many formed in the United States.[26] This is not to say that government is irrelevant to artistic and broader cultural excellence. But it has much more to do with the ways government may promote excellence in most endeavors, by facilitating creativity and innovation—by, for example, enforcing (up to a point) copyright protection. While the notion of art as economic product may grate on the sensibilities of some artists, the artist's process of creation occurs the same way as that of anything else produced that has value to society—by choosing on the basis of rewards and costs, personal or monetary.

The record producer Sam Phillips often recounted the story of hearing an unknown singer playing around in the studio with his bandmates, singing an unconventional version of a relatively well-known song, while waiting for Phillips to set up the equipment to record a song the singer planned to give to his mother. Upon hearing what they were playing, Phillips immediately told the singer to forget about what he came in to record and instead to record *that* song. He agreed, and the recording was made. That singer was Elvis Presley, the song was "That's All Right, Mama," and the rest is history. The ability of Phillips to spontaneously seize the artistic moment changed the course of twentieth-century culture. The contrast between market and state culture is the contrast between rock-and-roll as it spontaneously evolved, one cultural experiment at a time, and the music that would have resulted had Presley had to apply for a grant from the (then-nonexistent) National Endowment for the Arts instead. Presley himself served as early common ground between the music of southern American blacks and the broader white culture, from which young whites had been previously "protected" by their many cultural gatekeepers. The rock and roll he popularized was a classic example of a cultural mutation, building on work by earlier (mostly black) artists, opening the door to decades of further musical innovation, and made possible because of a bridging entrepreneurial institution—Phillips' Sun Records in this case. Some of the protectors of traditional American culture were subsequently horrified by this exercise in cultural experimentation, many of them depicting it as crassly pedestrian and lowbrow. This, ironically, is the same position which many anti-corporate activists take with respect to mass culture itself, even though much of that culture was radical in its day.

It is not difficult to understand why some people find the culture of exchange uncomfortable. Many of them are traffickers in ideas and like to think that their ideas and beliefs merit the confidence they themselves have in them. And so a frequent theme of those who criticize corporate globalization on cultural grounds is that the results are unedifying. The writer Anna Quindlen criticized the behavior of Afghans in the immediate aftermath of the fall of the Taliban, expressing dismay over their inexplicable choice of "celebrating the end of tyranny by buying consumer electronics."[27] That, of course, was hardly a fair description of the huge number of ways in which Afghans celebrated their new-found freedom from one of the world's most primitively oppressive governments. Traditional Afghan music, for example, has also undergone a revival with the end of the Taliban's blanket exercise of authority over what is legitimate artistic output (including the outright banning of music performance of any kind).

It is not clear what the aesthetic harm is when people several weeks removed from the most heartless and barbaric rule partake of things, such as the Indian movies some Afghans consumed voraciously, that the rest of the world takes for granted. But that the tastes of the average global citizen in such matters runs contrary to the tastes of those who write or agitate for a living is a problem given extraordinary attention by the latter groups. The ordinary behavior of hundreds of millions of people around the world who buy the mass-market products offered to them because they find them useful becomes somehow mentally aberrant or a moral failure. (The column from which the above Quindlen remark is taken is devoted, according to the secondary headline, to "America's crazed consumerism.") Quindlen herself was probably unaware when she wrote so disparagingly of the new Afghanistan that she herself is a major beneficiary of a previous outbreak of cultural freedom—in particular, the acceptance of the belief that writing for money is a legitimate activity. Until the mid-eighteenth century, most European intellectuals believed that only writing done without compensation was artistically pure; the rest was purely mercenary. This norm of course made it impossible for most of the population to even participate in the marketplace of ideas, because they lacked the means. It was ultimately simple protectionism on behalf of existing writers, and much of the elitist contempt for mass culture is the same—revulsion at the outcome of a competitive market because it poses a threat to culture and ideas that do not sell as well.

Much of the criticism of the new global culture has this feel. Gar Smith, the president of an environmental think tank and pressure group called the Earth Island Institute, bemoans what he has learned from no more evidence than how he has interpreted through the prism of his own tastes what he has seen in his travels through Africa. In lamenting the introduction of modernity to rural African villages full of people who desperately want it, he asserts that "[t]he idea that people are poor doesn't mean that they are not living good lives" and recounts that he has "seen villages in Africa that had vibrant culture and great communities that were disrupted and destroyed by the introduction of electricity."[28] In speaking this way, he is the inheritor of a long legacy of skepticism in certain quarters about how ordinary people organize their lives. The writer David Brooks has referred to this behavior as "bourgeoisophobia,"[29] which dates at least to the Romantic-era contempt of many in the hereditary elite for the rising fortunes of the new bourgeoisie, who appeared to be enjoying a prosperity and social station unjustified by their circumstances of birth. That attitude lives on among conservatives, particularly in Europe, but it has been merged in the anti-globalization movement with an ideology of primitivism that romanticizes grinding poverty, looks askance at popular middle-class culture, and seeks above all to prevent people in the rest of the world from making the choices that so many in the West and increasingly elsewhere have freely made.

In the end, the current global cultural system is vibrant, decentralized, constantly recombining, free of state control, and consequently superior to its alternatives. And corporations are not the force-feeders of unwilling or subservient cultures but the transmission channels of the global culture of exchange. Corporations merely pave the roads; artists and idea producers travel on them.

Cultural Institutions

The term "culture" does not just include such expressive works as music and literature, but also fundamental patterns of behavior and ways of looking at the world—habits, religious beliefs, family relations, and so on. How are these more fundamental aspects of culture likely to be affected by an increasingly interconnected, corporate-paved world? Here the story is more complex. Whereas greater connectivity will cause more experimentation with respect to cultural products, when it comes to patterns of belief and behavior there is without question some replacement of traditional ways by allegedly "Western" ones. And corporations are again a major facilitator of these changes. However, the idea of an imposed Western culture foisting itself on unwilling recipient cultures is as before a poor way of thinking about this phenomenon.

It is important to grant that a number of social behavior patterns began in the West, migrated elsewhere through trade and colonialism, and substantially displaced local competing practices. For example, agriculture, particularly small farming, has declined as a portion of the economy and labor force and a foundation of social organization wherever modernization has taken root. Countries rich and poor alike are far more urbanized in 2007 than in 1960, with the empty rural villages left behind mourned by both the traditionalist conservative and the anti-globalization, anti-corporate cultural protectionist alike.

But in the anti-corporate globalization argument, most (even all) local folkways will disappear and be replaced by a way of living that is more individualistic, more organized around modern commercial activity, that frays the ties of extended family, etc. These things happen, it is said, again not because of individuals freely choosing but because of pressures from the corporate above. The jarring clash of the modern with the traditional is illustrated by a controversy that recently erupted over the construction of a Wal-Mart approximately half a mile from one of Mexico's most important archaeological sites, a pyramid in the city of Teotihuacán. The opening of the store in 2004 caused a tremendous outcry among many of these activists. One group published an advertisement that made the store the very example of the cultural desecration brought about by corporate globalization:

> The struggle for Teotihuacán is a war of symbols. The symbol of ancient Mexico against the symbol of transnational commerce; genetically modified corn against the Feathered Serpent (the Aztec god Quetzalcoatl, Kukulcan in Mayan) and Mexico's traditional foods; the Day of the Dead against Halloween; skeletons against jack-o'-lanterns.[30]

A molecular biologist named Jaime Lagunez imputed immense, almost supernatural power to the superstore chain when telling the alternative newspaper *The Montreal Mirror* that Wal-Mart was with unusual clarity of purpose for a publicly listed company legally charged with maximizing shareholder value not doing these things but rather "trying to destroy our identity, our roots. This is the imposition of a new way of life, based on consumerism. I really believe this. Look, if the Spanish put churches on top of temples, why wouldn't the transnationals use the same strategy?"[31] That virtuous traditional cultures are replaced by mindless, uniformly consumption-oriented lives is a cornerstone of the cultural-institutions objection to globalization. A Wal-Mart would, its opponents complained, destroy many "traditional" local merchants (themselves often sustained in large part by the global tourist culture) and inculcate people holding more traditional (and morally superior) patterns of thought and behavior with inappropriate Western and especially American mores—the mores of market, of mass consumption, of turning all of life into tradable commodities to be bought and sold.

But seen in its entirety the Teotihuacán Wal-Mart is in fact revealing in another way. It is, most obviously, an opportunity for the people who live near the pyramid to achieve a higher standard of living via lower prices for a wider variety of goods, the essence of what Wal-Mart does. In the days after the store opened it was flooded with customers (as such "first-contact" Wal-Marts and McDonald's around the world invariably are). Its popularity with locals presumably ought to loom large in any philosophical assessment of the globalized culture. Like most modern retail corporations, Wal-Mart uses complex, centralized distribution systems to market ordinary (to prosperous Westerners) consumer goods at much lower prices, and this form of managing the desires of buyers and the wares of sellers far more efficiently than the traditional merchants it partially displaces plays a huge role in all prosperous societies. Wal-Mart's lower prices fight poverty every bit as effectively as higher incomes do, and thus Wal-Mart is a path to opportunity for those who have so little. So too with migration to cities, highly complex divisions of labor in production, the enthusiastic adoption of modern communications technology and other disruptions to traditional ways of doing things. And yet the comfortable anti-corporate activists will have none of it. As the writer Morris Berman complains to a German interviewer:

> Consider the use of cell phones as a single example: one sees this technology even in tiny villages in Italy. What is the result? It extends the world of work and business to every phase of human life, and it breaks down the barrier between public and private space. One can no longer sit in a café and have a quiet conversation with a friend, or just read a newspaper, without having to listen to someone loudly talking on a cell phone. It is an expression of extreme individualism; ultimately, it spells the death of community.[32]

Berman shares the same problem as Lagunez. He finds that the new, freely chosen habits of those around him are disagreeable, not to them but to him. As outlined in the introduction, resolving conflicts of will over how to organize society is one of the most fundamental problems any society faces. It is true that Mr. Berman cannot have the café experience that he believes he intrinsically deserves unless he is willing to look a little harder for a café where cell phones are scarce (or banned by the owner), but in the world before cell phones the patrons who disturb him did not even *have* the valuable communication opportunities they now enjoy. So too with the intellectuals (almost none of whom live there) who believe that whatever Wal-Mart provides to the residents of Teotihuacán cannot possibly be worth the aesthetic damage done to their own peculiarly exacting tastes by the store's continued presence.

But what such dissidents are up against is not some forcible incursion by militaristic, conquering multinationals bearing cultural uniformity to cram down the locals' throats. Rather, as the writer Mario Vargas Llosa has noted, these changes, which look similar wherever they occur around the world, are not even adoptions of Western cultural traits as such but of the universal requirements of modernization. The faster pace of life, the erosion of traditional social structures, and the like are essential for offering people the dramatically better life that modern opportunities, including those for which the global corporate form is indispensable, make available.[33] For example cities, much criticized by corporate-globalization opponents as wasteful islands of dependency on the surrounding countryside, are tremendous ways to accomplish extraordinary things in very little space.

Consider Manhattan Island. To a skeptic of modernization it is a city of extraordinary waste, requiring that the most basic items of sustenance (food, energy, etc.) be transported in from the outside if it is to survive at all. But in fact it is a mighty producer (and exporter) of things of immense value to the rest of humanity. In a mere twenty-six square miles of space, there is room for a garment district, a theater district, a media district, a financial district, a diamond district, a high-technology cluster, and many other forms of economic activity. People move efficiently from place to place, and an endless display of necessities (they are never more than a few minutes away from state-of-the-art medical care in an emergency) and luxuries is constantly available in various stores to anyone who needs them. The measured output of this tiny island exceeds that of roughly two-thirds of all countries.

This is in some sense what all cities are—an incredibly efficient way to organize a dizzying array of human activity. To think of a city as the destroyer of traditional lives and as something that is inefficient simply because food is transported in from elsewhere is to miss a gigantic forest for a vanishingly small tree. In that sense Berman's lamentations about the vanishing of his café ideals are part of a much broader phenomenon—modernization—that damages his peculiar interest because he dislikes cell phones, but facilitates the broader interests of huge numbers of people—the changes that are made so as to enable people to live longer, more dignified lives, to take control of their own future, to experience more of the world, to learn new things. Some older patterns of behavior (e.g., traditional village life or stifling social hierarchies) are largely thrown by the wayside through a sort of competitive cultural evolution, but what comes after is dramatically better than what was before.

Indeed, one other remaking of cultural behavior that has coincided with modern globalization and fits much more comfortably into the modernization model of what globalization is than the corporate-conquest model is the spread of consensual government. The number of liberal democracies is much larger now than in the early 1970s. The organization Freedom House has been rating countries on political-rights and civil-liberties protection since the early 1970s. They characterize countries as "not free," "partly free," and "free." In 1973, forty-seven, eighteen, and thirty-five percent of countries were not free, partly free, and free, respectively. In 2003, those percentages had changed to twenty-five, twenty-nine, and forty-six percent. The richest and most globalized countries are virtually all among the freest. Better governance, like all the cultural changes that accompany modernization, is something to celebrate rather than resent. In that sense it is illustrative that in its criticisms of cultural displacement the anti-corporate/anti-globalization movement seldom discusses the worldwide liberal democratic revolution. Like the other changes in cultural institutions that the movement so criticizes, consensual government is inextricably wound up with modernization, and like those changes it is a change for the better.

As in the previous evaluation of globalization, if we are interested in exploring whether people value the growing global culture of exchange, it is simple to ask. Table 7.1 shows the responses to a question from the Pew Center globalization survey used in Tables 6.2 and 6.3 regarding people's opinion of global cultural ties. Again, the approval/disapproval rating is extremely high. That so many in developing countries, on whose behalf the ACM claims to fight, all over the world are so receptive to global culture is particularly instructive. The global culture allows people to experience a world beyond the confined horizons of their ancestors, and they are (justifiably) excited about it.

The corporate culture, like the broader corporate world, is constantly evolving so as to better meet the goals of those whose interests it serves. A dynamic culture is sometimes a frightening one, particularly for those who have a great deal invested in the existing culture—intellectuals, clerics, rulers who rule merely because of tradition. Indeed, many of the

Table 7.1 Attitudes toward global cultural ties (percent saying "somewhat" or "mostly favorable"/"somewhat" or "mostly unfavorable").

N. America	
United States	78/15
Canada	80/8
Latin America	
Argentina	76/17
Bolivia	52/46
Brazil	78/18
Guatemala	72/25
Honduras	73/26
Mexico	75/18
Peru	63/30
Venezuela	86/11
W. Europe	
United Kingdom	87/8
France	91/8
Germany	86/11
Italy	78/14
E. Europe	
Bulgaria	84/10
Czech Republic	87/13
Poland	82/12
Russia	54/40
Slovak Rep.	69/20
Ukraine	76/28
Africa	
Angola	79/18
Ghana	73/21
Cote D'Ivoire	95/6
Kenya	66/29
Mali	77/22
Nigeria	90/8
Senegal	62/37
S. Africa	83/13
Tanzania	72/19
Uganda	78/18
Asia	
China	90/6
India	60/23
Japan	91/5
Philippines	75/22
S. Korea	78/19
Vietnam	87/11

Muslim-Majority Countries

Bangladesh	51/47
Egypt	46/36
Jordan	51/49
Indonesia	74/26
Lebanon	81/18
Pakistan	26/55
Turkey	78/15
Uzbekistan	71/28

Source: Pew Research Center for People and the Press, Views of a Changing World, How Global Publics View: War in Iraq, Democracy, Islam and Governance, Globalization.

most extreme anti-modernist social movements have drawn on this sentiment in their pursuit of power, the real power of armaments and police, not the imaginary power of successful business practices. But for those who are not so wedded to the existing system, the modern culture is an exciting one, and makes for an extraordinary time to be alive.

Chapter 8

Corporate Conclusions

The late environmental scientist, systems theorist, lead author of the early-1970s doomsday report *The Limits to Growth*, MacArthur Foundation "genius award" recipient, and anti-corporate campaigner Donella H. Meadows, while reviewing *When Corporations Rule the World*, summarized the anti-corporate agenda in 2000 as follows:

- Challenge the Supreme Court decision that gives corporations fictitious human rights. Persons in corporations should have all rights, but the corporation itself has no conscience, no moral accountability, no citizenship. Corporations, says Korten, "simply do not belong in people's political spaces."
- Take back the corporate charter. Corporations exist by public permission. If they break the law or act against the public good, their charters should be revoked.
- Flatly prohibit corporations from influencing the political process or "educating" the public on policy issues. Forbid false-front "citizen" lobbying organizations and even corporate "charitable" giving, through which firms often push their own agendas (for example, by threatening to withdraw public broadcasting contributions if shows are aired about clearcutting or overgrazing). If corporations want to serve society, says Korten, "let them provide good, secure jobs and safe products, maintain a clean environment, obey the law, and pay their taxes."
- Prohibit paid political advertising. The ads are misleading, and their huge cost makes candidates beholden to large donors.

Broadcasters, in return for the right to use the public airways, should be required to provide free, equal, in-depth exposure to all candidates.

- Pay for campaigns through a combination of strictly limited, small individual contributions and public funding. Corporations should be prohibited from using corporate resources in any way to favor any candidate.[1]

It is a provocative set of proposals, albeit disturbingly laden with words like "prohibit," "forbid," and so on. As we have seen, the general goal of anti-corporate thinkers is to bring profit-maximizing, shareholder-owned corporations more under the control of the public—to confine their activity to whatever the political process defines as permissible. To be sure, different constituencies in the ACM differ in how troubling they find the "private" in "private sector" to be. Some want the outright elimination of large corporations and the shareholder model; some merely want more voices for other stakeholders. But the general belief that corporations, particularly large ones, have grown so powerful that they must be reined in under the watchful eye of the government unites all wings of the movement. How did corporations come to be what they are? Why do anti-corporate campaigners hold these views? And, what would be the consequences if they prevailed? As anti-corporate thinking continues to grow, it is better to ask these questions now than later.

HOW DID WE GET HERE?

The modern corporation did not come from nowhere. Most of its key characteristics were introduced at various times and places, sometimes abandoned only later to be readopted because they were so useful. Over time, the modern corporate structure came into shape, with key contributions occurring particularly in the United States and Great Britain. In the future, it may be that other milestones in the development of the corporate form will occur in other places, as the corporation continues to spread worldwide.

As we saw, there are two explanations offered for the growth in both the number of total and the size of the largest corporations. One is that it is the outcome of an evolutionary process—with the word "evolution" connoting the survival of the fittest, implying that social institutions that fade away do so for good reason as do those that continue. The corporation is what it is and has been so enthusiastically embraced around the world because it is so useful for actual people, as opposed to "the people" as an abstraction. If true, this belief indicates that radically reshaping the modern limited-liability corporation is no more helpful or reasonable than trying to bring the dinosaurs back to life. But the ACM rejects this view out of hand. In their view, the corporate era and the public policies that have been promulgated during it are the results of a corporate power grab successfully executed, powered by the intrinsic incentives of shareholder-driven corporations and the economies of scale that they reap.

But in the end, the power-grab story is implausible. Recall that the special-privilege corporation, which involved far closer ties between corporations and governments than the modern era of open-access corporations, was ultimately displaced by the latter. The advent of the open-access corporation meant that any citizen, rich or poor, well-connected or not, from the dominant ethnic or religious group or not, could without having to satisfy a politician or king access the opportunities open-access incorporation made available. Indeed, while the era of early industrialization from roughly 1780 until approximately 1860 saw a radical overhaul of the basic nature of the corporation, the changes since then have been more modest. Given that this era saw perhaps the most dramatic economic revolution in history, it is unsurprising that it was accompanied by the most dramatic change to the corporate form. Once the most efficient form was settled on, corporate law became much more a matter of tinkering than of wholesale change. And most of the changes proposed by the ACM and outlined in Chapter 3 are nothing short of such radical change. They are thus a dramatic break with a form that has served society for well over a century. Even if enacted only in part, they would substantially reshape the world and its possibilities.

And the ACM's contrary diagnosis of a corporate takeover of society is not entirely new. Big business is frightening now and has been frightening in the past. In the nineteenth century, Marx believed that capitalists would drive his reserve army of the unemployed to the breaking point, because it was never rational for them to pay wages higher than subsistence level. But that prediction failed because Marx failed to see that once enough subsistence farmers and laborers had migrated from the countryside to the city during industrialization, workers became a truly scarce resource and business had to vigorously compete for them. Ever since that time, the standard of living has steadily risen in the West, with per capita income growth in the United States closely approximating an exponential growth curve for over a century. Each generation on both sides of the Atlantic has during this period had a standard of living roughly fifty percent higher than that of its parents, a pattern people in other parts of the world increasingly also enjoy.[2]

Why this has happened is a complex story, but stepping back from the quiet miracle that is modern society and observing it in historical perspective provide some hint of what our ancestors have accomplished in creating the world we take for granted and what we are accomplishing now every day across the United States as we reinvent the world yet again. Every day, millions of people get up and head to jobs—not jobs assigned to them by some master economic choreographer, but jobs that they sought out and sometimes created for themselves, and the performance of which makes their employers money. Every day all the goods they desire, not just for basic sustenance but to achieve things that were unimaginable to people even twenty or thirty years ago, are there. Anyone who goes to a grocery store finds that the actions of large numbers of unknown people all over the world have somehow been coordinated and, voilà, the food, the cars, the medicines, the books, and the computers are there. (Sometimes the prices are high, but prices are a rule for deciding who gets the goods and who doesn't.) The conflicting desires of the entire population are reconciled as efficiently as they can be. Lest anyone suppose that this is the normal state of things, a casual glance at the world around us suggests that this most basic of problems fails to be solved all the time—witness hours-long gas lines in countries such as Nigeria with substantial oil supplies, agriculturally blessed countries such as Zimbabwe that are unable to feed their people, countries that see per capita income stagnate or even regress over a period of several decades in which global technological progress soars, etc.

To take a hypothetical example of the quiet miracles of the corporate world, if a medical breakthrough—say, a cure for breast cancer—is discovered in a commercial laboratory owned by a corporation based in India, under the current system that corporation will quickly seek to maximize shareholder income by capitalizing on this breakthrough. (If a scientist in a publicly funded laboratory created the drug and a drug company representative learned of it at a scientific conference, the corporation would still seek to perfect and sell the drug, and the effect would be the same. Either way, the drug would end up in the hands of as many patients as possible given the costs to society of making it available to them.) The corporation will seek out distributors who will seek out vendors particularly in the richest countries and most particularly in the United States, the world's most lucrative market for most medical products. That revenue will fund further production and enable the company (and, eventually, competitors who invent similar drugs and ultimately generic manufacturers after the drug goes off-patent) to expand production and seek new markets, which is the economist's way of saying "cure more cancer."

But suppose it were a world shaped by the anti-corporate movement. Perhaps the company's ability to tap the capital markets would be restrained; perhaps the company would not be able to pay the best executives a salary sufficient to obtain their services; perhaps its ability to advertise the drug and hence inform potential beneficiaries about it would be restricted; perhaps governments in countries all around the world would annul the patent rights it had in good faith relied on in the course of developing the drug.

Every one of these steps the ACM might impose on our hypothetical corporation would make it less rational to try to discover the drug in the first place and to distribute it once it had been discovered. Every step in the corporate decision chain is risky and otherwise costly. The anti-corporate world tells that firm not to take those risks and incur those costs to begin with, because the long-established principles of basic contract and property law that it has taken for granted all along are not to be relied upon. And perhaps most damagingly, not only will existing firms refuse to take risks, but many such firms will never be formed to begin with. The hidden danger of anti-corporate thinking is the future that does not arise when such thinking triumphs—which is not a future of something as hackneyed as "corporate rule," but the missed opportunities to construct the networks of knowledge and personal ties that allow people with brilliant ideas in one place to be matched with those who will benefit from that knowledge somewhere else.

A big part of why such quiet miracles happen more in some places than in others is differences among countries in economic freedom— the protection of property rights, the sanctity of contracts, reasonable taxation rates and public-spending levels, restrained and nonarbitrary government regulations. The link between such freedom and economic growth is as well-established as any proposition in economics. The task of moving resources to where they can provide the greatest benefit for large populations with vastly diverse interests is an astonishingly complex one. For example, there is only so much oil to go around. Where should it go? For electricity? For gasoline? For plastics? If gasoline, which companies should get more and which should get less? From each selling company, which gas station should get it first and get the most?

Free markets—societies unencumbered by excessive deterrence of commerce—best solve this fundamental problem of who should get what, and they do so by simply allowing property owners to make bids on resources owned by other people. This takes decision-making authority away from politicians and gives it to producers and consumers, who sort it out for themselves in their buying and selling decisions. Anything that facilitates this process of efficient resource use, for example, the entire structure of corporate law, is something that helps societies solve these conflicts effectively and with a minimum of rancor. Corporate law is part of a long-term process of social evolution that has enabled us to live better, longer, more fulfilling lives. In this, the modern corporation resembles many such social institutions that persevere because they serve us well just as they are—the scientific method, universities dedicated to freedom of inquiry, the professionalization of medicine, the growth in legal respect for individual autonomy for women and previously oppressed minority groups, and so on. Any evaluation of the corporate place in society must take account of this fact.

WHERE MIGHT WE BE GOING?

The alternative to deferring to free markets, including corporations, large and small, to decentralize problem-solving is to solve them by drawing up plans at the top of society and then imposing them on lower levels—by relying on the government, in other words—not necessarily to produce goods but, as the ACM freely confesses, to limit the capacity of corporations to act and especially to grow if they are successful.[3] Like any large organization, government relies on a hierarchical chain of command. And like any organization, it finds that the gap between what it wishes to be transmitted down the chain of command and what actually happens is quite different. But unlike other large organizations, it has the police and taxation power to back up its wishes, whether the outcomes it expects when using them are actually likely to happen or not. This unfortunate combination means that when its top-down plans do not work as intended, the natural response of politicians and civil servants, particularly those higher up the chain of command, is to blame society for not functioning as they or the experts on whom they relied predicted, and hence to pass yet more laws and regulations, i.e., more restrictions on commercial freedom, to force people to behave as the plan assumed they would. The entrepreneur's freedom of maneuver declines more and more, and his ability to solve problems declines, including problems that are not even on the radar screen before the entrepreneur applies his genius to them.

It is instructive to note that many of the industries where people complain the most about quality and availability in the United States are those where the government is most entangled—medicine and insurance, to take two obvious examples. In each case, relatively modest intervention—once-small government programs like Medicare or Medicaid established to provide medical care for a small part of the population, or state regulatory commissions whose only goal is to trim abusive insurance excesses—quickly becomes completely ensnared in the conflicting demands of providers and customers. Public complaints—medical treatments cost too much, home insurers don't provide enough coverage in highly earthquake or hurricane-prone areas—quickly follow. And so government entanglement deepens, producers are further constrained from efficiently meeting the goals of consumers, and the problem feeds on itself. Businesses that behave this way in an environment free of regulation quickly die, replaced by firms that can do things better. While Wal-Mart and Nike have plenty of criticism from activists who have no financial stake in them and neither work there or buy their products, they receive few from their customers. But businesses heavily regulated by the state find themselves in eternal combat with other pressure groups, each struggling to gain control over the government regulatory apparatus.

Diverting productive decisions to the political sphere is a recipe for disaster, because politics can never solve these problems to everyone's satisfaction because of its zero-sum nature.

And yet that is where the anti-corporate campaigners, whether moderate or extreme, would take us. The mindset of the ACM—its belief in the dominance of the corporate interest in setting public policy, its opposition to the otherwise obvious public interest, its conviction that rights are vested in groups rather than individuals—leads it inescapably to try to restrict contractual freedom. The details differ from campaigner to campaigner, but among the most common recommendations are limits on executive compensation, limits on financial trading, limits on the freedom to contract or not with workers, higher corporate taxes, and restrictions on involvement of corporations in political activism. Fortunately, some ACM proposals are a pipe dream. It is, for example, difficult to imagine any combination of events that will lead to an overturning of the corporate-personhood doctrine; as we saw, it has roots that date back centuries, and is well-entrenched as law. (The ACM's theory of how this doctrine came to be is important in its own right and discussed below.)

But much of the rest of the ACM's agenda becomes more plausible, if not necessarily immediately likely, with every passing year. Note first that hostility to business, especially big business, is (contrary to some stereotypes about what Americans believe) far from unknown in American politics. Even now, data from the University of Chicago's General Social Survey indicate that "major businesses" are far from the most respected American social institutions. (In 2004, 18.77 percent of Americans had "a great deal of confidence" in "major business." Of eleven nonbusiness institutions assessed, the figure was higher for seven of them.[4]) A 2005 Harris poll showed that "big business" was the institution that the greatest percentage of respondents thought had "too much power or influence in Washington," one of only two institutions to have seen an increase in that percentage since 1994. This suggests a rising populism, defined as belief in using the government to protect the "little guy," whether small business owner, consumer, or worker, from big business. This is a tendency that has waxed and waned over time in American politics.

And globalization and increasing income inequality in industrial countries, while driven by technological changes and (as we saw in Chapter 6) ultimately one of the more important events in human history in terms of the actual positive difference made in the lives of large numbers of people, may in the short term be driving a significant amount of this sentiment. But the new anti-corporatism is very capable of merging with and reinforcing these preexisting tendencies. If we assume that politicians in democratic societies are followers rather than leaders, we would expect anti-corporate beliefs to show up in the way political campaigns are manufactured, and increasingly they do. The campaigns against

Wal-Mart, for example, have taken years to shape and have now lured many leading politicians of the American center-left and left into their wake.[5] As we saw in the introduction, anti-corporate sentiment played a significant role in the 2004 Democratic presidential nominating process. And shortly after the 2006 election, Rahm Emmanuel, a Democratic representative from Illinois and an influential member of the party's central decision-making apparatus, said that "[p]rescription drugs, gas prices and economic populism are no longer associated with blue-collar downscale voters. Office park workers can be just as populist as industrial workers—they are struggling under rising college and health care costs too. They resent giveaways to H.M.O.s; they don't want subsidies to oil companies when oil is 68 bucks a barrel."[6]

To be sure the future is not as bright for anti-corporatism in the United States as in the most economically troubled societies of Western Europe. There are several reasons for this. The first is that in Europe much more than the United States, people are more inclined to attribute outcomes in life to grand social forces only remediable by the state. Particularly in the central spine of the EU (European Union), the large economies of Germany, France, and Italy, there is a strong tendency to believe that, in the words of a 2003 survey by the Pew Global Attitudes Project, "[s]uccess in life is pretty much determined by forces outside our control."[7] While thirty-one percent of Americans agreed with the statement (the lowest percentage of all forty-four countries surveyed), agreement among Germans, Italians, and French was sixty-eight, forty-four, and fifty-four percent, respectively. Americans tend to believe they can make their own way in life, and Europeans tend to believe that impersonal social forces drive history. Such reliance on all-encompassing theories of society to explain individual outcomes has long been present in European thought (think of Marx as the ultimate example), and such beliefs naturally lend themselves to agitation for countervailing action by the state against whatever villain the population has settled on. The perceived machinations of global corporations now provide just such a compelling theory for many Europeans.

Much of Europe is also less competitive and hence more under threat by globalization and more committed even without this effect to restraint of business in the name of "social justice." On the one hand, globalization is exerting pressures for the trimming back of social justice for reality's sake, a process which has already taken hold in countries such as Britain, Denmark, and the Netherlands. But on the other, power to regulate economic affairs in Europe is increasingly flowing from the national level to the superstructure of the less democratically accountable EU. Like bureaucracies everywhere, the EU's bureaucracy, Brussels' European Commission, may be prone to supposing that any problem, even lack of competitiveness caused by excessive regulation from on high, is best addressed by even more regulation from on even higher.[8] There is an active movement (of still uncertain strength) within the corridors of power in the EU to try (futilely) to regulate globalization itself, making it more amenable to the increasingly obsolete European social model. Combined, these factors may make Europe even friendlier territory for anti-corporate thinking. And the temporary negative effects of globalization on people in the United States who are most damaged by it in the short run may increasingly make anti-globalization sentiment in particular, which has many of the same practical effects as purely anti-corporate activism, a more important political force here. The slowdown in further trade liberalization in the last several years because of rising protectionist pressures in both the United States and Europe is perhaps the most vivid evidence of this.

In the rest of the world, things are not so bleak. As we saw in Chapter 6, both multinational corporations and globalization are wildly popular in much of the developing world because of the potential deliverance they promise from corruption and brutally incompetent governance. (Portions of Latin America, driven by the populism of the Venezuelan president Hugo Chavez, itself an echo of that region's historical and ideological demons, may be an exception.) And so the sad irony is that anti-corporate thinking and anti-business thinking more generally pose the greatest threat in the developed world, which is developed to begin with in part because of what the corporate structure has allowed people to achieve there.

It may be that anti-corporatism is, along with skepticism of American power, more and more the single unifying principle of the global left. (To the extent that globalization is seen as an American plan, the two beliefs intersect.) Increasingly, the obstacles to *everything* that progressives believe in—decent health care and retirement for all through the welfare state, world peace, a clean environment—are being interpreted exclusively through the anti-corporate prism. The ease with which politicians and activists drop some form of the word "corporate" into their language is a striking sign of the times. Together with whatever support progressives can pick up from the nativist and traditionalist right in Europe and the United States uncomfortable with the cultural disruptions brought about by global commerce and migration, this means that anti-corporatism is likely to be an ideology with a bright future.

If the movement does achieve political viability, what is likely to happen? In the long term, it is difficult to believe that policies that are so hostile to the human drive to excel and achieve, and to the gains that free commerce can create, are sustainable absent the dictatorial powers necessary to make them work. As Hayek noted, there is no exercising substantial "public" (i.e., government) control over economic activity without extending its control over noneconomic activity as well.[9] Open-access corporations are formed because someone perceives an unfulfilled human need. To use the power of the state to restrain this basic desire, even if initially couched in the anodyne language of wanting to restrain only "big business" rather than commerce itself, is ultimately to bring more and more human activity under the purview of that power when things don't work out as planned.

But partial though still costly restraints on "corporate power" are easily imaginable in the current political climate. And *all* anti-corporate proposals are ultimately about restriction or annulment of agreements voluntarily worked out by others. Limits on corporations' ability to contract with potential executives, to use any financial instruments that someone is willing to buy to raise funds, to bargain freely with workers and suppliers, and, perhaps most importantly, to defend themselves in the political arena will ultimately have disastrous effects on their ability to do what they do best. And as we have seen, what they do best is solve human problems by connecting people in a position, often without knowing it, to help one another.

THE PHILOSOPHICAL CONFUSION OF ANTI-CORPORATISM

In its promiscuous use of such politically charged phrases as "corporate power," the ACM evinces a lamentable lack of clear thinking about what power is and what it means to be free. Recall that in Chapter 3, I defined "power" as the ability to limit the opportunities of others. "Freedom," then, is the absence of power of some *individuals* over others. Clearly, the vast majority of what corporations do is the precise opposite of that—the expansion of opportunities of other people. Corporations provide customers with choices they didn't have before, workers with employment options they didn't have before, residents of ill-governed countries the potential for charting their own destiny, members of despised social groups the possibility of being compensated by what they can contribute rather than by their tribal identity. The modern global corporation provides people all over the world with the opportunity to partake of the vast array of offers that other people all over the world are willing to make. The corporation, in this conception, cannot help but increase freedom and decrease the arbitrary application of power, if these things are properly defined.

Of course, corporations do frequently limit individual choice when they are able to use the government to obtain special privileges that come at the expense of others. Every special tax break or limit on competition that serves a particular corporation or group of corporations deprives other people of options. But this of course derives ultimately from the fact that the state has this power to begin with, not that corporations may use it effectively. And it is this power possessed by government that generates the ACM's (unreflective) notion of power, which reduces to "the ability to outmaneuver us in the political process." But if the ACM got its way, the measures that would result would be a dramatic exercise of power over not an abstract component of a system but flesh-and-blood individuals—by limiting their freedom to transact in the marketplace, to draw up contracts, to be willing to let others make them better offers than the ones they currently possess as consumers, workers, or investors.

The philosophical underpinnings of the rising tide of anti-corporate thinking are worth explicitly teasing out. As we saw, the notion of trust in the individual, a belief in his capability for self-direction and self-ownership, is nowhere to be found. Instead, there is a belief in, first, groups as the fundamental unit of society and, second, in reliance on grand plans to limit and regulate the ways in which flesh-and-blood individuals might otherwise consensually interact with one another. The monolithic "corporate interest" is to be balanced out against the equally monolithic interests of other groups if "the system"—political, ecological, or otherwise—is to function effectively. And if, in the judgment of a sufficiently large number of politicians, the corporate interest is doing too well and the other interests are not doing well enough, then laws must be written to reshuffle the wealth.

That individuals transact with corporations for mutual benefit is impossible for a true anti-corporate believer to accept. Businesses are in this conception not vehicles for individuals to pursue their own interests as free agents but a tool used by a group—corporate elites—to beat all the other groups in society into submission. This group-based thinking is simply flatly inconsistent with a free society. The legal scholar Henry G. Manne has written that fundamentally every corporation starts with an idea and only grows thenceforth (if it survives) one contract at a time. In every step on the ladder from mere idea to multinational colossus, individuals are using the corporation to freely transact with one another. Unless there is some coercive infringement on the possibilities for others—a negative externality—there is no "public" interest at stake:

> But what has happened to implicate public involvement in the management or governance of these enterprises as they grew from a mere idea? Nothing. And if that nothing be multiplied by tens or hundreds or thousands, the product is still zero. So where along the line to enormous size and financial heft has the public-private nexus necessarily changed? True, there are now a large number of complex and specialized private contracts, but every single one of these transactions is based on private property, freedom of contract, and individual risk and reward. If one apple is a fruit, even a billion apples do not become meat.
>
> The origins of this transformation lie in the minds of people who do not like or appreciate the genius of capitalist success stories,

including always politicians, who will generally make any argument in order to control more private wealth. Of course, the social responsibility of corporations is always tied to the proponents' own views of compassion or justice or avoidance of a cataclysm. But the logic of their own arguments requires that essentially private corporations be viewed as somehow "public" in nature. That is, the public, or the preferred part of it, often termed "stakeholders" (another shameful semantic play, this time on the word "shareholders"), has a pseudo-ownership interest in every large corporation. Without that dimension in their argument, free market logic would prevail. [10]

That the "public interest," at least as used by the ACM, has no clear meaning that is logically distinguishable from raw majoritarian force, that grand government plans so often turn out to have unexpected negative consequences for the public (and that politicians and bureaucrats who make such mistakes cannot easily be disciplined by competition in the way a businessman who makes a mistake can), and that these plans entail a gross insult to human progress and freedom makes the rising tide of anti-corporate thought and action cause for concern.

IS ANTI-CORPORATISM A CONSPIRACY THEORY?

Anti-corporate thought, in whatever form, argues that a coherent, sinister force—corporate power—is substantially responsible for the contemporary state of politics in most societies. In anti-corporate literature, corporate power and its use have all the elements of a good mystery story—a well-defined structure, a motive, a series of historical clues as to how the murder of democracy happened and replete with extensive documentation. Its current strength is depicted in a coherent and internally consistent (if not necessarily empirically defensible) narrative. It is a cohesive, meticulously documented story.

But this does not make it a sensible story. In his classic work on conspiracy theories, the historian Richard Hofstadter argued that "[o]ne of the impressive things about the paranoid literature is precisely the elaborate concern with demonstration it almost invariably shows. One should not be misled by the fantastic conclusions that are so characteristic of this political style into imagining that it is not, so to speak, argued out along factual lines."[11] Recall the way the ACM describes the *Santa Clara* case, which is occasionally cited even now by courts as establishing that corporations have the rights that persons do. Several leading lights in the ACM such as Ted Nace and the radio talk host Thom Hartmann have offered an elaborate tale purporting to establish that this principle was decided on, at a minimum, procedurally mistaken grounds, and more likely as a result of subterfuge by the court reporter J.C. Bancroft Davis and the testimony of Congressman Roscoe Conkling, with both persons corrupted by corporate interests. In particular, Davis is said to have inserted a note into the official documentation accompanying the case (the preparation of which was his job) which indicated that Chief Justice Morrison R. Waite told those present when the case was argued that personhood was a settled doctrine, and the Court did not wish to hear argument on it. Supposedly primary in this decision was testimony of Conkling in *San Mateo County v. Southern Pacific Railroad* four years prior. This misstatement, combined with the legally erroneous decision by future Supreme Courts to accept Davis' note as binding law, meant that subsequent jurisprudence would erroneously magnify what had been decided in *Santa Clara* beyond what even the Court had then intended. This mistaken at best, corrupt at worst decision has since become cemented into American law, with disastrous consequences.

This reasoning has all the makings of a good conspiracy theory: hidden, corrupt malefactors, specific, real, plausibly relevant incidents spawning major changes in American society (similar to the original meeting of the Bavarian Illuminati that some conspiracy aficionados assert orchestrated the French Revolution), and sweeping control of society by a monolithic, secret, powerful entity (similar to previous accounts of, e.g., Freemasons or the hierarchy of the Catholic Church). That much of this literature posits an ignorant but good-hearted public that would know the right thing to do were it not so completely led astray by the conspirators (think of the anti-corporate tirades against popular entertainment and thinktank corporate shills) is also a hallmark of classic conspiracy theories. If only the public knew, these theories generally hold, decency would be restored and all would be well.[12] The notion of an Eden spoiled by secret conspirators is widespread both in anti-corporate literature (here, virtuous democracy destroyed by corporate rule) and in grand conspiracy theories more generally.

Anti-corporate language too is revealing. David Korten has described (in, recall, a series of works very popular in higher education and elsewhere) the corporation as "as repressive as any totalitarian state."[13] To anyone with either historical acquaintance or firsthand experience with totalitarianism this is of course ludicrous. While (perhaps sensing the vulnerability it exposes him to) Korten denies that the groups foster an explicit master plan, the usual conspiracist suspects of the Trilateral Commission, the Bilderberg Group, and the Council on Foreign Relations loom surprisingly large in his tale of how corporate rule came to be. His work is replete with references to "Memorandum E-B34" and other "secret memos" and exact meeting dates of government officials.[14] As we saw in Chapter 3, angry references to "pathology," corporate "gangs," and the like are also common. Dissent is "squelched," and new immigrants to America are "branded" with corporate consumption patterns.

Perhaps this is simple rhetorical excess. But perhaps not. This kind of abstract theorizing—society is the way it is because of secret plotting by a small group acting in opposition to the rest of society—is seldom politically productive. That in anti-corporatism the subject of the anger is an abstract entity rather than a group of people per se (even though the entities are of course a human institution employing, earning income for and serving real people) probably extends the kind of damage this kind of thinking can do—it is easier to be angry at a "corporation" than, say, a person who may come from an ethnic group familiar to you from the neighborhood or office. And it is no defense to say, as some anti-corporate campaigners do, that they are not positing a sweeping, Illuminati-like plot but merely describing a historical process. Historically many conspiracy theories have spread without requiring specific dates or plans, merely a pattern of behavior by a group with a common anti-social interest.

To be sure, there are conspiracy theories and then there are conspiracy theories. Anti-corporate conspiracism is not as malicious as older conspiracy theories and is not motivated by the primal tribal urges that have characterized so many instances in which such theories are hurled against various tribal groups (the Ottoman Armenians, the Indian entrepreneurs expelled by Uganda's democidal dictator Idi Amin in the 1970s, etc.). And yet the ease with which anti-corporate activists ignore the idea that politics is a messy compromise among all sides and slide into the belief in one all-powerful faction pulling the strings is troubling. As it continues to develop, anti-corporate thinking will almost certainly not degenerate into violence; the checks and balances of Western society are too robust for that. (Although scattered violence against corporate officials is not unknown, as in the campaigns in the 1970s and 1980s by the Italian Red Brigades and the German Baader-Meinhof gang.) But if it succeeds in getting even a fraction of its agenda enacted, the consequences, particularly for the world's poorest, will be substantial.

SOME PRINCIPLES FOR A (PARTLY) CORPORATE WORLD

It is in the end a corporate world, not in the sense of corporations exercising authority over the rest of us, but of the corporate form helping to power an unprecedented advance in the human condition. And it is a fact that large corporations are a significant social institution with great impact on huge numbers of people around the world, whose influence thus understandably prompts public discussion of the extent to which they should be controlled through the political process. But how? The ideas developed in this book suggest several principles that ought to guide corporate–state interaction.

Decentralize corporate regulation. A key agenda item for the ACM for decades in the United States has been a federal law of incorporation, which does not currently exist. (In the United States, corporations are chartered exclusively by states.) The reason for this is that at the national level the power of a highly motivated minority to defeat a diffuse majority with much more at stake in total but much less per capita is greatest. Factional struggles reward small groups with a lot at stake per factional member. Sugar farmers with huge amounts of money at stake if foreign sugar imports continue to be sharply limited will have much more incentive to lobby, make campaign contributions, and otherwise fight political warfare than sugar consumers (including people who consume products with sugar in them), for whom the damage per person is light but total damage to the group is large.

This is just as true at the state level as the federal, but when corporate chartering is done at the state rather than federal level, mistakes are less costly and successes can be duplicated. If California makes a mistake in amending its laws regarding corporate operations, Texas and New York can observe the consequences and avoid the same mistake. When Congress does so, the mistake is immediately borne by the entire country. Since narrow pressure groups such as anti-corporate activists are more able to politically outmuscle shareholders, product buyers, and other broad groups, laws enacted at the federal level are more likely to be poorly constructed to begin with. The same arguments would apply even more emphatically to any attempt to standardize corporate chartering across national borders (through the World Trade Organization, say). A federal corporate-chartering law would be a gigantic mistake.[15]

Think in terms of individuals, not groups. The single most disturbing weakness of anti-corporate thinking (and for that matter, anti-business thinking generally) is its reduction of citizens to nothing more than group members. In this, it is far from alone. For example, pressure groups organized on ethnoreligious lines (and whose continued vitality depends on the continued public perception of the importance of ethnoreligious conflict or discrimination) may encourage people to define themselves primarily around their ethnic and religious aspects of their identities. (And the principle that laws should be debated and enacted with individuals rather than groups in mind in no way precludes much modern government activity; income transfers motivated by a desire to fight poverty and a recognition of the right of individuals to form collective-bargaining units are examples.) When the citizen begins to interpret politics entirely as "the rich vs. the poor," "labor vs. management" (or, worse, "labor vs. capital"), or "corporations versus the public," politics ceases being about ways to give individuals the means to pursue happiness and becomes an endless redistributive war.

Simplifying the world is essential in both natural and social science. Indeed, science would be impossible if we could not make limiting assumptions about the world to enable us to create hypotheses about it. But in politics group-based abstraction—interpreting your life and society in terms of group conflict—is dangerous, and such abstraction is the heart of the modern anti-corporate movement. Corporations are fundamentally a collection of *individuals.* To the extent that particular constituents of a single corporation have similar interests, we may sometimes plausibly speak of individual corporations using the state to promote their interests. To a much lesser extent, we may sometimes speak of a common "corporate interest." But once some individuals are identified in the law, or in the politics that shapes it, as being defined purely as a member of the "corporate" class, the law has ceased to be about protecting the sanctity and dignity of individuals, which is its primary function. To be sure, this is not a danger unique to anti-corporate thought. But, especially given the importance of individual entrepreneurs in dynamic societies, it is foolish to aggravate the problem by reducing all citizens exclusively to "shareholders," "workers," etc. (let alone to "shareholders" and "everybody else").

When corporations impose negative externalities, they should be controlled. Of course, an individual who is a contracting party to a corporation may still commit breaches of the law in its name, and like anyone else he and his corporation should be held accountable for them. Corporations are treated as a single legal entity for contracting and other purposes and can and should be held accountable for such breaches, without accepting the larger anti-corporate argument that the primary fulcrum of politics is between corporations on one side and the rest of us on the other. When someone under corporate authority engages in an act that harms an external party without that party's consent—for which pollution is overwhelmingly the most common example—then that corporation should clearly be held responsible for the full social consequences of that decision. Whether the better penalty is individual liability (civil or criminal) for the decision-maker or collective liability for the firm is a somewhat arcane question for the economic theorists to sort out. But nothing in this work suggests that anyone operating under corporate authority should be capable of escaping the consequences of such actions. And any political discussion that has reached the point at which someone makes a "corporations impose negative externalities, and should pay" argument would benefit from a (lengthy) list of the immense *positive* effects, many of them external, of free commerce that were outlined in Chapter 4.

Equality before the law. This principle, outlined in Chapter 5, is one of the most important yet misunderstood in all of political thought. It requires, in the words of Steven E. Landsburg, that "people in analogous situations should be treated analogously."[16] This is a simple principle that almost anyone would agree with in the abstract, but which most discard when they enter the political arena. Currently, most taxation and much government spending is based on inequality before the law—the use of the government's taxation and spending authority to treat different kinds of citizens differently because of choices they have made that are irrelevant to their duties as citizens. To take a recent example, former French President Jacques Chirac persuaded the French legislature to impose a tax on airline tickets to fund efforts against various illnesses such as AIDS and tuberculosis that currently wreak a heavy toll on developing countries, an idea that is now spreading to other countries. Everyone agrees that these illnesses are one of the world's most serious problems; the objections to the proposal were primarily that it would replace other foreign aid and that the aid would focus too much on providing more medicine and divert resources from providing more health-care workers or funding preventive measures.[17] But no one asked a basic philosophical question: serious though the problem is, why should air travelers be the ones primarily responsible for addressing it? If this is a proper function for government, why not spread the burdens equally among the citizenry?

The obvious answer, although one seldom confessed to, is "because that's where the money is." An equally cynical but true answer is that the tax is significantly invisible to the purchasers of air tickets. But this is an appalling moral basis for a tax; good government is based on justice (however defined), not opportunism. Whether it maximizes government revenue is not the proper starting point in evaluating a tax system. Rather, a society must first independently decide how much government spending is needed, and then to impose taxes needed to find that expenditure. Any tax chosen should treat citizens as uniformly as possible. And spending that benefits only a few citizens while imposing burdens on the rest of them is equally objectionable. Spending benefiting particular groups because they have the most political influence serves only to further turn the government into an instrument of redistributive warfare and to inculcate cynicism about the government.

In the debate over corporations and society, equality before the law means that the ACM is right to harshly criticize "corporate welfare," but criticizes it for the wrong reasons and fails to extend the logic of equal treatment. Corporate special privileges are objectionable not because they are corporate, but because they are special. True equality requires first that *no corporation be treated differently from any other.* Massive subsidies for ethanol production or domestic oil drilling or to auto companies looking for a location for their latest factory are wrong because they are special privileges provided only to specific types of citizen associations. Many Congressmen have become experts in writing benefits not even for an entire industry but a specific company into the fine print of appropriations bills. The standard argument in favor of such subsidies is that they promote some positive effect beyond the mere market value of the output—a positive externality.[18]

But the actual subsidies we get out of the political process bear no resemblance to those an economist might draw on his chalkboard; they are crafted substantially to reward political supporters and punish political opponents rather than theoretical need, and the arguments used to justify the alleged externalities often border on the preposterous.[19] The argument for subsidies to particular corporations or types of corporations on the grounds of broader benefits to society has been used to the point of uselessness and should be ignored. Indeed, at least some corporate political activism (and special-interest political activism generally) is simply self-defense, employed because the government has already arrogated the privilege of using its unique powers to impose special privileges (which harm the competitors of the group to whom the privilege has been awarded). If labor unions lobby in favor of, say, guaranteed representation for them on boards of directors, then business in self-defense will unavoidably lobby the other way. So too will some businesses lobby against special tax breaks or other privileges given to others. A government that prioritizes ending the habit of handing out special privileges and burdens to begin with will be one where corporate (or anti-corporate) welfare is not a concern.

But an even more profound implication of taking equality before the law seriously is that for-profit and nonprofit corporations should also be treated equally, that *corporations formed for profit receive the same rights as corporations formed for other reasons.* For-profit corporations obviously exist to make money for shareholders, and nonprofit corporations at least nominally exist for other purposes. Each organization is fundamentally the same—it is formed to advance the interests of the members who control it. But of course only for-profit corporations are taxed. It is questionable whether any organization should be taxed directly, rather than taxing the income derived by its members, because of the double-taxation problem discussed in Chapter 5. But even granting this, a corporation designed to advance, say, anti-corporate legislation ought to be as subject to taxation as one formed to make money for shareholders. If the anti-corporate corporation gets its way, its members will see their interests furthered, just as surely as shareholders in a for-profit corporation do when a corporation makes money. (Recall that like many nonprofit—which is not to say nonspecial interest—groups, anti-corporate groups incorporate.) The only difference is in the way interests are defined. The for-profit corporation is formed to make money for its shareholders, and the nonprofit anti-corporate corporation is formed to reduce other people's ability to make money. There is no argument in favor of taxing only for-profit corporations that does not reduce to "because that's where the money is," which as we have already seen is a morally dubious proposition. The most obvious way to slice through this difficulty is simply not to tax any organizations at all, only individuals. This also has the nice property of eliminating double taxation of corporate income.

For-profit corporations are social creations like any other. As Milton Friedman argued many years ago, they do not have any extraneous "social responsibility" other than the most basic one, to maximize shareholder value subject to basic morality and legal constraints necessitated by the threat of negative externalities.[20] If any other group of citizens wants to advance their interests by restricting the freedom of corporate shareholders and managers to behave in a particular way, the proper way to do this (such externalities aside) is to rely on negotiation outside of politics (including, certainly, such hardball tactics as boycotts) and not legislation. It is no more proper for anti-corporate campaigners to use the law to force (under threat of punishment) people who contract with a for-profit corporation to pursue the campaigners' purpose (by paying higher wages or foregoing political donations or not producing overseas, for example) than it is for corporate shareholders to use the law to force anti-corporate campaigners to work on behalf of the corporation's profits. In either case, the law is being used to put one set of people to work for someone else's interest rather than their own. In either case, that is generally an inappropriate function of the law.

Corporate officials are no less moral than anyone else. Perhaps the biggest mistake of anti-corporate thinkers is to imagine corporations as sharing no important common features, and many critical differences, with every other form of social organization and to think of the people who run them as somehow different from the rest of humanity when behaving as moral agents. This is simply nonsense. Corporate shareholders and executives are like politicians, farmers, doctors, lawyers, and like those who make up the ACM itself—sinners all, but disciplined by the same moral code as anyone else. Spinning wild stories about how corporate officials must as a matter of law abandon all scruples to maximize shareholder value simply will not do. The more it is assumed that corporate decision-makers are uniquely prone to venality and malevolence, the easier it will be to mobilize politics against them. Any contemplation of the corporate role in society should begin by assuming that such decision-makers are as moral—no more, no less—as those criticizing them.

The "corporate social responsibility" campaigners Stephen Fenichell and Jeffrey Hollender have claimed that the public will increasingly demand that corporations do many things beyond providing high-quality, low-cost products—pay responsible wages, show good environmental stewardship, etc. In this view, the public will demand this not so much through laws but through such nonlegislative options as boycotts, shareholder activism, negative publicity, and so on. Maybe so, and something they have every right to do. But that option is possible only in a society that upholds the freedom to contract, including the freedom not to contract with someone making demands that cut against your interests. Once corporate governance becomes primarily a struggle over what the law should permit and require corporations to do for every interest group in the country, the ability for people to pursue their interests by associating with those who will advance them and refusing to associate with those who will not shrinks, and the power to conscript others into pursuing your interest rather than their own correspondingly grows. Anti-corporate campaigners, in other words, have a powerful arsenal in a free society that shareholders and customers (and, ultimately, everyone) will lack in a society governed by the principles of the ACM. Appealing to the moral sensibilities of corporate decision-makers, who are fundamentally as moral as their ideological opponents, is a major weapon in this arsenal. This is how free societies work.

CONCLUSION

For all its contributions to human progress, liberal democracy is not without its frustrations. The essence of idealized representative democracy is that the citizen goes out into the marketplace of ideas and collects the information he needs to decide what is best. He and his fellow citizens are then explicitly asked for their views in the form of an election. Collectively, the public knows what is best for it, and so elections are the key to sound governmental decision-making and, as a result, social progress. But for most citizens their voice will be an infinitesimally small one, even if they are extremely active politically. Each person's vote is one among millions, and it will be weighted the same as those of voters who have drawn opposite conclusions, whether or not they have read the same books or attended the same rallies as that person, or even read anything at all. Naturally, each citizen is convinced that his view of things is the right one, the more so when he tends only to congregate with others of like mind.

When the political world makes decisions that a public-spirited voter with out-of-the-mainstream views does not like, he tends to fault "the system" or the ignorance or manipulation of his fellow citizens. Sometimes, such gaps between the beliefs of a small but committed movement and those of the larger society generate some of the greatest moments in American history—for example, the civil-rights revolution, which took decades of groundwork before its seemingly sudden triumph in the 1960s. But sometimes, when the larger society is not initially receptive to the pleas of the ideological minority, the possibility that the government has been captured by mysterious, malevolent, powerful forces is more comforting than the possibility that your view of what constitutes good public policy is not shared by many of your fellow citizens. Such a view is even more tempting when you do not share (or actually have contempt for) mainstream bourgeois tastes in housing, food, culture and entertainment, etc.

That liberal democracy is the secular religion of the United States, taught in schools as the way of enshrining the highest moral good that is the public will, makes being out of step all the more discomforting. To believe in overwhelming corporate power, and to see that many of your citizens do not seem concerned about it when "democracy" is taught as the highest principle of politics (often at the expense of other equally important founding principles such as checks and balances as a way of preserving individual liberty), makes those holding views away from the mainstream all the more frustrated. The only way of reconciling your own normality with the objective rejection of your own worldview is then to engage in an elaborate self-deception whereby the government in fact does not currently reflect the public will. If the world around you is the result of a secret plan rather than a citizenry that does not share your values, you may both be more secure in those views and be more confident that things will change. Hard-line anti-corporatism—the anti-corporatism that runs so deeply among the movement's most committed thinkers—is, like all the conspiracy theories that the United States produces in such abundance, perhaps best seen in this light.

Left to itself, this way of seeing the world would be harmless. But if true believers are committed enough and persuasive enough, it has the potential to do tremendous damage. A combination of a persuasive story and a receptive audience is the key to achieving political change. And while we are not there yet, particularly in the countries most benefiting from the corporate, global and technological revolution, we might easily arrive at such a moment in some parts of the world if we are not careful. The global economic transformation that is so dramatically expanding what is possible for so many is nonetheless costly for those who are currently competitively disadvantaged, often through no fault of their own. Anti-business sentiment often runs highest in a society when it is undergoing a macroeconomic crisis or period of painful adjustment. That there is so much of that about in the world these days means that run-of-the-mill populism, so common throughout history since the dawn of the industrial era, may, as it were, profitably synergize with the new anti-corporate thought. If so, the damage to the world's weakest, standing on the threshold of an unprecedented independence from *real* power—the power of arbitrary bureaucracy or dream-destroying social custom—that prosperity brings, and to the human future more generally, may be great. Anti-corporatism will crest one day, and the primary mission of those concerned about the human future is to work to make that day come soon.

Notes

CHAPTER 1. THE CONCEPT OF THE CORPORATE REGIME

1. Christian de Brie, "Transatlantic Wheeling and Dealing: Watch Out for MAI Mark Two," *Le Monde Diplomatique,* May 1999, http://mondediplo.com/1999/05/13mai.

2. The references to Manchurian Global's activities are from a Web site, since discontinued, actually created by the movie producers to imitate that of a real multinational corporation (http://www.manchurianglobal.com). When it was still active it contained no signs of simply being a promotional adjunct of the film.

3. In the movies, another recent example is 2005's *The Constant Gardener,* which depicts big pharmaceutical companies in league with Western governments to engage in experimentation on unwitting Africans. The director, Fernando Meirelles, has called such firms "perfect bad guys." From literature there is the novel *Jennifer Government* by Max Barry (New York: Vintage, 2003), in which corporations have taken over almost all the functions once performed by the state. Some of the work of the acclaimed novelist Thomas Pynchon depicts corporate power as almost Orwellian totalitarianism, and even something as globally mainstream as the Star Wars movie series depicts corporations as scheming, subversive monopolists. Artistic conceptions of the corporation are discussed in further detail in Chapter 3.

4. United Nations, Economic and Social Council, Commission on Human Rights, Sub-Commission on the Promotion and Protection of Human Rights, "Transnational Corporations and Human Rights," Document E/CN.4/Sub.2/2002/NGO/10, July 19, 2002. The document is not a publication of the commission itself but a submitted statement by numerous nongovernmental organizations, including such fairly mainstream ones as the Danielle Mitterand Foundation and the 26 million-member World Confederation of Labor.

5. Library of Congress, letter by Thomas Jefferson to William H. Crawford, June 20, 1816, available via http://memory.loc.gov/ammem/mtjhtml/mtjhome. html.

6. Lee Drutman, "The History of the Corporation," March 25, 2003, http:// www.citizenworks.org/corp/dg/s2r1.pdf.

7. If "power" means the ability to influence the government, which *does* have the power to do those things, this is certainly a hypothesis worth exploring, as it will be in Chapter 5.

8. Lee Drutman, "America the Fat," *Alternet*, December 18, 2001, http:// www.alternet.org/story/12110. See also Joel Bakan, *The Corporation: The Pathological Pursuit of Profit and Power* (New York: Free Press, 2004), 123–24.

9. Donnie Dugger, "How They Could Steal the Election This Time," *Nation*, August 16–23, 2004, 11–24. Paul Krugman, "Fear of Fraud," *New York Times*, July 27, 2004.

10. Stephen Kinzer, *Overthrow: America's History of Regime Change from Hawaii to Iraq* (New York: Times Books, 2006).

11. Neil Clark, "The Spoils of Another War," *Guardian*, September 21, 2004.

12. William Hartung and Michelle Ciarocca, "The Military-Industrial-Think Tank Complex: Corporate Think Tanks and the Doctrine of Aggressive Militarism," *Multinational Monitor* 24, no. 1–2 (January/February 2003), http:// multinationalmonitor.org/mm2003/03jan-feb/jan-feb03corp2.html.

13. John Kenneth Galbraith, "A Cloud Over Civilisation," *Guardian*, July 15, 2004.

14. The remarkably elastic nature of the Unocal/Taliban story is laid out in Seth Stevenson, "Pipe Dreams: The Origin of the 'Bombing Afghanistan for Oil Pipelines' Theory," *Slate*, December 6, 2001, http://www.slate.com/id/205 9487.

15. The Pew Research Center for the People and the Press, "Public Sours on Government and Business; DeLay, Rove Viewed Unfavorably," press release, October 25, 2005. The Pew Research Center for the People and the Press, *The 2004 Political Landscape: Evenly Divided and Increasingly Polarized* (Washington: The Pew Research Center for the People and the Press, 2003), 59–65.

16. Adolph Reed Jr., "Ebony and Ivory Fascists," *Progressive* 60, no. 4 (April 1996): 20–22.

17. Kathryn Shattuck, "Artists Display Confessions of Passers-by on a 44th Street Storefront," *New York Times*, May 6, 2006.

18. Virginia Postrel, *The Future and its Enemies: The Growing Conflict Over Creativity, Enterprise and Progress* (New York: Touchstone, 1999), 204. To Postrel, a stasist is someone who is uncomfortable with social and economic change, and is willing to use the government to prevent it. A dynamist, on the other hand, is someone who is willing to let individuals experiment with social and economic change without hindrance by the government.

CHAPTER 2. A BRIEF HISTORY OF THE CORPORATION

1. The historical facts in this chapter, unless otherwise noted, comes from three sources: John Micklethwait and Adrian Wooldridge, *The Company: A Short History of a Revolutionary Idea* (New York: Modern Library, 2003); William J. Bernstein,

The Birth of Plenty: How the Prosperity of the Modern World Was Created (New York: McGraw-Hill, 2004); David A. Moss, *When All Else Fails: Government as the Ultimate Risk Manager* (Cambridge, MA: Harvard University Press, 2004), especially chap. 2.

2. Much of the information in this paragraph is from the Library of Congress, Country Study—India, 1995, http://lcweb2.loc.gov/frd/cs/intoc.html.

3. Micklethwait and Wooldridge, *Company*, 32.

4. The Camden and Amboy railroad, for example, was chartered by New Jersey in 1830 and given a monopoly of the northeast–southwest rail traffic connecting New York City and Philadelphia by running through that state, in exchange for a large donation of stock to the state government. And the Martin Van Buren political machine in New York State handed out bank charters exclusively to political allies.

5. The term was invented in Anne Krueger, "The Political Economy of the Rent-Seeking Society," *American Economic Review* 64, no. 3 (June 1974): 291–303.

6. Simeon Djankov and others, "The Regulation of Entry," *Quarterly Journal of Economics* 117, no. 1 (February 2002): 1–37.

7. See, for example, Kevin Danaher and Jason Mark, *Insurrection: Citizen Challenges to Corporate Power* (New York: Routledge, 2003), 26.

8. Moss, *When All Else Fails*, 56.

9. Among other places in the anti-corporate literature, the Boston Tea Party is depicted as an anti-corporate episode in David Korten, *When Corporations Rule the World* (San Francisco: Berrett-Koehler Publishers, 2001), 307 and Ted Nace, *Gangs of America: The Rise of Corporate Power and the Disabling of Democracy* (San Francisco: Berrett-Koehler Publishers, 2003).

10. *Trustees of Dartmouth College v. Woodward*, 17 U.S. 518 (1819).

11. Ibid., 647.

12. Djankov and others, "Regulation of Entry."

13. For an example of this sort of naïve thinking in an academic-journal setting, see Charlie Cray and Lee Drutman, "Corporations and the Public Purpose," *Seattle Journal of Social Justice* 4, no. 1 (Fall/Winter 2005). For an example from the general literature see many of the works cited in much of the new anti-corporate work cited in Chapter 3.

14. *Santa Clara County v. Southern Pacific Railroad Co.*, 118 U.S. 394 (1886).

15. Cited in Micklethwait and Wooldridge, *Company*, 4.

16. William J. Carney, "The Political Economy of Competition for Corporate Charters," *Journal of Legal Studies* 26, no. 1 (1997): 303–29.

17. In *Gangs of America*, for example, Ted Nace attributes the rise of general incorporation primarily to the machinations of a few powerful railroad barons such as Tom Scott of the Pennsylvania Railroad, who worked behind the scenes in the 1860s and 1870s for legal changes that would make it considerably easier to do business in one state while incorporating in another. In attaching so much importance to one individual he neglects the entire loosening of special-privilege law that had occurred in prior decades. The broader notion of a race to the bottom caused by globalization is a common indictment of that phenomenon, and will be explored further in Chapter 6.

18. Tobias J. Moskowitz, "The Political Economy of Financial Regulation: Evidence from U.S. State Usury Laws in the 18th and 19th Century" Working paper W12851 (National Bureau of Economic Research, January 2007). He finds in particular that resistance to open-access incorporation coincides with the continued presence of anti-usury laws (which protect entrenched domestic firms against competition from new lenders willing to back higher-risk projects) and the absence of free banking laws (i.e., the protection of in-state banks from competition against banks from out of state, who also were less subject to rent-seeking demands by in-state politicians).

19. John Joseph Wallis, "Constitutions, Corporations, and Corruption: American States and Constitutional Change, 1842 to 1852," *Journal of Economic History* 65, no. 1 (March 2005): 211–56.

20. Micklethwait and Wooldridge emphasize the importance of the British adoption of the open-access process, because of Britain's importance as the first and, then, mightiest industrial power. But the importance of American jurisdictional competition in the development of open-access incorporation should not be underestimated. The controversy is not of critical importance here, in that most laws ended at roughly the same place— open-access incorporation without discrimination by the state. Micklethwait and Wooldridge, *Company*.

21. Robert W. Hillman, "Limited Liability in Historical Perspective," *Washington and Lee Law Review* 54, no. 2 (Spring 1997): 615–27.

22. Cited in Paul Halpern, Michael Trebilcock, and Stuart Turnbull, "An Economic Analysis of Limited Liability in Corporation Law," *University of Toronto Law Journal* 30, no. 2 (Spring 1980): 117–50, 117.

23. Atsushi Tokuda, "The Origin of the Corporation in Meiji Japan," Discussion Paper DP 21 (University of London Center for Financial and Management Studies), http://www.cefims.ac.uk/documents/research-9.pdf.

24. Naomi R. Lamoreaux and Jean-Laurent Rosenthal, "Legal Regime and Contractual Flexibility: A Comparison of Business's Organizational Choices in France and the United States During the Era of Industrialization," *American Law and Economics Review* 7, no. 1 (Spring 2005): 28–61.

25. The cultural historian Jacques Barzun credits the railroads with introducing standardized time—the idea that clocks should display precisely the same time throughout an entire region. Previously the local time could differ significantly from one location to the next. Jacques Barzun, *From Dawn to Decadence: 500 Years of Western Cultural Life* (New York: HarperCollins, 2000), 544.

26. Adolf A. Berle and Gardiner C. Means, *The Modern Corporation and Private Property* (New Brunswick, NJ: Transaction Publishers, 1991), 30–32.

27. One author argues that the managerial class was not new, and that its progenitor could be found in medieval monasteries, which were often run much like modern sophisticated corporations. Rodney Stark, *The Victory of Reason: How Christianity Led to Freedom, Capitalism, and Western Success* (New York: Random House, 2005), 57–61.

28. For a sketch of the influence of German (and British and French) corporate law on other societies, see Rafael La Porta and others, "Law and Finance," *Journal of Political Economy* 106, no. 6 (December 1998): 1113–55.

CHAPTER 3. A BRIEF HISTORY OF THE ANTI-CORPORATE MOVEMENT

1. Michael L. Budde and Robert L. Brimlow, *Christianity Incorporated: How Business Is Buying the Church* (Grand Rapids, MI: Brazos Press, 2002).

2. Library of Congress, http://memory.loc.gov/cgi-bin/query/r?ammem/ mtj:@field(DOCID+@lit(tj010010)).

3. Adam Smith, *An Inquiry into the Nature and Causes of the Wealth of Nations* (Chicago: University of Chicago Press, 1976), 264–65.

4. Karl Marx and Friedrich Engels, *Manifesto of the Communist Party* (Rendelsham: The Merlin Press, 1998), 3.

5. The latter argument can be found in Mancur Olson, *The Rise and Decline of Nations: Economic Growth, Stagflation, and Social Rigidities* (New Haven: Yale University Press, 1982).

6. His legacy in scholarship outside of social science is also (sometimes inexplicably) profound, having transformed literary criticism, anthropology and other fields far removed from political economy.

7. The process involved the selling of bonds that could be converted into stock to allies of Drew and his cohort Jay Gould. John C. Coffee Jr., "The Rise of Dispersed Ownership: The Roles of Law and the State in the Separation of Ownership and Control," *Yale Law Journal* 111, no. 1 (October 2001): 1–82.

8. Ibid., 27.

9. The full entry reads "Mayor Hewitt, of New York, is complimented by the newspapers for brave words spoken on the labor question. They are all in criticism of the Labor men. Some obvious blunders of the leaders and mistakes in methods are easily pointed out. But there is no bravery in it, and I suspect not much wisdom. The real difficulty is with the vast wealth and power in the hands of the few and the unscrupulous who represent or control capital. Hundreds of laws of Congress and the state legislatures are in the interest of these men and against the interests of the workingmen. These need to be exposed and repealed. All laws on corporations, on taxation, on trusts, wills, descent, and the like, need examination and extensive change. This is a government of the people, by the people, and for the people no longer. It is a government of corporations, by corporations, and for corporations.—how is this?" The diary itself is unpublished, but the entry is from March 11, 1888, according to a conversation on June 7, 2006, with Merv Hall of the Rutherford B. Hayes Presidential Center.

10. Charles Francis Adams and Henry Adams, *Chapters of Erie, and Other Essays* (Boston: J.R. Osgood, 1871); Richard T. Ely, "Social Sciences I—the Nature and Significance of Corporations," *Harper's* 74, no. 444 (May 1887): 970–77; Ely, "Social Sciences II—the Growth of Corporations," *Harper's* 74, no. 445 (June 1887): 71–79; Ely, "Social Sciences III—the Future of Corporations," *Harper's* 74, no. 446 (July 1887): 259–66.

11. In one of his columns during this period ultimately compiled in *The Devil's Dictionary* (New York: World, 1911), Ambrose Bierce defined the corporation as "an ingenious device for obtaining individual profit without individual responsibility."

12. George Stigler, "The Theory of Economic Regulation," *Bell Journal of Economics and Management Science* 2, no. 1 (Spring 1971): 3–21.

13. Woodrow Wilson, *The New Freedom: A Call for the Emancipation of the Generous Energies of a People* (New York: Doubleday, Page & Co., 1913), 20.

14. Herbert David Croly, *The Promise of American Life* (Boston: Northeastern University Press, 1989).

15. Thorstein Veblen, *Absentee Ownership and Business Enterprise in Recent Times: The Case of America* (New Brunswick, NJ: Rutgers University Press, 1997).

16. A view that is, while probably held by a majority, strenuously disputed. One alternative suggests that the Depression was a natural reaction to the introduction of radical new technologies whose ultimate best uses had to be sorted out by the market. Eugene N. White. "Are There Any Lessons from History?" in *Crashes and Panics: The Lessons from History,* ed. Eugene N. White (Homewood, IL: Dow Jones-Irwin, 1990), 235–40. Another holds that the Depression was a fairly conventional crash that became what it was only because of miserable economic policy by both the Hoover and Franklin Roosevelt administrations. Different versions of this view can be found in Milton Friedman and Anna Jacobson Schwartz, *Monetary History of the United States: 1867–1960* (Princeton, NJ: Princeton University Press, 1963) and in Murray Rothbard, *America's Great Depression* (Auburn, AL: Mises Institute, 2000).

17. Adolph A. Berle and Gardiner C. Means, *The Modern Corporation and Private Property* (New York: Macmillan, 1932).

18. The Pure Food and Drug Act, which authorized federal regulation of food and drug safety, was enacted in 1906. The Food and Drug Administration was established (under a different name) in 1927.

19. Most recently reissued as Peter F. Drucker, *The Concept of the Corporation* (New Brunswick, NJ: Transaction Publishers, 1993).

20. Drucker, *The Concept of the Corporation* (New York: New American Library, 1946), 26.

21. Galbraith wrote that "[t]here is no more pleasant fiction than that technical change is the product of the matchless ingenuity of the small man forced by competition to employ his wits to better his neighbor. Unhappily, it is a fiction. Technical development has long since become the preserve of the scientist and the engineer. Most of the cheap and simple inventions have, to put it bluntly and unpersuasively, been made. Not only is development now sophisticated and costly but it must be on a sufficient scale so that successes and failures will in some measure average out." John Kenneth Galbraith, *American Capitalism: The Concept of Countervailing Power* (New York: Houghton-Mifflin, 1956), 86. While the statement describes some activities reasonably well (this is in fact an argument frequently offered for protecting patents or even extending their lengths for pharmaceuticals), it brushes aside the possibility that the "small man"—Steven Jobs or the college students who created Google or Yahoo—may completely remake the existing way of doing things.

22. John Kenneth Galbraith, *The New Industrial State* (New York: Houghton-Mifflin, 1971).

23. Galbraith, *American Capitalism.*

24. Such research is different from basic scientific research. Galbraith is referring to knowledge about how to improve sophisticated manufactured goods rather, than, say discoveries about bosons.

25. Occasionally what exactly qualified as "countervailing power" became counterintuitive. Homebuilders tended to be relatively small firms, but faced powerful building-trades unions. It was the latter who possessed the "original power," and hence the blanket exemption of unions from the antitrust laws was in Galbraith's view a mistake.

26. Galbraith, *The New Industrial State*, 321.

27. Institutional economics still lives on in vestigial form. Interested readers may consult its primary journal, *Journal of Economic Issues*. Infuriatingly for its few remaining adherents, the term itself has been appropriated. "Institutional economists" are now not those who use institutions to explain preferences and constraints but preferences and constraints to explain institutions, exploring such questions as why societies do or do not develop property-rights protection.

28. John Kenneth Galbraith, *The Affluent Society* (New York: Houghton-Mifflin, 1956).

29. Ralph Nader, *Unsafe at Any Speed: The Designed-In Dangers of the American Automobile* (New York: Grossman, 1965).

30. Micklethwait and Wooldridge indicate that Bismarck forced employers to begin contributing to pensions for workers in the 1850s, and instituted co-determination in 1891. Micklethwait and Wooldridge, *Company.*

31. Masaru Yoshimori, "Whose Company Is It? The Concept of the Corporation in Japan and the West," *Long Range Planning* 28, no. 6 (December 1995): 33–44.

32. E. Merrick Dodd, "For Whom Are Corporate Managers Trustees?" *Harvard Law Review* 45, no. 7 (May 1932): 1145–63.

33. Cited in Robert Reich, "Broken Faith: Why We Need to Renew the Social Compact," *Nation*, February 16, 1998, 11. The stakeholder model eventually found its way into government, at least to the extent of Reich's brief term as Secretary of Labor during the first term of President Bill Clinton.

34. The plural "corporations" is used to attempt to filter out stories about a single firm. So this may understate the total.

35. Peter Drucker, *The New Realities: In Government and Politics, in Economics and Business, in Society and World View* (New York: Harper & Row, 1989); Thomas Friedman, *The World Is Flat: A Brief History of the Twenty-first Century* (New York: Farrar, Straus and Giroux, 2005); Kenichi Ohmae, *The Borderless World: Power and Strategy in an Interlinked Economy*, 2nd ed. (New York: HarperBusiness, 1999).

36. Marjorie Kelly, *The Divine Right of Capital: Dethroning the Corporate Aristocracy* (San Francisco: Berrett-Koehler Publishers, 2001); Danaher and Mark, *Insurrection*; Naomi Klein, *No Logo* (New York: Picador, 2000). Klein, it should be noted, is a Canadian rather than an American rabble-rouser.

37. Ted Nace, *Gangs of America*; Charles Derber, *Regime Change Begins at Home: Freeing America from Corporate Rule* (San Francisco: Barrett-Koehler, 2004); Bakan, *Corporation*. Clint Willis, ed., *The I Hate Corporate America Reader: How Big Companies from McDonald's to Microsoft Are Destroying Our Way of Life* (New York: Thunder's Mouth Press, 2005). Despite its intemperate title, Bakan's book cheerfully acknowledges it never would have been possible without the corporations that made his computer, published the book, etc.

38. Bakan's and Klein's books were published under the imprints of major firms.

39. See, for example, Madeline Bunting, "Fall of the Arrogant," *Guardian*, January 28, 2002.

40. The Duke of Wellington, who later in life after his defeat of Napoleon at Waterloo was a Tory prime minister, is said to have objected to the introduction of the railroads, a dramatic technological revolution in its time, on the grounds that it would "cause the lower classes to move about needlessly."

41. The American edition of the book was Fred A. McKenzie, *The American Invaders: Their Plans, Tactics, and Progress* (New York: Street & Smith, 1902).

CHAPTER 4. CORPORATE ECONOMICS

1. Frank H. Easterbrook and Daniel R. Fischel, *The Economic Structure of Corporate Law* (Cambridge, MA: Harvard University Press, 1991).

2. Amy E. Knaup, "Survival and Longevity in the Business and Employment Dynamics Data," *Monthly Labor Review* 128, no. 5 (May 2005): 50–56.

3. These were the large drug corporations responsible for creating human insulin, an improvement over the insulin made from cows and pigs, and later human insulin whose release in the body after injection more closely approximates the pattern in a nondiabetic. Both innovations significantly enhanced the ability of diabetics to forestall the disease's potentially catastrophic consequences.

4. On Scotland, see Robin Mackie, "Family Ownership and Business Survival: Kirkcakly, 1870–1970," *Business History* 43, no. 3 (July 2000): 1–32. On England, John F. Wilson and Andrew Popp, ed., *Industrial Clusters and Regional Business Networks in England, 1750–1970* (Burlington, VT: Ashgate, 2003); Herbert Shannon, "The Coming of Limited Liability," *Economic History* 2, no. 6 (January 1931): 267–91. On the United States, David Blumberg, "Limited Liability and Corporate Groups," *Journal of Corporation Law* 11, no. 4 (Summer 1986): 573–631. On Germany, Michael Horvath and Michael Woywode, "Entrepreneurs and the Choice of Limited Liability," *Journal of Institutional and Theoretical Economics* 161, no. 4 (December 2005): 1–27.

5. Even customers can be thought of as "investing" in the firm to the extent they rely on its performance. A restaurant owner is investing in a food supplier to the extent that he relies on it and not other suppliers, and a consumer invests in this sense in a computer platform to the extent he relies on it, and not alternative platforms, to do useful work.

6. The anti-corporate campaigner might object that mere money cannot compensate for a tort of the magnitude of the Bhopal tragedy or the Exxon Valdez oil spill. Recalling that corporate managers are already criminally liable, that is no objection at all, because money is simply the measure of legally assessed damage. It is no more reasonable to assert that money cannot compensate for a mass tort than that inches cannot be used to measure an object that is too tall. Indeed, for noncorporate defendants money is the only measure the legal system has for even the most severe torts—for example, medical malpractice resulting in a fatality. Corporate defendants are no different in this respect.

7. Elected judges have been found to be more likely to favor in-state defendants against out-of-state plaintiffs, and to make larger awards, than appointed ones. This suggests, clearly, a motivation grounded in political concerns rather than legal principles. Alexander Tabarrok and Eric Helland, "Court Politics:

The Political Economy of Tort Awards," pt. 1, *Journal of Law and Economics* 42, no. 1 (April 1999): 157–88.

8. Cindy R. Alexander and Mark A. Cohen, "New Evidence on the Origins of Corporate Crime," *Managerial and Decision Economics* 17, no. 4 (July–August 1996): 421–35; Cindy R. Alexander and Mark A. Cohen, "Why do Corporations Become Criminals? Ownership, Hidden Actions, and Crime as an Agency Cost," *Journal of Corporate Finance* 5, no. 1 (March 1999): 1–34.

9. Nuno Garoupa, "Corporate Criminal Law and Organization Incentives: A Managerial Perspective," *Managerial and Decision Economics* 21, no. 6 (September 2000): 243–52.

10. John Hicks, "Limited Liability: The Pros and Cons," in *Limited Liability and the Corporation,* ed. Tony Orhnial (London: Croom Helm, 1982), 11–21, 12.

11. "Governor's Speech," June 2, 1825, in *Resolves of the General Court of the Commonwealth of Massachusetts,* May 25–June 18, 1825, 192–94. Cited in Moss, *When All Else Fails,* 64.

12. The Zogby survey is cited in Richard Nadler, "Portfolio Politics: Nudging the Investor Class Forward," *National Review,* December 4, 2000, 38–40.

13. This argument is offered, with empirical evidence to support it, in Jack L. Carr and G. Frank Mathewson, "Unlimited Liability as a Barrier to Entry," *Journal of Political Economy* 96, no. 4 (August 1988): 766–84.

14. Coffee Jr., "The Rise of Dispersed Ownership," 1–82.

15. For evidence on the value of a Morgan man on the board of directors, see J. Bradford De Long, "Did Morgan's Men Add Value? An Economist's Perspective on Financial Capitalism," in *Reputation: Studies in the Voluntary Elicitation of Good Conduct,* ed. Daniel B. Klein (Ann Arbor: University of Michigan Press, 1997), 191–223. The argument on the unexpected consequences of populist anti-corporate measures is in Mark J. Roe, *Strong Managers, Weak Owners: The Political Roots of American Corporate Finance* (Princeton, NJ: Princeton University Press, 1994).

16. As I write this, the law firm Milberg Weiss Bershad & Schulman is under indictment, along with two of its partners, for recruiting plaintiffs by paying them. At least one article paraphrases the New York University law professor Burt Neuborne as asserting that "it [is] common practice for law firms to pay lead plaintiffs in class actions for their time and trouble, but such payments should be disclosed." David Cay Johnston, "Judge's Wide Disclosure Order Could Tie Up Litigation Firm," *New York Times,* July 21, 2006.

17. Angus Maddison, *The World Economy: A Millennial Perspective* (Paris: OECD Development Center, 2001).

18. The economist Thomas Sowell notes that earthquakes of almost equal size and less than a week apart killed many thousands in Iran and fewer than ten people in California. The difference was not that Iran didn't have strict building codes (it did), but that the poverty of Iranians made the law meaningless—the price of any housing many residents could afford to buy was too low to pay for seismic safety. Thomas Sowell, "Two Earthquakes," Townhall.com, December 30, 2003, http://www.townhall.com/columnists/ThomasSowell/2003/12/30/two_earthquakes.

19. Robert W. Fogel, "Changes in the Process of Aging During the Twentieth Century," Lecture (Department of Labor Economics—School of Industrial and

Labor Relations, Cornell University, October 18, 2004), http://www.ilr.cornell.edu/FogelVisit2004/Lecture.pdf.

20. Robert W. Fogel, *The Escape from Hunger and Premature Death, 1700–2100* (Cambridge: Cambridge University Press, 2004).

21. David S. Landes, *The Wealth and Poverty of Nations* (New York: W.W. Norton, 1999), 24.

22. Janette Rutterford and Josephine Maltby, "'The Widow, the Clergyman, and the Reckless': Women Investors in England, 1830–1914," *Feminist Economics* 12, no. 1–2 (January/April 2006): 111–38.

23. Ralph Blumenthal, "Thinking Outside the Cellblock: Inmates with Ambition," *New York Times*, July 1, 2006.

24. "Racing to the Top: How Global Competition Disciplines Public Policy," in *2005 Annual Report* (Federal Reserve Bank of Dallas, 2005), 3–18, http://www.dallasfed.org/fed/annual/2005/index.html.

25. Susan Rose-Ackerman, *Corruption and Government: Causes, Consequences and Reforms* (Cambridge: Cambridge University Press, 1999).

26. Sharon LaFraniere, "Business Joins African Effort to Cut Malaria," *New York Times*, July 29, 2006.

27. Micklethwait and Wooldridge, *Company*, 86.

28. I use "tribe" as a catch-all term for race, ethnicity, religion, caste, and sex.

29. Many examples of this phenomenon do not come from the United States. Countries as far-flung as Malaysia, India, and recently France have grappled with these problems. For further investigation of the way tribally dispensed government privileges can worsen tribal conflict, see Evan Osborne, "Diversity, Multiculturalism, and Ethnic Conflict: A Rent-Seeking Perspective,"*Kyklos* 53, no. 4 (2000): 509–26. For an investigation of the destructive effects of such zero-sum competition in India in particular see Evan Osborne, "Culture, Development, and Government: Reservations in India," *Economic Development and Cultural Change* 49, no. 3 (April 2001): 659–85.

30. Of fifty-eight countries where both variables can be measured, forty-four have a higher percentage of women in management than in the legislature. The average percentage of female managers among 157 countries is 22.3, and the average percentage of female legislators among 66 countries is 13.3.

31. The idea that competition can overcome prejudice is owed to Gary S. Becker, *The Economics of Discrimination*, 2nd ed. (Chicago: University of Chicago Press, 1971). For evidence that competition was overcoming racism in the South until racists took control of Southern governments and restricted commerce through mandated segregation, see Robert Higgs, *Competition and Coercion: Blacks in the American Economy, 1854–1914* (Cambridge: Cambridge University Press, 1977).

32. Some procedures are necessary; there can be no property titling if steps are not taken to register the title with the state. But sometimes these steps reach absurd proportions, motivated by officials' desires to have more opportunities to demand bribes. People who are naïve enough to follow all the procedures rather than paying a bribe to cut through the red tape could in principle take years to do so. Research conducted by Peru's Institute for Liberty and Democracy finds that to follow all the legal steps necessary to buy and register all the permits and titles needed to build on a plot of land takes almost twelve years and costs over

$9,000 in Guatemala, which is over twice the per capita income there. "Black Market, Big Market," *Latin Business Chronicle,* June 19, 2006, http://www.latinbusiness chronicle.com/app/article.aspx?id=95 (subscription only).

33. The overall correlation between the two measures is 0.5184. A value of one would mean that each pair of measures moves exactly together, a value of -1 means each pair moves exactly oppositely, and a rating of zero means their movements are completely unrelated. In most social-science settings the correlation here is high.

34. Paul D. Moreno, *Black Americans and Organized Labor: A New History* (Baton Rouge, LA: Louisiana State University Press, 2006), 39.

35. Moreno, *Black Americans and Organized Labor.*

36. BBC News, "India 2026: What Will Life Be Like?" http://news.bbc.co.uk/2/hi/business/4773425.stm.

CHAPTER 5. CORPORATE POWER

1. Korten, *When Corporations Rule the World,* 142.

2. Quoted in Bakan, *Corporation,* 146.

3. Robert Dahl, "The Concept of Power," *Behavioral Science* 2, no. 3 (July 1957): 201–15, 202–3; Bertran Russell, *Power* (London: George Allen & Unwin, 1938); Robert Bierstedt, "An Analysis of Social Power," *American Sociological Review* 15, no. 6 (December 1950): 730–38.

4. Paul Heyne, *The Economic Way of Thinking,* 9th ed. (New York: Prentice-Hall, 2000), especially chap. 14.

5. This is apart from the question of defining what a "monopoly" is. No producer is a monopoly in the sense that consumers have no opportunity in part or in total to substitute away from its product if the price is too high. On the other hand, if the "product" is defined sufficiently narrowly, every producer is a monopolist. Thus the term, while widely used, is not particularly helpful.

6. Friedrich Hayek, *The Road to Serfdom* Fiftieth Anniversary ed. (Chicago: University of Chicago Press, 1994), 80.

7. The people who want it to be used for timber harvests are not just those affiliated directly with timber companies, but anyone who would buy the products made from the timber and are fully aware of how their products were made.

8. The ability of the Constitution to constrain factional warfare and therefore preserve liberty is a key theme in Madison's *Federalist 10,* among the most important of the Federalist papers.

9. Carola Hoyos, "The New Seven Sisters: Oil and Gas Giants Dwarf Their Western Rivals," *Financial Times,* March 11, 2007.

10. Note that this violates the assumption of equality before the law. Workers are not only free to collude in setting the price of their labor, but firms may not legally punish them for doing so. Firms that collude in setting prices for their output violate the federal criminal code.

11. On regulatory employees see Susan E. Dudley, *The Hidden Tax of Regulation* (Mercatus Center, George Mason University, January 15, 2004), http://mercatus.org/repository/docLib/20060809_The_Hidden_Tax_of_Regulation.pdf. On Federal Register pages see Susan E. Dudley, *Primer on Regulation* (Mercatus Center,

George Mason University, 2005), http://www.mercatus.org/repository/docLib/20060510_Primer_on_Regulation_Dudley_Dec_2005_Final_as_Posted.pdf.

12. Austan Goolsbee, "The Impact and Inefficiency of the Corporate Income Tax: Evidence from State Organizational Form Data," *Journal of Public Economics* 88, no. 11 (September 2004): 2283–99.

13. For a favorable view of such changes see William M. Landes and Richard A. Posner, "A Positive Economic Analysis of Product Liability," *Journal of Legal Studies* 14, no. 3 (December 1985): 535–67. A skeptical account is found in George Priest, "The Invention of Enterprise Liability: A Critical History," *Journal of Legal Studies* 14, no. 3 (December 1985): 461–527.

14. A. T. Kearney, "Preparing for Global Change in the Petroleum Supply Chain," University of Nevada/COPPEAD Petroleum Executives Logistics Course Presentation, June 30, 2005, www.unr.edu/coba/logis/executive_education/University%20of%20Nevada_05.06.30%20v2.pdf.

15. Arie de Gues, *The Living Company: Habits for Survival in a Turbulent Business Environment*(Cambridge, MA: Harvard Business School Press, 1997).

16. "Case Study: Why Good Companies Fail," *Times,* November 17, 2005, http://www.timesonline.co.uk/article/0,,8543-1873798,00.html.

17. Corrado Guilmi, Mauro Gallegati, and Paul Ormerod, "Scaling Invariant Distribution of Firms' Exit in OECD Countries," *Physica A* 334, no. 1–2 (March 1, 2004): 267–73.

18. Jerry Mander, "The Rules of Corporate Behaviour," in *The Case Against the Global Economy and for a Turn Toward the Local,* ed. J. Mander and E. Goldsmith (San Francisco: Sierra Club Books, 1996): 309–22; Kenneth A. Gould, David M. Pellow, and Allan Schnaiberg, "Interrogating the Treadmill of Production: Everything You Wanted to Know About the Treadmill but Were Afraid to Ask," *Organization and Environment* 17, no. 3 (September 2004): 296–316; David C. Korten, *The Post-Corporate World: Life After Capitalism* (San Francisco: Berrett-Koehler Publishers, 2000).

19. Edward N. Wolff, "Changes in Household Wealth in the 1980s and 1990s in the U.S.," in *International Perspectives on Household Wealth,* ed. Edward N. Wolff (Northampton, MA: Edward Elgar, 2006),

20. Jerry Mander, *In the Absence of the Sacred* (San Francisco: Sierra Club Books, 1991), 97–98.

21. Richard Sennett, *The Culture of the New Capitalism* (New Haven: Yale University Press, 2006). This work is not strictly speaking of the anti-corporate variety, although analysis of corporations plays a big part in it.

22. Thomas Greco, "The Trouble with Money," *Yes! Magazine,* Summer 1997, http://www.yesmagazine.org/article.asp?ID=883.

23. Cited in James W. Ceasar, "A Genealogy of Anti-Americanism," *Public Interest* 152 (Summer 2003): 3–18.

24. Martin Heidegger, *Introduction to Metaphysics* (New Haven, CT: Yale University Press, 1959), 46.

25. Friedrich Nietzsche, *The Gay Science,* ed. Bernard Williams, trans. Josefine Nauckhoff (Cambridge: Cambridge University Press, 2001), 183.

26. Friedrich Engels, "The Condition of the Working Class in England" (Palo Alto, CA: Stanford University Press, 1868).

27. Klein, *No Logo,* 2002; Juliet B. Schor, *Born to Buy: The Commercialized Child and the New Consumer Culture* (New York: Scribner, 2004).

28. Karen Freeman, "Amos Tversky, Expert on Decision Making, Is Dead at 59," *New York Times,* June 6, 1996.

29. Thomas Sowell, "Digital Disgust," July 14, 2004, http://www.townhall.com/columnists/ThomasSowell/2004/07/14/digital_disgust.

30. Gary S. Becker and Kevin M. Murphy, "A Simple Theory of Advertising as a Good or Bad,"*Quarterly Journal of Economics* 108, no. 4 (1993): 941–64.

31. Stephen Leacock, *The Garden of Folly* (New York: Dodd, Mead, 1924), 123.

32. Sidney Wolfe, "Direct to Consumer Advertising: Education or Emotion Promotion?" *New England Journal of Medicine* 346, no. 7 (2002): 524–26.

33. Klein, *No Logo.*

34. Naomi Klein, "Reclaiming the Commons," Talk at Centre for Social Theory & Comparative History, UCLA, April 2001, http://home.mira.net/~deller/ethicalpolitics/blackwood/klein.htm. José Bové is a French anti-globalization activist who rose to fame on an afternoon spent vandalizing a McDonald's after a protest against French farm policy.

35. Timothy Sandefur, "The Common Law Right to Earn a Living," *Independent Review* 7, no. 1 (Summer 2002): 69–90.

36. It was arguably a corporation, albeit a special-privilege one, that introduced democracy to these shores when the Virginia Company decided to allow its members to elect its officers.

37. Kelly, *The Divine Right of Capital,* 15.

38. The number of stakeholders is irrelevant; if anything, a greater number would make the problem worse.

39. A good primer on cycling and other problems of democratic governance is found in Dennis C. Mueller, *Public Choice III* (New York: Cambridge University Press, 2003).

40. Gordon Tullock, *On Voting: A Public Choice Approach* (Northampton, MA: Edward Elgar, 1998).

41. The World Bank, *Doing Business 2004: Understanding Regulations* (Washington: World Bank and Oxford University Press, 2004).

42. Leora Klapper, Luc Raeven, and Raghuram Rajan, "Entry Regulation as a Barrier to Entrepreneurship," *Journal of Financial Economics* 82, no. 3 (December 2006): 591–629.

43. For evidence on stagnation, see Edmund Phelps and Gylfi Zoega, "The Rise and Downward Trend of the Natural Rate," *American Economic Review, Papers and Proceedings* 87, no. 2 (May 1997): 283–89. For evidence on corruption, see Alberto Ades and Rafael Di Tella, "National Champions and Corruption: Some Unpleasant Interventionist Arithmetic," *Economic Journal* 107, no. 443 (July 1997): 1023–42.

44. On the first point, that more complex rules generate more corruption to allow people to escape them, the Roman historian Tacitus is often quoted as saying that "[t]he laws were most numerous when the commonwealth was most corrupt" (Tacitus, *Annales* 27.3).

CHAPTER 6. CORPORATE GLOBALIZATION

1. Boanaventura de Sousa Santos, "The Fall of the Angelus Novus: Beyond the Modern Game of Roots and Options," *Eurozine,* October 15, 1999, http://www.eurozine.com/article/1999-10-15-santos-en.html; Jeremy Seabrook, "Localizing Cultures," *Korea Herald,* January 13, 2004. Asfour is quoted in Bassam Za'Za', "Arab Speakers See Threat to Culture by Globalization," *Gulf News,* March 21, 2002.

2. Jagdish N. Bhagwati, *In Defense of Globalization* (New York: Oxford University Press, 2004); Thomas Friedman, *The Lexus and the Olive Tree* (New York: Farrar, Strauss, Giroux, 2000); Salman Rushdie, "Rethinking the War on American Culture," *New York Times,* March 5, 1999.

3. Medicine provides a good example of further specialization over time. In medieval Europe, the same person who cut your hair (or foretold your future astrologically) might treat your breathing difficulties. (How effectively is of course another story.) Ultimately medicine reemerged as a distinct specialty, as did pediatrics, then pediatric surgery, then pediatric cardiac surgery, and so on.

4. "Misplaced" because regional integration comes at the expense of far more valuable efforts toward global free trade. Deepak Lal, "Trade Blocs and Multilateral Free Trade," *Journal of Common Market Studies* 31, no. 3 (September 1993): 349–58. In addition, there are recent signs that some leaders, particularly in Latin America, wish to use regional trading blocs to limit rather than promote trade with industrial countries. For a fuller description of Prebisch's views on international trade, see John Toye, "60 Years of Development Economics," paper presented at the "50 years of Development Economics: Taking Stock of Controversies" conference of the Development Studies Association, July 2003, http://www.devstud.org.uk/studygroups/economics/50yrs_toye.pdf.

5. Immanuel Maurice Wallerstein, *The Modern World-System; Capitalist Agriculture and the Origins of the European World-Economy in the Sixteenth Century* (New York: Academic Press, 1974); Immanuel Maurice Wallerstein, *World-Systems Analysis: An Introduction* (Durham: Duke University Press, 2004).

6. Leslie Sklair, *Sociology of the Global System,* 2nd ed. (Baltimore: Johns Hopkins University Press, 1995), 9.

7. Leslie Sklair, "Competing Conceptions of Globalization," *Journal of World-Systems Research* 5, no. 2 (1999), 143–62, 156.

8. Lou Dobbs, *Exporting America: Why Corporate Greed Is Shipping America's Jobs Overseas* (New York: Warner Business Books, 2004), 1.

9. Michael C. Dreiling, "The Class-Embeddedness of Corporate Political Action: Leadership in Defense of the NAFTA," *Social Problems* 47, no. 1 (February 2000): 21–48.

10. Linda McQuaig, *All You Can Eat: Greed, Lust and the New Capitalism* (New York: Penguin Books, 2001).

11. Marc Levinson, *The Box: How the Shipping Container Made the World Smaller and the World Economy Bigger* (Princeton, NJ: Princeton University Press, 2006).

12. This charge is not strictly accurate, in that WTO panels are free to accept *amicus curiae* briefs from nongovernmental organizations, a rule identical to that of the U.S. Supreme Court. World Trade Organization, *A Handbook on the WTO Dispute Settlement System* (Cambridge: Cambridge University Press, 2004). Some

governments actually have legislation allowing the government to file WTO claims on the basis of complaints by domestic pressure groups.

13. For (unevidenced) arguments that globalization promotes child labor, see Bernard Schlemmer, ed., *The Exploited Child* (London: Zed Books, 2000); "Fighting Corporate Globalization After Seattle: A Tikkun Roundtable," *Tikkun* 15, no. 2 (March/April 2000): 28–30, 48–50.

14. For a skeptical account of the benefits of open trade policies, see Francisco Rodriguez and Dani Rodrik, "Trade Policy and Economic Growth: A Skeptic's Guide to the Cross-National Evidence," in *NBER Macroeconomics Annual 2000* (Cambridge, MA: MIT Press, 2001), 261–325. For a similar account of opening to foreign portfolio investment, see Joseph E. Stiglitz, "Capital Market Liberalization and Exchange Rate Regimes: Risk Without Reward," *Annals of the American Academy of Political and Social Science* 579, no. 1 (January 2002): 219–48.

15. David Dollar and Art Kraay, "Trade, Growth, and Poverty," *Economic Journal* 114, no. 493 (February 2004): F22–F49.

16. Colin Hines, *A Global Look to the Local* (London: International Institute for Environment and Development, 2003), 30. See also William Kingston, "A Spectre is Haunting the World—the Spectre of *Global* Capitalism" (emphasis in original), *Journal of Evolutionary Economics* 10, no. 1–2 (January 7, 2000): 83–108.

17. Korten, *When Corporations Rule the World*, 47.

18. James S. Dusenberry, *Income, Saving and the Theory of Consumer Behavior* (Cambridge, MA: Harvard University Press, 1949). Richard A. Easterlin, "Will Raising the Incomes of All Increase the Happiness of All?" *Journal of Economic Literature* 27, no. 1 (June 1995): 35–47.

19. David G. Blanchflower and Andrew J. Oswald, "Well-Being Over Time in Britain and the USA," *Journal of Public Economics* 88, no. 7–8 (July 2004): 1359–86.

20. William J. Bernstein, *The Birth of Plenty: How the Prosperity of the Modern World Was Created* (New York: McGraw-Hill, 2004), especially 322–26.

21. Bernt Bratsberg, "Legal Versus Illegal U.S. Immigration and Source Country Characteristics," *Southern Economic Journal* 61, no. 3 (January 1995): 715–27.

22. Eric D. Ramstetter, "Labor Productivity, Wages, Nationality, and Foreign Ownership Shares in Thai Manufacturing, 1996–2000," *Journal of Asian Economics* 14, no. 6 (January 2004): 861–84; Robert E. Lipsey and Frederik Sjöholm, "Foreign Direct Investment, Education, and Wages in Indonesian Manufacturing," *Journal of Development Economics* 73, no. 1 (February 2004): 415–22; Sourafel Girma, Steve Thompson, and Peter W. Wright, "Why are Productivity and Wages Higher in Foreign Firms?" *Economic and Social Review* 33, no. 1 (Spring 2002): 93–100; Frank Barry, "Export-Platform Foreign Direct Investment: The Irish Experience," *EIB Papers* 9, no. 2 (2004): 8–37; Dirk Willem te Velde and Oliver Morrissey, "Do Workers in Africa Get a Wage Premium If Employed in Firms Owned by Foreigners?" *Journal of African Economies* 12, no. 1 (March 2003): 41–73; Arjun S. Bedi and Andrzej Cieślik, "Wages and Wage Growth in Poland: The Role of Foreign Direct Investment," *Economics of Transition* 10, no. 1 (March 2002): 1–27.

23. Drusilla K. Brown, Alan V. Deardorff, and Robert M. Stern, "The Effects of Multinational Production on Wages and Working Conditions in Developing Countries," in *Challenges to Globalization: Analyzing the Economics*, ed. Robert E. Baldwin and L. Alan Winters (Chicago: University of Chicago Press, 2004), 279–326.

24. Human Right Watch, for example, has many such reports. See, for example, *Inside the Home, Outside the Law Abuse of Child Domestic Workers in Morocco* (New York: Human Rights Watch, 2005), http://hrw.org/reports/2005/morocco1205.

25. Dana Frank, "Our Fruit, Their Labor and Global Reality," *Washington Post,* June 2, 2002.

26. UNICEF, *The State of the World's Children 1997,* pt. 2 (New York: UNICEF, 1997), 67–71.

27. "Largely," because even now child labor exists in advanced countries, often with the full consent of the parents. For example, farm parents in the United States often put their children to work on their own farms. This suggests that referring to "child labor" without elaboration is empirically unhelpful. Some forms of child labor are abhorrent, some are not.

28. For the beneficial effects of trade on child labor, see Eric V. Edmonds and Nina Pavcnik, "International Trade and Child Labor: Cross-Country Evidence," *Journal of International Economics* 68, no. 1 (January 2006): 115–40; Eric V. Edmonds and Nina Pavcnik, "The Effect of Trade Liberalization on Child Labor," *Journal of International Economics* 65, no. 2 (March 2005): 401–19. For the particular effect of investment by multinationals, see Eric Neumayer and Indra De Soysa, "Trade Openness, Foreign Direct Investment, and Child Labor," *World Development* 33, no. 1 (January 2005): 43–63.

29. Korten, *When Corporations Rule the World,* 245–47.

30. Rich Pirog and Andrew Benjamin, *Checking the Food Odometer: Comparing Food Miles for Local Versus Conventional Produce Sales to Iowa Institutions,* Leopold Center for Sustainable Agriculture, July 2003, http://www.leopold.iastate.edu/pubinfo/papersspeeches/food_travel072103.pdf.

31. Helena Norberg-Hodge, "Break Up the Monoculture: Why the Drive to Create a Homogenized World Must Inevitably Fail," *Nation* 263, no. 3 (July 15, 1996): 20–23.

32. While largely free of industrial pollution, such societies can generate environmental problems of other sorts, for example, massive forest and species destruction. See Jared Diamond, *Collapse: How Societies Choose to Fail or Succeed* (New York: Viking Adult, 2004).

33. Gene Grossman and Alan Krueger, "Environmental Impacts of a North American Free Trade Agreement," in *The U.S.–Mexico Free Trade Agreement,* ed. Peter Garber (Cambridge, MA: MIT Press, 1993), 13–56. Gene Grossman and Alan Krueger, "Economic Growth and the Environment," *Quarterly Journal of Economics* 110, no. 2 (May 1995): 353–77.

34. Rachel Carson, *Silent Spring* (New York: Houghton-Mifflin, 1962).

35. For evidence that transfer of environmentally superior technology is a significant benefit, see Gunnar S. Eskeland and Ann E. Harrison, "Moving to Greener Pastures? Multinationals and the Pollution Haven Hypothesis," *Journal of Development Economics* 70, no. 1 (February 2003): 1–23.

36. David I. Stern, "The Rise and Fall of the Environmental Kuznets Curve," *World Development* 32, no. 8 (August 2004): 1419–1439. The World Bank Group, "Is Globalization Causing a 'Race to the Bottom' in Environmental Standards?" pt. 4 of *Assessing Globalization* series (Washington: The World Bank, 2000). Jeffrey Frenkel, "The Environment and Globalization," in *Globalization: What's New,* ed.

Michael Weinstein (New York: Columbia University Press, 2005), 129–69. For a survey of the literature that argues that prosperity is promoting environmental improvement even faster than Grossman and Krueger had posited in the work cited in Note 33 above, see Susmita Dasgupta and others, "Confronting the Environmental Kuznets Curve," *Journal of Economic Perspectives* 16, no. 1 (Winter 2002): 147–68.

37. David Wheeler, "Racing to the Bottom? Foreign Investment and Air Pollution in Developing Countries," *Journal of Environment and Development* 10, no. 3 (September 2001): 225–45.

38. Thomas G. Rawski, "Urban Air Quality in China: Historical and Comparative Perspectives" Working paper 282 (University of Pittsburgh, Department of Economics).

39. Daniel L. Millimet and John A. List, "A Natural Experiment on the 'Race to the Bottom' Hypothesis: Testing for Stochastic Dominance in Temporal Pollution Trends," *Oxford Bulletin of Economics and Statistics* 65, no. 4 (September 2003): 395–420; Daniel L. Millimet, "Assessing the Impact of Environmental Federalism," *Journal of Regional Science* 43, no. 4 (November 2003): 711–33; Matthew Potoski, "Clean Air Federalism: Do States Race to the Bottom?" *Public Administration Review* 61, no. 3 (May/June 2001): 335–42. A similar argument has been used to dispute claims that alleged jurisdictional competition promotes lower standards of living from investment mobility, with the authors finding instead convergence to a much higher standard of living. See Kris James Mitchener and Ian W. McLean, "U.S. Regional Growth and Convergence, 1880–1980," *Journal of Economic History* 59, no. 4 (December 1999): 1016–42.

40. Indra de Soysa and Eric Neumayer, "False Prophet, or Genuine Savior? Assessing the Effects of Economic Openness on Sustainable Development, 1980–1999," *International Organization* 59, no. 3 (Summer 2005): 731–72.

41. Mark T. Heil and Thomas M. Selden, "Carbon Emissions and Economic Development: Future Trajectories Based on Historical Experience," *Environment and Development Economics* 6, no. 1 (February 2001): 63–83; J. Timmons Roberts and Peter E. Grimes, "Carbon Intensity and Economic Development 1962–91: A Brief Exploration of the Environmental Kuznets Curve," *World Development* 25, no. 2 (February 1997): 191–98. The latter study attributes the improved environmental quality since the early 1970s almost entirely to wealthy countries, which has occurred not due to shifts from industry to services, but to "other social and political factors" (196). For our purposes the distinction is irrelevant. As long as the public in richer countries is more willing to make the sacrifices necessary for lower CO_2 emissions via the political process, growth brings them to this moment faster. For evidence of growth promoting sustainability more generally, see de Soysa and Neumayer, "False Prophet or Genuine Savior?".

42. Bjorn Lomborg, ed., *Global Crises, Global Solutions* (Cambridge: Cambridge University Press, 2007).

43. For the fascinating tale of how the creation of individual property rights in trees (which had been the property of the state since French colonial times) gave people an incentive to grow them and therefore rolled back desertification, see Lydia

Polgreen, "In Niger, Crops and Trees Turn Back the Desert," *New York Times,* February 11, 2007.

44. Friends of the Earth International, *Business Rules: Who Pays the Price* (London: Friends of the Earth International, 2003), 26–27; Amnesty International, *Business and Human Rights: A Geography of Risk* (London: Amnesty International and Prince of Wales International Business Leaders Forum, 2002).

45. Marta Bengoa and Blanca Sanchez-Robles, "Foreign Direct Investment, Economic Freedom and Growth: New Evidence from Latin America," *European Journal of Political Economy* 19, no. 3 (September 2003): 529–45.

46. Freedom House, *Freedom in the World 2004,* http://www.freedomhouse.org /research/freeworld/2004/methodology.htm.

47. The overall correlation coefficient of the Heritage and democracy measures is 0.6913. The Freedom House measures as used here range from 0 to 14, with 14 indicating more freedom. The Heritage measure ranges from 0 to 100, with 100 denoting more economic freedom.

48. For theoretical arguments why dictatorships would be unfriendly to property rights, see Christopher Clague and others, "Democracy, Autocracy and the Institutions Supportive of Economic Growth," in *Institutions and Economic Development: Growth and Governance in Less-Developed and Post-Socialist Countries,* ed. Christopher Clague (Baltimore: John Hopkins University Press,1997), 91–119; Mancur Olson Jr., "Autocracy, Democracy and Prosperity," in *Strategy and Choice,* ed. Richard J. Zeckhauser (Cambridge, MA: MIT Press, 1991), 131–57. For empirical evidence see Christopher Clague and others, "Property and Contract Rights in Autocracies and Democracies," *Journal of Economic Growth* 2, no. 1 (June 1996): 243–76. They find that democracies tend to protect property rights better than autocracies, and that both long-term autocracies and democracies tend to protect them the best. They report no evidence that autocracies protect property rights better than democracies.

49. Mathias Busse, "Transnational Corporations and Repression of Political Rights and Civil Liberties: An Empirical Analysis," *Kyklos* 57, no. 1 (2004): 45–65.

50. Debi Barker, "Globalization and Industrial Agriculture," in *The Fatal Harvest Reader: The Tragedy of Industrial Agriculture,* ed. Andrew Kimbrell (Sausolito, CA: Island Press, 2002), 249–63.

51. Kevin Shear McCann, "The Diversity-Stability Debate," *Nature* 405, no. 6783 (May 2000): 228–33.

52. David Schap and Andrew T. Young, "Enterprise and Biodiversity: Do Market Forces Yield Diversity of Life?" *Cato Journal* 19, no. 1 (Spring/Summer 1999): 49–67.

53. Helena Norberg-Hodge, "Global Monoculture: The Worldwide Destruction of Diversity," in *The Fatal Harvest Reader: The Tragedy of Industrial Agriculture,* ed. Andrew Kimbrell (Sausalito, CA: Foundation for Deep Ecology, 2002), 58–64, 60.

54. United Nations Development Program, *Human Development Report 2003* (New York: United Nations Development Program, 2003), 51.

55. Stephen Pollard and others, *EU Trade Barriers Kill* (Brussels: Centre for the New Europe, 2003).

56. Pew Research Center for the People and the Press, *Views of a Changing World, How Global Publics View: War in Iraq, Democracy, Islam and Governance, Globalization* (Washington: Pew Research Center for the People and the Press, 2003).

57. Ibid., 71.

58. Johan Norberg, "The Noble Feat of Nike," in *The New World Reader*, ed. Gilbert H. Muller (New York: Houghton-Mifflin, 2005): 173–77. http://www. johannorberg.net/?page=articles&articleid=53.

CHAPTER 7. CORPORATE CULTURE

1. Cornel West, "The Role of Law in Progressive Politics," in *The Cornel West Reader* (New York: Basic Books, 2000), 269–70.

2. Mark Crispin Miller, "What's Wrong with This Picture?" *Nation*, January 7, 2002, http://www.thenation.com/doc/20020107/miller.

3. Douglas Kellner, "Critical Theory and British Cultural Studies: The Missed Articulation," in *Cultural Methodologies*, ed. Jim McGuigan (Thousand Oaks, CA: Sage, 1997), 12–41.

4. Russell Kirk, "Neoconservatives: An Endangered Species," The Heritage Lecture 178 (The Heritage Foundation, December 15, 1988), http://www. heritage.org/Research/PoliticalPhilosophy/HL178.cfm.

5. Ralph Nader, "The Diversion of Discontent" (speech, Boulder, Colorado, March 31, 1998).

6. Thomas Frank, *What's the Matter With Kansas? How Conservatives Won the Heart of America* (New York: Metropolitan Books, 2004).

7. Thomas Frank, "Dark Age," in *Commodify Your Dissent: Salvos from the Baffler*, ed. Thomas Frank and Matt Weiland (New York: W.W. Norton, 1997), 272, 274.

8. Chris Anderson, *The Long Tail: Why the Future of Business Is Selling Less of More* (New York: Hyperion, 2006).

9. New music acts often set up pages on social networking sites such as Myspace to enable them to communicate with potential and actual fans.

10. Soleil Securities Group, "'The Long Tail' Drives Entertainment Industry Growth," December 15, 2005, http://www.lifgroup.com/Long_Tail_Implica tions_for_Stocks.pdf.

11. Ben Bagdikian, *The Media Monopoly* (Boston: Beacon Press, 1997), 1.

12. Ben Compaine, "Domination Fantasies: Does Rupert Murdoch Control the Media? Does Anyone?" *Reason*, January 2004, http://www.reason.com/news/ show/29001.html.

13. At least one book even encodes this zero-sum, conflict-ridden view of political speech in its title. Robert W. McChesney and John Nichols, *Our Media, Not Theirs: The Democratic Struggle against Corporate Media* (New York: Seven Stories Press, 2002).

14. Ambrose Evans-Pritchard, "French an Also-Ran as English Tops the EU," *Daily Telegraph*, April 24, 2004.

15. Herbert I. Schiller, *Communication and Cultural Domination* (White Plains, NY: International Arts and Sciences Press, 1976).

16. Benjamin R. Barber, "Democracy at Risk: American Culture in a Global Culture," *World Policy Journal* 15, no. 2 (Summer 1998): 29–41, 37–38.

17. Benjamin R. Barber, *Jihad vs. McWorld: Terrorism's Challenge to Democracy* (New York: Ballantine, 1996), 71.

18. Tappan Raj, interview, BBC World Service, broadcast February 5, 2007.

19. Tyler Cowen, *Creative Destruction: How Globalization is Changing the World's Cultures* (Princeton, NJ: Princeton University Press, 2004).

20. Joseph Schumpeter, *Capitalism, Socialism, and Democracy* (New York: Harper Perennial, 1962). Ironically Schumpeter viewed the creative destruction of capitalism as temporary, to be replaced upon completion with socialist planning. What he failed to see is that creative destruction never ends, and thank goodness.

21. Ben McConville, "Black Music from Scotland? It Could be the Gospel Truth," *The Scotsman,* August 31, 2003.

22. Howard W. French, "Sushi Comes Home, With Cream Cheese and Chili," *New York Times,* April 4, 2002.

23. Janelle Gelfand, "Passionate About the Piano," *Cincinnati Enquirer,* February 1, 2002.

24. Jean-Francois Revel, "The Anti-American Obsession," *New Criterion* 22, no. 2 (October 2003): 12–19.

25. Adam Smith, *The Wealth of Nations,* 309.

26. The Church of Jesus Christ of Latter-Day Saints and Reform Judaism are two examples of religions largely created or nurtured in the United States. More generally, see Laurence Iannaccone, "Introduction to the Economics of Religion," *Journal of Economic Literature* 36, no. 3 (September 1998): 1465–96.

27. Anna Quindlen, "Honestly—You Shouldn't Have," *Newsweek,* December 3, 2001, 76.

28. Quoted in Marc Marano, "Environmentalist Laments Introduction of Electricity," Cybercast News Service, August 26, 2002, http://www.cnsnews.com/ViewCulture.asp?Page=\Culture\archive\200208\CUL20020826b.html.

29. David Brooks, "Among the Bourgeoisophobes," *Weekly Standard* 7, no. 30 (April 15, 2002): 20–72.

30. Knight-Ridder News, October 29, 2004. Appearing in *Billings Gazette* as "Mexican Traditionalists Fight Wal-Mart Close to Pyramids," October 29, 2004.

31. "Where Wal-Mart Turns into God," *Montreal Mirror* 20, no. 20 (November 4–10, 2004).

32. Jurgen Sander, interview with Morris Berman, *Büchergilde,* 200, http://www.buechergilde.de/archiv/exklusivinterviews/berman_englisch.shtml.

33. Mario Vargas Llosa, "The Culture of Liberty," *Foreign Policy* 122 (January/February 2001): 502–6.

CHAPTER 8. CORPORATE CONCLUSIONS

1. Donella H. Meadows, "The Global Citizen: Corporations Already Rule the World," http://www.sustainabilityinstitute.org/dhm_archive/index.php?display_article=vn629kortened.

2. In some European countries since the early 1980s, this pattern has slowed down considerably, owing to the growth of regulations imposed on businesses

in the form of taxation and labor-market and wage regulation. One commentator has described this as the transformation of Western Europe into "stagnant societies where mass unemployment and falling living standards are accepted as permanent facts of life." Anatole Kaletsky, "Europeans Are Shouting 'No' for One Reason: It's Their Economies, Stupid," *Times,* May 26, 2005.

3. Recall that some government is not only not harmful, but actually essential to allowing markets to work—the enforcement of property rights in particular. Here I refer to government decisions about how resources are specifically to be used, including price controls, restrictions on competition that benefit well-connected businesses, etc.

4. Author analysis of General Social Survey data. To be fair, two of the four institutions with lower levels of confidence were governmental—the federal executive branch and Congress.

5. New York Democratic Senator Hillary Rodham Clinton was on the board of directors of Wal-Mart during her years in Arkansas in the 1980s. By 2006 she was refusing its contributions and casting her lot with activists who were asking the company, with the undercurrent threat of legal action, to increase worker compensation.

6. Cited in Thomas B. Edsall, "Risk and Reward," *New York Times,* December 5, 2006.

7. Pew Global Attitudes Project, *Views of a Changing World, June 2003* (Washington: Pew Research Center for the People and the Press, 2003). The reported percentages are for those who "completely agree" or "mostly agree" with the statement.

8. It is noteworthy in this respect that in 2000, the EU called for substantial free-market reform over the next ten years via what came to be known as the Lisbon Process, but that an interim report in 2005 found that this process had substantially failed. European Commission, *Working Together for Growth and Jobs: A New Start for the Lisbon Strategy* (Brussels: European Commission, February 2, 2005).

9. Hayek, *The Road to Serfdom.*

10. Henry G. Manne, "Milton Friedman was Right," *Wall Street Journal,* November 24, 2006.

11. Richard Hofstadter, *The Paranoid Style in American Politics and Other Essays* (New York: Alfred A. Knopf, 1966), 135–36.

12. As in the title of William Greider, *Who Will Tell the People? The Betrayal of American Democracy* (New York: Simon & Schuster, 1992).

13. Korten, *When Corporations Rule the World,* 211.

14. Ibid., 135–37.

15. The financial markets are regulated at the federal level via the Securities and Exchange Commission and the Commodity Futures Trading Commission, but must be regulated that way given the ways in which anonymous individuals of different jurisdictions trade financial assets with complete indifference to borders.

16. Steven E. Landsburg, *Fair Play: What Your Child Can Teach You About Economics, Values, and the Meaning of Life* (New York: The Free Press, 1997), 87.

17. Celia Dugger, "Five Nations to Tax Airfare to Raise Funds for AIDS Drugs," *International Herald Tribune,* September 19, 2006.

18. For example, domestic drilling should be subsidized because more expensive domestic production is preferable to cheaper foreign oil, or ethanol is preferable to gasoline because of national security and climate-change reasons.

19. For example, federal subsidies for sheep farmers were originally introduced in response to a shortage of mohair, used to make military uniforms, during the Korean War. The military dropped mohair soon after, but for decades one could observe congressmen from sheep-laden districts arguing in the well of the House with a straight face that national security demanded that such subsidies continue.

20. Milton Friedman, "The Social Responsibility of Business Is to Increase Its Profits," *New York Times Magazine,* September 1, 1970.

Index

About the Author

EVAN OSBORNE is Professor of Economics at Wright State University. He has written for such publications as *Journal of Legal Studies, Public Choice, Cato Journal, Journal of Sports Economics, and Economic Development and Cultural Change*. Among others, the AP, Reuters, *Christian Science Monitor, Newsweek* (International), Bloomberg Radio, and Forbes.com have featured his views.

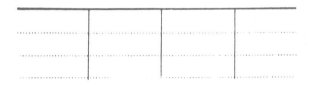